The New Deal

Edited and with an introduction by

David E. Hamilton
University of Kentucky, Lexington

Houghton Mifflin Company   Boston   New York

Editor-in-Chief: Jean Woy
Associate Editor: Leah Strauss
Associate Project Editor: Rebecca Bennett
Associate Production/Design Coordinator: Jodi O'Rourke
Assistant Manufacturing Coordinator: Andrea Wagner
Marketing Manager: Sandra McGuire

Cover Designer: Sarah Melhado
Photo Researcher: Rose Corbett Gordon
Cover Image: President Roosevelt at CCC camp receiving cake.
          (UPI/Corbis-Bettman)

Printed in the U.S.A.

Library of Congress Catalog Card Number: 98-72036

ISBN: 0-395-87075-5

123456789—QF—02 01 00 99 98

The New Deal

PROBLEMS IN AMERICAN CIVILIZATION

For Ellis W. Hawley

The Editor

Born in Pontiac, Michigan, David E. Hamilton is associate professor of history at the University of Kentucky, Lexington, where he has taught since 1984. He earned his degrees at Iowa State University (1976) and the University of Iowa (1985). He has written *From New Day to New Deal: American Farm Policy from Hoover to Roosevelt, 1928–1933* (1991) and his articles have appeared in the *Journal of American History*, the *Journal of Southern History*, and *Agricultural History*. He has received the Theodore Saloutos Book Prize and the Fred Carstensen Article Prize from the Agricultural History Society. He has also been awarded fellowships by the National Endowment for the Humanities and the American Council on Learned Societies.

Contents

Preface

The New Deal political order may be dead, but the historical debate over the New Deal and its meaning remain vital to understanding modern America. Historians continue to ask what was the New Deal, what did it achieve, and what were its limits. More recent scholarship investigates how the New Deal was part of larger developments in American society; what the New Deal meant for women, African Americans, and Native Americans; and why the New Deal state took the shape it did. Older histories debate whether the New Deal was "pragmatic" or whether it was a "watershed." Newer studies explore how the New Deal was constrained by cultural values, how New Deal liberalism was transformed late in the 1930s and during World War II, and what the New Deal meant for the American people. This burgeoning literature and the many diverse points of view make any neat summary of New Deal scholarship impossible. With the greater complexity, however, has come a richer and more exciting understanding of New Deal America.

This volume offers students a selection of important work from the 1960s combined with a sampling of more recent interpretations. Part I includes differing conclusions and analyses of the New Deal. Part II looks at the different forms of New Deal state building and New Deal conceptions of the role of the central government in American life. Part III includes assessments of New Deal policies and programs. Part IV analyzes the New Deal's relationship with different groups in American society.

I wish to thank the authors and publishers of the works reprinted in this collection for their cooperation. Valuable comments provided by the following reviewers aided me in putting the volume together: Richard S. Kirkendall, University of Washington; Mark H. Leff, University of Illinois; and George T. McJimsey, Iowa State University. Leah Strauss, Becky Bennett, and Jean Woy of Houghton Mifflin were helpful throughout the many stages of the project. My great thanks to them.

D. E. H.

Introduction

"I pledge you, I pledge myself to a new deal for the American people." So spoke Franklin Delano Roosevelt to the Democratic Party convention the evening of July 2, 1932, when he shattered political tradition by appearing in person to accept his nomination. When a political cartoonist used the phrase "new deal" for a caption the next day, Roosevelt's dramatic speech supplied, without ever intending to, the name for his campaign and then the first two terms of his presidency. The New Deal became a reform movement that redefined American liberalism, instituted the greatest changes in America's political institutions since the Constitution, and forged a political order that lasted into the 1960s.

Roosevelt's 1932 pledge came during the worst year of the Great Depression. Factories across the country stood silent, a quarter or more of the nation's workers were unemployed, millions more worked but a day or two a week, and thousands of banks had failed. In the countryside, farmers by the tens of thousands could no longer pay taxes or mortgage debts because their crops and livestock were selling for the lowest prices of the century.

The crisis had overwhelmed the nation's public and private institutions. Families, charities, and local governments struggled to aid the unemployed and the destitute, but depleted budgets and timid imaginations had rendered them helpless to meet the nation's needs. Herbert Hoover threw his immense energy into stemming the deflation but in time he became as much the depression's victim as the men and women who stood huddled in city breadlines. When the glum Hoover and the confident Roosevelt rode together in the inaugural motorcade, it was Hoover who appeared the invalid.

Roosevelt took office on March 4, 1933, amidst a national banking panic. Just hours after telling the nation in his inaugural address that it had "nothing to fear but fear itself," he declared a national bank holiday and called Congress into special session. This began what would soon be known as the First Hundred Days during which Congress passed fifteen pieces of legislation. The bills included legalizing the sale of beer; taking the United States off the gold standard; and creating "alphabet agencies" such as the National Recovery Administration (NRA), the Public Works Administration

(PWA), the Agricultural Adjustment Administration (AAA), the Federal Emergency Relief Administration (FERA), and the Tennessee Valley Authority (TVA). Two years later came a new burst of legislation, or the Second Hundred Days. It included some of the most important laws in American history, measures such as the Wagner National Labor Relations Act, which established National Labor Relations Board (NLRB); the Public Utilities Holding Company Act; the Revenue Act; and the Social Security Act.

The agencies and programs created by this legislative flurry had many purposes. Some were intended to provide relief for families in need and aid for farmers and homeowners threatened with foreclosure. Some were aimed at sparking economic recovery and others at reforming an economy too prone to collapse; still others were established to employ out-of-work artists, reverse American Indian policy, and bring about labor-capital peace. Much of the New Deal was shortlived; the NRA barely lasted two years and the arts programs of the Works Progress Administration (WPA) lasted only slightly longer. But even today much remains, including Social Security, unemployment insurance, banking and financial regulation, and the TVA.

With the New Deal came important changes in American politics and government. The presidency emerged as the center of the national government. The labor movement, finally able to begin organizing mass-production industries such as steel and automobiles, emerged as a powerful voice. Aided by New Deal programs, the urban working class, northern African Americans, and middle-class reformers forged loyal bonds to the Democratic Party that made it the majority party for over thirty years. When the Supreme Court began to uphold the constitutionality of New Deal legislation in 1937, it commenced a constitutional revolution that legitimized a more expansive federal government.

When Roosevelt began his presidency, he had hoped to win support for the New Deal by appealing for national cooperation and unity. After 1933, however, cooperation gave way to furious conflict and partisanship. Conservative critics charged the New Deal with wasteful spending and destroying traditions of limited government, individualism, and free enterprise. Critics on the left faulted it for offering timid expedients, bowing too readily to the demands of powerful interests, and ignoring capitalism's defects.

In Roosevelt's second term, the New Deal stalled. Some important legislation was passed: a second Agricultural Adjustment Act, the Fair Labor Standards Act, and the 1939 amendments expanding the Social Security Act. More often, however, Roosevelt and liberal reform met defeat. The ill-advised "court-packing" plan, the recession of 1937–1938, the controversial "sit-down" strikes, and the unsuccessful attempt to "purge" conservative Democrats from Congress gave new support to a "conservative coalition" of white southern Democrats and conservative Republicans in Congress. The crumbling of Europe's peace, meanwhile, shifted the nation's focus from depression to war.

Spurred by easy access to Roosevelt's papers and the still raging political struggles over the New Deal, historians following World War II began a massive outpouring of New Deal books and articles. Generally, they admired, even celebrated, New Deal reform. They credited it with rescuing millions of Americans from destitution, stimulating a modest recovery, and restoring a sense of hope and optimism among the American people. Just as important, it had toppled a Republican-led oligarchy wedded to defeating liberal reform while protecting corporate power and privileged wealth. After 1933, the American government was more open with a greater voice for farm, labor, ethnic, and racial groups. And by vesting the national government with new regulatory and social-welfare functions, New Deal reform had established a "mixed" economy with a "modern" state capable of correcting capitalism's abuses and creating new forms of economic security. Above all, this reform had sustained and enlarged democratic government when such government was disappearing in Europe.

Led by Arthur Schlesinger, Jr., these historians saw liberal reform as an ongoing battle that pitted defenders of laissez-faire government and unchecked private power against farmers, workers, and reformers seeking to use public power to humanize and bring order to an unstable system of industrial capitalism. Roosevelt, they argued, had pursued "pragmatic" reform in order to redefine the "vital center" of American politics.

Until the mid-1960s, much of the "debate" over the New Deal centered on whether it marked a "revolution" or a "watershed" in American thought and politics. Nevertheless, some scholars, most notably the former New Dealer Rexford G. Tugwell and Roosevelt biographer James MacGregor Burns, argued that the New Deal could have achieved greater changes than it did. Why, they asked, had it not curtailed corporate power, adopted Keynesian fiscal policies, built national planning systems, ended mass unemployment, or transformed completely the Democratic Party into a reform party? Burns and others argued that the New Dealers, and especially Roosevelt, had been too practical, too willing to improvise, too ready to compromise, too politically opportunistic. Roosevelt had lacked a clear vision of social and economic reform and had misspent his immense personal popularity.

The most influential appraisal of the New Deal's mixed record of accomplishment and failure was William E. Leuchtenburg's *Franklin D. Roosevelt and the New Deal* (1963). Much of the New Deal, Leuchtenburg noted, had been inadequate and flawed. He noted the limited coverage of Social Security, the treatment of the South's tenant farmers and sharecroppers, the ambiguous commitment to unionization, and the inability to end the depression. On balance, however, Leuchtenburg's appraisal was decidedly favorable. By transforming the presidency, vesting the federal government with new responsibilities, creating economic stabilizers, and shifting the focus of national political debate, the New Deal had achieved, he wrote, a "half-way revolution" in American politics.

Tugwell, Burns, and Leuchtenburg all shared the assumptions of the "liberal consensus" of the 1950s and early 1960s. A stronger national government, they believed, could achieve the other "half" of the New Deal revolution by expanding social-welfare systems, further harnessing corporate power, and attacking race discrimination. Future liberal "activist" presidents would build on Roosevelt's New Deal to achieve a more just and democratic America.

These assumptions came under withering attack during the second half of the 1960s by "revisionist" historians critical of the New Deal and of postwar liberalism. In the view of social democratic and "New Left" historians such as Paul Conkin and Barton Bernstein, the New Deal was no half-way revolution; it was a capitalist rescue operation intended to protect class and corporate privilege. It had failed to restore prosperity, embrace movements of social protest, address poverty, or attack racial injustice. At best it had created a system of "interest-group liberalism" that doled out subsidies to businesses, banks, and commercial farmers, while to tenant farmers, sharecroppers, the urban poor, and the unemployed, the New Deal's help was skimpy and demeaning. Roosevelt and the leading New Dealers, they argued, had opposed redistributing wealth and power in American society. As a result, they had bequeathed to post–World War II America the racism, inequalities, and corporate concentration of the prewar period. The turmoil of the 1960s, they implied, had its roots in the 1930s.

The revisionist critique of the New Deal exerted much less influence than did the revisionism of the origins of the Cold War, but it did signal important shifts in New Deal scholarship. One of these was to see the often sharp limits to what the New Deal had achieved. Another was a greater willingness to highlight the conservatism of Roosevelt and the New Dealers. As Mark Leff and Nancy Weiss have shown, the New Deal did not press for either progressive taxation or civil rights legislation for African Americans. Historians studying labor policies have made similar arguments about the New Deal's commitment to granting workers greater control over the workplace.

Another shift has been the efforts of historians to explain the external constraints to more far-reaching reform, constraints that made impossible the changes desired by Bernstein and Conkin. Among the most important of these obstacles was the nature of America's political institutions. The division of power between state governments and the federal government and the decentralized party system over which Roosevelt exercised little control were important roadblocks. So too was the South where conservative opposition by southerners in Congress acted to stymie bolder reform, and building support for an urban-based liberalism rooted in the labor movement and the ethnic working classes was impossible to develop. In a political system that vested large amounts of power with city bosses, reactionary governors, and racist southern congressmen, even modest reform, let alone radical change, was easily thwarted.

More recently, sociologists and political scientists studying the process of "state-building" and state and society relations have emphasized yet another constraint to New Deal reform. Led by Theda Skocpol, they have explored how the prior development of governing institutions, or "state capacity," explains why the New Deal intervened in the way it did and why some programs were more successful than others. A major theme of this work is that the meager scope of the federal government before 1933 acted to impede the New Deal after 1933.

Some historians, meanwhile, have pointed to an even more formidable constraint: the virulent antistatism of America's political culture. Ellis W. Hawley and Barry Karl have argued that twentieth century America has been torn by conflicting desires for the abundance and material progress possible through greater organization and centralization while also yearning for the openness and opportunity of fragmented political power and a small-scale competitive economy. Because these competing value systems were so difficult to reconcile, the New Deal patched over the differences. One example of this patchwork was the New Deal's attack on monopoly, which Hawley described as "a study in economic ambivalence." What emerged from the 1930s, so Karl argued, was not so much a "modern state" as an "uneasy state" shaped by the contradictory quest for planned efficiency and freedom from public and private power.

By emphasizing the New Deal's limits, its conservative aspects, and the constraints it labored to overcome, more recent New Deal scholarship has abandoned the simplistic notions of a New Deal "revolution." At the same time, however, this scholarship suggests the significance of the New Deal's achievement. Faced with the cultural opposition to state-building and a governing system marked by diffused power, what is impressive about the New Deal is not what it failed to bring about but what it in fact managed to accomplish. Out of the turmoil and despair of the 1930s it is easy to imagine a much darker outcome.

This is not to suggest, however, that a new consensus has emerged. Indeed, conflicting views of the New Deal continue to appear. Some scholars argue that business and corporate influence shaped the electoral realignment and the labor policies of the New Deal. Others, however, argue that New Deal policies made possible a more balanced and fairer national economic development. Some argue that women reformers developed a powerful network that was crucial in winning passage of Social Security and other social-welfare policies, but others argue that these same measures marginalized women by further institutionalizing gender barriers. Some contend that the Wagner Act undermined traditions of worker control, while still others argue that the New Deal encouraged a new militancy among workers. And some see Roosevelt poised to launch a "third New Deal" in his second term while others see him pulling away from bolder commitments to restructuring the economy.

The coherence that once characterized historical writing on the New Deal is gone. In its place is a richer, if more confusing, picture, and this volume offers students the opportunity to study at least a part of it. The essays reprinted represent both older and newer work. Part I includes three assessments of Roosevelt and the New Deal. The first is William E. Leuchtenburg's "The Triumph of Liberal Reform," which argues that the New Deal rebuilt American politics and government to create a more humane and democratic society. The New Deal's success, Leuchtenburg believes, was evidence of liberal reform's ability to resolve the nation's social and economic problems. The second is Barton Bernstein's influential "New Left" critique, which challenges Leuchtenburg's conclusions about both the New Deal and liberal reform. Finally, Anthony J. Badger's essay neither laments nor celebrates the New Deal but rather tries to assess its accomplishments, failures, and constraints and to understand why New Deal consequences differed so markedly from New Deal intentions. The New Deal, in his view, is best seen as a "holding operation" that stabilized the economy and made possible the spectacular recovery of World War II.

The selections in Part II discuss New Deal ideas about "state-building" during the 1930s. In his essay, Alan Brinkley argues that following the recession of 1937–1938 and the experience of economic mobilization during World War II, liberal New Dealers changed their ideas about the rightful scope and functions of the federal government. They abandoned trying to reorganize and restructure capitalism and instead sought to create the fiscal tools needed to encourage high rates of economic growth and consumption. What emerged by the end of the war was a liberal doctrine far less critical of industrial capitalism and more content with limited tools of economic management. In the second selection, Ellis Hawley offers a very different explanation of how the New Deal state came to take the shape it did. Hawley stresses the powerful impact of antistatist and "anti-bureaucratic" ideas in shaping the New Deal government. Much of the New Deal, he notes, was designed to create an alternative to centralized regulatory and social-welfare systems. Hence while there was much growth in the size of the federal government during the 1930s, there did not emerge a government with strong planning and managerial capabilities. Instead, at the center of the New Deal state was a "hollow-core."

The pieces included in Part III examine very different sets of New Deal programs and policies. In the first, Mark Leff argues that Roosevelt adopted the highly regressive payroll tax for Social Security because of his conservative views on deficit spending. Pete Daniel explores how New Deal farm policies and rural relief measures affected southern agriculture and encouraged the South's economic transformation. He emphasizes the great disparity in benefits between landowners and tenants and sharecroppers. Jane De Hart examines the arts programs of the Works Progress Administration and how they sought—with mixed results—to democratize American culture.

Recent scholarship has made clear the difficulties of generalizing about the New Deal and its consequences. There were in effect, many New Deals, for these consequences varied by community and region, class and gender, race and ethnic group. Part IV contains four examples of these different experiences. Lizabeth Cohen examines how Chicago's ethnic working class made its "new deal" during the 1930s, and Nancy Weiss examines why African Americans shifted their allegiance to the Democratic Party. Graham Taylor explores the results of the Wheeler-Howard Act of 1934, which began the "Indian New Deal," and Winifred Wandersee reviews the meaning of the New Deal for women.

From these selections emerges no easily summarized analysis. In some Roosevelt appears conservative, in others bold. Some portray New Deal programs as well-intentioned, helpful, and innovative. Others see serious flaws and unfortunate consequences. Workers in Chicago experienced a very different New Deal than did southern black sharecroppers.

Many of the essays also call into question widely held perceptions of Roosevelt and the New Deal. The selection by Mark Leff on the Social Security tax, for instance, hardly conforms to the idea of Roosevelt as a free-spender. Ellis Hawley's essay makes clear that the New Dealers were not uniformly committed to centralized government. Throughout many of the selections, in fact, a recurring theme is the New Deal's desire to develop local administrative systems that would encourage citizen participation. Graham Taylor and Jane De Hart in particular emphasize how the New Deal hoped to strengthen local communities and local self-government. Cohen and Weiss, meanwhile, show how the New Deal encouraged marginalized citizens to participate in American politics.

The coalition of voters who made possible the "New Deal order" has long since fallen apart. The historical debate over the New Deal, however, remains vibrant. What did the New Deal achieve? Was it a "half-way revolution," a protector of corporate capitalism, or a "holding operation"? Did Roosevelt and the New Dealers, by their own conservatism, short-circuit the New Deal? Or were they constrained by the decentralized party system, conservative cultural values, and the minuscule size of the national government in 1933? Did it give workers real economic power or simply entangle them in bureaucratic systems? Did it reinforce the racism and sexism of modern America or did it act as a catalyst for civil rights and greater equality? Did it establish "big government" or a larger government with such limited managerial powers that it had a "hollow core" at its center? Did it make possible a better society after the Great Depression or did it contribute to the problems of more recent decades?

Now, more than a half century after Roosevelt's death, the questions of how and why the New Deal took the shape it did, what its impact was, and what its legacy is remain among the most enduring problems of modern American history. It is these questions that the following essays explore.

Chronology

1932 *July:* Roosevelt won the Democratic Party nomination. *November:* Roosevelt defeated Hoover by winning 57.4 percent of the popular vote and 472 electoral votes to Hoover's 59.

1933 *February:* Attempted assassination of Roosevelt in Miami; start of national banking crisis. *March:* Inauguration, national bank holiday, and Congress called into special session; start of First Hundred Days; Emergency Banking Act; first "fireside chat"; act establishing the Civilian Conservation Corps (CCC); Economy Act. *April:* Act abandoning the gold standard; *May:* Agricultural Adjustment Act created the Agricultural Adjustment Administration (AAA); Emergency Farm Mortgage Act provided for the refinancing of farm mortgages and debts; the Federal Emergency Relief Act established the Federal Emergency Relief Administration (FERA) and a national relief system; Tennessee Valley Authority Act created the Tennessee Valley Authority (TVA). *June:* Home Owners' Loan Act created the Home Owners Loan Corporation (HOLC); National Industrial Recovery Act provided for the creation of the National Recovery Administration (NRA) and the Public Works Administration (PWA); Glass-Steagall Banking Act created the Federal Deposit Insurance Corporation (FDIC). *June–July:* London Economic Conference. *October:* Roosevelt established Civil Works Administration (CWA).

1934 *April:* Bankhead Cotton Control Act. *June:* Securities and Exchange Act created the Securities and Exchange Commission (SEC); Indian Reorganization Act (Wheeler-Howard). *August:* American Liberty League founded. *November:* In the mid-term congressional elections, pro–New Deal Democrats triumphed and Democrats enlarged their margins in both the House and Senate by nine seats. *November:* Father Coughlin formed National Union of Social Justice; Congress passed National Housing Act.

1935   *April:* Emergency Relief Appropriation Act, Resettlement Administration (RA) established. *May:* Rural Electrification Administration (REA) and Works Progress Administration (WPA) established; Supreme Court in *United States* v. *Schechter* decision invalidated the NRA. *July:* Start of Second Hundred Days (July 5–August 30); Wagner National Labor Relations Act created the National Labor Relations Board (NLRB). *August:* Social Security Act; Revenue Act ("Soak the Rich Tax"); Wheeler-Rayburn Public Utility Holding Company Act. *September:* Huey Long assassinated in Louisiana. *October:* Congress of Industrial Organizations (CIO) split with American Federation of Labor (AFL).

1936   *January:* Supreme Court in *United States* v. *Butler* declared the AAA's processing tax unconstitutional. *March:* Soil Conservation and Domestic Allotment Act replaced the Agricultural Adjustment Act. *November:* Roosevelt defeated Kansas governor Alfred M. Landon. Roosevelt carried all but two states and won 60.8 percent of the popular vote. *December:* Start of General Motors' sitdown strike in Flint, Michigan. The strike ended in February of 1937.

1937   *February:* Roosevelt submitted his court reform plan, and the "court packing" fight continued until August. *April:* Supreme Court upheld constitutionality of Wagner Act in *NLRB* v. *Jones & Laughlin Steel Corp. July:* Bankhead-Jones Farm Security Act created the Farm Security Administration (FSA). *August–September:* "Roosevelt Recession" began and lasted until June 1938.

1938   *February:* Second Agricultural Adjustment Act. *June:* Fair Labor Standards Act established minimum wage and maximum hours standards. *June–August:* Roosevelt unsuccessfully tried to "purge" conservative Democrats by seeking their defeat in primary elections. *November:* Republicans and anti–New Deal Democrats made dramatic gains in the congressional elections. The election marked the emergence of a "conservative coalition" in Congress hostile to New Deal liberalism.

1939   *April:* Marian Anderson concert on Easter Sunday, Lincoln Memorial; Reorganization Act of 1939 established the Executive Office of the President. *August:* Major amendments to the Social Security Act. *September:* Start of World War II in Europe when Germany invaded Poland.

1940   *May:* German conquest of France. *July:* FDR nominated for an unprecedented third term with Henry A. Wallace as his vice-presidential running mate. *November:* Roosevelt defeated the maverick industrialist Wendell Willkie with 55 percent of the popular vote.

The New Deal

I

Interpreting Roosevelt
and the New Deal

One reason for Roosevelt's powerful bond with many millions of Americans during the 1930s was the perception that he was a caring, compassionate leader. These qualities, as well as Roosevelt's determination to pursue a life in politics, were strengthened when polio destroyed his leg muscles in 1921. He could stand or take a few painful steps only by wearing heavy steel leg braces and using crutches or canes. Usually Roosevelt moved about in a wheelchair, but news reporters and photographers agreed not to take pictures revealing his crippled condition. This 1941 photograph of Roosevelt was a private photo taken by his cousin. He is with a grandniece and is holding Fala, his Scotch terrier. (Franklin D. Roosevelt Library)

William E. Leuchtenburg

The Triumph of Liberal Reform

William E. Leuchtenburg's *Franklin D. Roosevelt and the New Deal* (1963) is one of the finest and most influential histories of the New Deal. More so than other historians who sympathized with liberal reform, Leuchtenburg explored the New Deal's defects and disappointments, the flaws in its ideas and administration, and its often cautious and conservative actions. More impressive to Leuchtenburg, however, were Roosevelt's and the New Deal's successes. He credited Roosevelt with revitalizing the American presidency and the New Deal with transforming and expanding the responsibilities of the federal government. The result, he argued in his concluding chapter, was a more effective government, a more vigorous democracy, and a political system more attuned to the needs of America's weaker citizens. All told, the changes wrought by the New Deal marked, so Leuchtenburg believed, "a radically new departure" in American life.

William Leuchtenburg is Kenan Professor of History emeritus at the University of North Carolina. His many books include: *In Search of Roosevelt: From Harry Truman to Bill Clinton* (1993); *The Supreme Court Reborn: The Constitutional Revolution in the Age of Roosevelt* (1995); and *The FDR Years: On Roosevelt & His Legacy* (1995).

In eight years, Roosevelt and the New Dealers had almost revolutionized the agenda of American politics. "Mr. Roosevelt may have given the wrong answers to many of his problems," concluded the editors of *The Economist*. "But he is at least the first President of modern America who has asked the right questions." In 1932, men of acumen were absorbed to an astonishing degree with such questions as prohibition, war debts, and law enforcement. By 1936, they were debating social security, the Wagner Act, valley authorities, and public housing. The thirties witnessed a rebirth of issues politics, and parties split more sharply on ideological lines than they had in many years past. "I incline to think that for years up to the present juncture thinking Democrats and thinking

From Chapter 14: "The Roosevelt Reconstruction: Retrospect" from *Franklin D. Roosevelt and the New Deal, 1932–1940* (New American Nation Series) by William E. Leuchtenburg. Copyright © 1963 by William E. Leuchtenburg. Reprinted by permission of HarperCollins Publishers, Inc.

Republicans had been divided by an imaginary line," reflected a Massachusetts congressman in 1934. "Now for the first time since the period before the Civil War we find vital principles at stake." Much of this change resulted simply from the depression trauma, but much too came from the force of Roosevelt's personality and his use of his office as both pulpit and lectern. "Of course you have fallen into some errors—that is human," former Supreme Court Justice John Clarke wrote the President, "but you have put a new face upon the social and political life of our country."

Franklin Roosevelt re-created the modern Presidency. He took an office which had lost much of its prestige and power in the previous twelve years and gave it an importance which went well beyond what even Theodore Roosevelt and Woodrow Wilson had done. Clinton Rossiter has observed: "Only Washington, who made the office, and Jackson, who remade it, did more than [Roosevelt] to raise it to its present condition of strength, dignity, and independence." Under Roosevelt, the White House became the focus of all government—the fountainhead of ideas, the initiator of action, the representative of the national interest.

Roosevelt greatly expanded the President's legislative functions. In the nineteenth century, Congress had been jealous of its prerogatives as the lawmaking body, and resented any encroachment on its domain by the Chief Executive. Woodrow Wilson and Theodore Roosevelt had broken new ground in sending actual drafts of bills to Congress and in using devices like the caucus to win enactment of measures they favored. Franklin Roosevelt made such constant use of these tools that he came to assume a legislative role not unlike that of a prime minister. He sent special messages to Congress, accompanied them with drafts of legislation prepared by his assistants, wrote letters to committee chairmen or members of Congress to urge passage of the proposals, and authorized men like Corcoran to lobby as presidential spokesmen on the Hill. By the end of Roosevelt's tenure in the White House, Congress looked automatically to the Executive for guidance; it expected the administration to have a "program" to present for consideration.

Roosevelt's most important formal contribution was his creation of the Executive Office of the President on September 8, 1939. Executive Order 8248, a "nearly unnoticed but none the less epoch-making event in the history of American institutions," set up an Executive Office staffed with six administrative assistants with a "passion for anonymity." In 1939, the President not only placed obvious agencies like the White House Office in the Executive Office but made the crucial decision to shift the Bureau of the Budget from the Treasury and put it under his wing. In later years, such pivotal agencies as the Council of Economic Advisers, the National Security Council, and the Central Intelligence Agency would be moved into the Executive Office of the President. Roosevelt's decision, Rossiter has concluded, "converts the Presidency into an instrument of twentieth-century government; it gives the incumbent a sporting chance to stand the strain and fulfill his constitutional mandate as a one-man branch of our three-part government; it deflates even the most forceful arguments, which are still raised occasionally, for a plural executive; it assures us that the Presidency will survive the advent of the positive state. Executive Order 8248 may yet be judged to have saved the Presidency from paralysis and the Constitution from radical amendment."

Roosevelt's friends have been too quick to concede that he was a poor administrator. To be sure, he found it difficult to discharge incompetent aides, he procrastinated about decisions, and he ignored all the canons of sound administration by giving men overlapping assignments and creating a myriad of agencies which had no clear relation to the regular departments of government. But if the test of good administration is not an impeccable organizational chart but creativity, then Roosevelt must be set down not merely as a good administrator but as a resourceful innovator. The new agencies he set up gave a spirit of excitement to Washington that the routinized old-line departments could never have achieved. The President's refusal to proceed through channels, however vexing at times to his subordinates, resulted in a competition not only among men but among ideas, and encouraged men to feel that their own beliefs might win the day. "You would be surprised, Colonel, the remarkable ideas that have been turned loose just because men have felt that they can get a hearing," one senator confided. The President's "procrastination" was his own way both of arriving at a sense of national consensus and of reaching a decision by observing a trial by combat among rival theories. Periods of indecision—as in the spring of 1935 or the beginning of 1938— were inevitably followed by a fresh outburst of new proposals.

Most of all, Roosevelt was a successful administrator because he attracted to Washington thousands of devoted and highly skilled men. Men who had been fighting for years for lost causes were given a chance: John Collier, whom the President courageously named Indian Commissioner; Arthur Powell Davis, who had been ousted as chief engineer of the Department of the Interior at the demand of power interests; old conservationists like Harry Slattery, who had fought the naval oil interests in the Harding era. When Harold Ickes took office as Secretary of the Interior, he looked up Louis Glavis—he did not even know whether the "martyr" of the Ballinger-Pinchot affair was still alive—and appointed him to his staff.

The New Dealers displayed striking ingenuity in meeting problems of governing. They coaxed salmon to climb ladders at Bonneville; they sponsored a Young Choreographers Laboratory in the WPA's Dance Theatre; they gave the pioneer documentary film maker Pare Lorentz the opportunity to create his classic films *The Plow That Broke the Plains* and *The River.* At the Composers Forum-Laboratory of the Federal Music Project, William Schuman received his first serious hearing. In Arizona, Father Berard Haile of St. Michael's Mission taught written Navajo to the Indians. Roosevelt, in the face of derision from professional foresters and prairie states' governors, persisted in a bold scheme to plant a mammoth "shelterbelt" of parallel rows of trees from the Dakotas to the Panhandle. In all, more than two hundred million trees were planted—cottonwood and willow, hackberry and cedar, Russian olive and Osage orange; within six years, the President's visionary windbreak had won over his former critics. The spirit behind such innovations generated a new excitement about the potentialities of government. "Once again," Roosevelt told a group of young Democrats in April, 1936, "the very air of America is exhilarating."

Roosevelt dominated the front pages of the newspapers as no other President before or since has done. "Frank Roosevelt and the NRA have taken the place of love nests," commented Joe Patterson, publisher of the tabloid New York *Daily News.* At his very first press conference, Roosevelt abolished the written question and told reporters they could interrogate him without warning. Skeptics predicted the free and easy exchange would soon be abandoned, but twice a week, year in and year out, he threw open the White House doors to as many as two hundred reporters, most of them representing hostile publishers, who would crowd right up to the President's desk to fire their questions. The President joshed them, traded wisecracks with them, called them by their first names; he charmed them by his good-humored ease and impressed them with his knowledge of detail. To a degree, Roosevelt's press conference introduced, as some observers claimed, a new institution like Britain's parliamentary questioning; more to the point, it was a device the President manipulated, disarmingly and adroitly, to win support for his program. It served too as a classroom to instruct the country in the new economics and the new politics.

Roosevelt was the first president to master the technique of reaching people directly over the radio. In his fireside chats, he talked like a father discussing public affairs with his family in the living room. As he spoke, he seemed unconscious of the fact that he was addressing millions. "His head would nod and his hands would move in simple, natural, comfortable gestures," Frances Perkins recalled. "His face would smile and light up as though he were actually sitting on the front porch or in the parlor with them." Eleanor Roosevelt later observed that after the President's death people would stop her on the street to say "they missed the way the President used to talk to them. They'd say 'He used to talk to me about my government.' There was a real dialogue between Franklin and the people," she reflected. "That dialogue seems to have disappeared from the government since he died."

For the first time for many Americans, the federal government became an institution that was directly experienced. More than state and local governments, it came to be *the* government, an agency directly concerned with their welfare. It was the source of their relief payments; it taxed them directly for old age pensions; it even gave their children hot lunches in school. As the role of the state changed from that of neutral arbiter to a "powerful promoter of society's welfare," people felt an interest in affairs in Washington they had never had before.

Franklin Roosevelt personified the state as protector. It became commonplace to say that people felt toward the President the kind of trust they would normally express for a warm and understanding father who comforted them in their grief or safeguarded them from harm. An insurance man reported: "My mother looks upon the President as someone so immediately concerned with her problems and difficulties that she would not be greatly surprised were he to come to her house some evening and stay to dinner." From his first hours in office, Roosevelt gave people the feeling that they could confide in him directly. As late as the Presidency of Herbert Hoover, one man, Ira Smith, had sufficed to take care of all the mail the White House received. Under Roosevelt, Smith had to acquire a staff of fifty people to handle the thousands of letters written to the President each week. Roosevelt gave people a sense of membership in the national community. Justice Douglas has written: "He was in a very special sense the people's President, because he made them feel that with him in the White House they shared the Presidency. The sense of sharing the Presidency gave even the most humble citizen a lively sense of belonging."

When Roosevelt took office, the country, to a very large degree, responded to the will of a single element: the white, Anglo-Saxon, Protestant property-holding class. Under the New Deal, new groups took their place in the sun. It was not merely that they received benefits they had not had before but that they were "recognized" as having a place in the commonwealth. At the beginning of the Roosevelt era, charity organizations ignored labor when seeking "community" representation; at the end of the period, no fund-raising committee was complete without a union representative. While Theodore Roosevelt had founded a lily-white Progressive party in the South and Woodrow Wilson had introduced segregation into the federal government, Franklin Roosevelt had quietly brought the Negro into the New Deal coalition. When the distinguished Negro contralto Marian Anderson was denied a concert hall in Washington, Secretary Ickes arranged for her to perform from the steps of Lincoln Memorial. Equal representation for religious groups became so well accepted that, as one priest wryly complained, one never saw a picture of a priest in a newspaper unless he was flanked on either side by a minister and a rabbi.

The devotion Roosevelt aroused owed much to the fact that the New Deal assumed the responsibility for guaranteeing every American a minimum standard of subsistence. Its relief programs represented an advance over the barbaric predepression practices that constituted a difference not in degree but in kind. One analyst wrote: "During the ten years between 1929 and 1939 more progress was made in public welfare and relief than in the three hundred years after this country was first settled." The Roosevelt administration gave such assistance not as a matter of charity but of right. This system of social rights was written into the Social Security Act. Other New Deal legislation abolished child labor in interstate commerce and, by putting a floor under wages and a ceiling on hours, all but wiped out the sweatshop.

Roosevelt and his aides fashioned a government which consciously sought to make the industrial system more humane and to protect workers and their families from exploitation. In his acceptance speech in June, 1936, the President stated: "Governments can err, Presidents do make mistakes, but the immortal Dante tells us that divine justice weighs the sins of the cold-blooded and the sins of the warm-hearted in different scales.

"Better the occasional faults of a Government that lives in a spirit of charity than the constant omission of a Government frozen in the ice of its own indifference.". . .

The federal government expanded enormously in the Roosevelt years. The crisis of the depression dissipated the distrust of the state inherited from the eighteenth century and reinforced in diverse ways by the Jeffersonians and the Spencerians. Roosevelt himself believed that liberty in America was imperiled more by the agglomerations of private business than by the state. The New Dealers were convinced that the depression was the result not simply of an economic breakdown but of a political collapse; hence, they sought new political instrumentalities. The reformers of the 1930's accepted almost unquestioningly the use of coercion by the state to achieve reforms. Even Republicans who protested that Roosevelt's policies were snuffing out liberty voted overwhelmingly in favor of coercive measures.

This elephantine growth of the federal government owed much to the fact that local and state governments had been tried in the crisis and found wanting. When one magazine wired state governors to ask their views, only one of the thirty-seven who replied announced that he was willing to have the states resume responsibility for relief. Every time there was a rumored cutback of federal spending for relief, Washington was besieged by delegations of mayors protesting that city governments did not have the resources to meet the needs of the unemployed. . . .

Under the New Deal, the federal government greatly extended its power over the economy. By the end of the Roosevelt years, few questioned the right of the government to pay the farmer millions in subsidies not to grow crops, to enter plants to conduct union elections, to regulate business enterprises from utility companies to air lines, or even to compete directly with business by

generating and distributing hydroelectric power. All of these powers had been ratified by the Supreme Court, which had even held
that a man growing grain solely for his own use was affecting interstate commerce and hence subject to federal penalties. The President, too, was well on his way to becoming "the chief economic
engineer," although this was not finally established until the Full
Employment Act of 1946. In 1931, Hoover had hooted that some
people thought "that by some legerdemain we can legislate our-
selves out of a world-wide depression." In the Roosevelt era, the
conviction that government both should and could act to forestall
future breakdowns gained general acceptance. The New Deal left a
large legacy of antidepression controls—securities regulation, banking reforms, unemployment compensation—even if it could not
guarantee that a subsequent administration would use them.

In the 1930's, the financial center of the nation shifted from
Wall Street to Washington. In May, 1934, a writer reported:
"Financial news no longer originates in Wall Street." That same
month, *Fortune* commented on a revolution in the credit system
which was "one of the major historical events of the generation."
"Mr. Roosevelt," it noted, "seized the Federal Reserve without fir-
ing a shot." The federal government had not only broken down
the old separation of bank and state in the Reserve system but had
gone into the credit business itself in a wholesale fashion under the
aegis of the RFC, the Farm Credit Administration, and the housing agencies. Legislation in 1933 and 1934 had established federal
regulation of Wall Street for the first time. No longer could the
New York Stock Exchange operate as a private club free of national
supervision. In 1935, Congress leveled the mammoth holding-
company pyramids and centralized yet more authority over the
banking system in the federal government. . . .

Despite this encroachment of government on traditional business prerogatives, the New Deal could advance impressive claims to
being regarded as a "savior of capitalism." Roosevelt's sense of the
land, of family, and of the community marked him as a man with
deeply ingrained conservative traits. In the New Deal years, the
government sought deliberately, in Roosevelt's words, "to energize
private enterprise." The RFC financed business, housing agencies
underwrote home financing, and public works spending aimed to
revive the construction industry. Moreover, some of the New Deal

reforms were Janus-faced. The NYA, in aiding jobless youth, also served as a safety valve to keep young people out of the labor market. A New Deal congressman, in pushing for public power projects, argued that the country should take advantage of the sea of "cheap labor" on the relief rolls. Even the Wagner Act and the movement for industrial unionism were motivated in part by the desire to contain "unbalanced and radical" labor groups. Yet such considerations should not obscure the more important point: that the New Deal, however conservative it was in some respects and however much it owed to the past, marked a radically new departure. As Carl Degler writes: "The conclusion seems inescapable that, traditional as the words may have been in which the New Deal expressed itself, in actuality it was a revolutionary response to a revolutionary situation."

Not all of the changes that were wrought were the result of Roosevelt's own actions or of those of his government. Much of the force for change came from progressives in Congress, or from nongovernmental groups like the C.I.O., or simply from the impersonal agency of the depression itself. Yet, however much significance one assigns the "objective situation," it is difficult to gainsay the importance of Roosevelt. If, in Miami in February, 1933, an assassin's bullet had been true to its mark and John Garner rather than Roosevelt had entered the White House the next month, or if the Roosevelt lines had cracked at the Democratic convention in 1932 and Newton Baker had been the compromise choice, the history of America in the thirties would have been markedly different.

At a time when democracy was under attack elsewhere in the world, the achievements of the New Deal were especially significant. At the end of 1933, in an open letter to President Roosevelt, John Maynard Keynes had written: "You have made yourself the trustee for those in every country who seek to mend the evils of our condition by reasoned experiment within the framework of the existing social system. If you fail, rational change will be gravely prejudiced throughout the world, leaving orthodoxy and revolution to fight it out." In the next few years, teams of foreigners toured the TVA, Russians and Arabs came to study the shelterbelt, French writers taxed Léon Blum with importing "Rooseveltism" to France, and analysts characterized Paul Van Zeeland's program in Belgium as a "New Deal." Under Roosevelt, observed a Montevideo newspaper, the United States had become "as it was in the eighteenth century, the victorious emblem around which may rally the multitudes thirsting for social justice and human fraternity."

In their approach to reform, the New Dealers reflected the tough-minded, hard-boiled attitude that permeated much of America in the thirties. In 1931, the gangster film *Public Enemy* had given the country a new kind of hero in James Cagney: the aggressive, unsentimental tough guy who deliberately assaulted the romantic tradition. It was a type whose role in society could easily be manipulated; gangster hero Cagney of the early thirties was transformed into G-man hero Cagney of the later thirties. Even more representative was Humphrey Bogart, creator of the "private eye" hero, the man of action who masks his feelings in a calculated emotional neutrality. Bogart, who began as the cold desperado Duke Mantee of *Petrified Forest* and the frightening Black Legionnaire, soon turned up on the right side of anti-Fascist causes, although he never surrendered the pose of noninvolvement. This fear of open emotional commitment and this admiration of toughness ran through the vogue of the "Dead End Kids," films like *Nothing Sacred,* the popularity of the St. Louis Cardinals' spike-flying Gas House Gang, and the "hardboiled" fiction of writers like James Cain and Dashiell Hammett.

Unlike the earlier Progressive, the New Dealer shied away from being thought of as sentimental. Instead of justifying relief as a humanitarian measure, the New Dealers often insisted it was necessary to stimulate purchasing power or to stabilize the economy or to "conserve manpower." The justification for a better distribution of income was neither "social justice" nor a "healthier national life," wrote Adolf Berle. "It remained for the hard-boiled student to work out the simple equation that unless the national income was pretty widely diffused there were not enough customers to keep the plants going." The reformers of the thirties abandoned— or claimed they had abandoned—the old Emersonian hope of reforming man and sought only to change institutions. This meant that they did not seek to "uplift" the people they were helping but only to improve their economic position. "In other words," Tugwell stated bluntly, "the New Deal is attempting to do nothing to *people,* and does not seek at all to alter their way of life, their wants and desires."

Reform in the 1930's meant *economic* reform; it departed from the Methodist-parsonage morality of many of the earlier Progressives, in part because much of the New Deal support, and many of its leaders, derived from urban immigrant groups hostile to the old Sabbatarianism. While the progressive grieved over the fate of the prostitute, the New Dealer would have placed Mrs. Warren's profession under a code authority. If the archetypical progressive was Jane Addams singing "Onward, Christian Soldiers," the representative New Dealer was Harry Hopkins betting on the horses at Laurel Race Track. When directing FERA in late 1933, Hopkins announced: "I would like to provide orchestras for beer gardens to encourage people to sit around drinking their beer and enjoying themselves. It would be a great unemployment relief measure." "I feel no call to remedy evils," Raymond Moley declared. "I have not the slightest urge to be a reformer. Social workers make me very weary. They have no sense of humor."

Despite Moley's disclaimer, many of the early New Dealers like himself and Adolf Berle did, in fact, hope to achieve reform through regeneration: the regeneration of the businessman. By the end of 1935, the New Dealers were pursuing a quite different course. Instead of attempting to evangelize the Right, they mobilized massive political power against the power of the corporation. They relied not on converting industrial sinners but in using sufficient coercion. New Dealers like Thurman Arnold sought to ignore "moral" considerations altogether; Arnold wished not to punish wrongdoers but to achieve price flexibility. His "faith" lay in the expectation that "fanatical alignments between opposing political principles may disappear and a competent, practical, opportunistic governing class may rise to power." With such expectations, the New Dealers frequently had little patience with legal restraints that impeded action. "I want to assure you," Hopkins told the NYA Advisory Committee, "that we are not afraid of exploring anything within the law, and we have a lawyer who will declare anything you want to do legal."

In the thirties, nineteenth-century individualism gave ground to a new emphasis on social security and collective action. In the twenties, America hailed Lindbergh as the Lone Eagle; in the thirties, when word arrived that Amelia Earhart was lost at sea, the *New Republic* asked the government to prohibit citizens from engaging in such "useless" exploits. The NRA sought to drive newsboys off the streets and took a Blue Eagle away from a company in Huck Finn's old town of Hannibal, Missouri, because a fifteen-year-old was found driving a truck for his father's business. Josef Hofmann urged that fewer musicians become soloists, Hollywood stars like Joan Crawford joined the Screen Actors Guild, and Leopold Stokowski canceled a performance in Pittsburgh because theater proprietors were violating a union contract. In New York in 1933, after a series of meetings in Heywood Broun's penthouse apartment, newspapermen organized the American Newspaper Guild in rebellion against the disspiriting romanticism of Richard Harding Davis. "We no longer care to develop the individual as a unique contributor to a democratic form," wrote the mordant Edgar Kemler. "In this movement each individual sub-man is important, not for his uniqueness, but for his ability to lose himself in the mass, through his fidelity to the trade union, or cooperative organization, or political party.". . .

Commentators on the New Deal have frequently characterized it by that much-abused term "pragmatic." If one means by this that the New Dealers carefully tested the consequences of ideas, the term is clearly a misnomer. If one means that Roosevelt was exceptionally anti-ideological in his approach to politics, one may question whether he was, in fact, any more "pragmatic" in this sense than Van Buren or Polk or even "reform" Presidents like Jackson and Theodore Roosevelt. The "pragmatism" of the New Deal seemed remarkable only in a decade tortured by ideology, only in contrast to the rigidity of Hoover and of the Left.

The New Deal was pragmatic mainly in its skepticism about utopias and final solutions, its openness to experimentation, and its suspicion of the dogmas of the Establishment. Since the advice of economists had so often been wrong, the New Dealers distrusted the claims of orthodox theory—"All this is perfectly terrible because it is all pure theory, when you come down to it," the President said on one occasion—and they felt free to try new approaches. Roosevelt refused to be awed by the warnings of economists and financial experts that government interference with the "laws" of the economy was blasphemous. "We must lay hold of the fact that economic laws are not made by nature," the President stated, "They are made by human beings." The New Dealers denied that depressions were inevitable events that had to be borne stoically, most of the stoicism to be displayed by the most impoverished, and they were willing to explore novel ways to make the social order more stable and more humane. "I am for experimenting . . . in various parts of the country, trying out schemes which are supported by reasonable people and see if they work," Hopkins told a conference of social workers. "If they do not work, the world will not come to an end."

Hardheaded, "anti-utopian," the New Dealers nonetheless had their Heavenly City: the greenbelt town, clean, green, and white, with children playing in light, airy, spacious schools; the government project at Longview, Washington, with small houses, each of different design, colored roofs, and gardens of flowers and vegetables; the Mormon villages of Utah that M. L. Wilson kept in his mind's eye—immaculate farmsteads on broad, rectangular streets; most of all, the Tennessee Valley, with its model town of Norris, the tall transmission towers, the white dams, the glistening wire strands, the valley where "a vision of villages and clean small factories has been growing into the minds of thoughtful men." Scandinavia was their model abroad, not only because it summoned up images of the countryside of Denmark, the beauties of Stockholm, not only for its experience with labor relations and social insurance and currency reform, but because it represented the "middle way" of happy accommodation of public and private institutions the New Deal sought to achieve. "Why," inquired Brandeis, "should anyone want to go to Russia when one can go to Denmark?"

Yet the New Deal added up to more than all of this—more than an experimental approach, more than the sum of its legislative achievements, more than an antiseptic utopia. It is true that there was a certain erosion of values in the thirties, as well as a narrowing of horizons, but the New Dealers inwardly recognized that what they were doing had a deeply moral significance however much they eschewed ethical pretensions. Heirs of the Enlightenment, they felt themselves part of a broadly humanistic movement to make man's life on earth more tolerable, a movement that might someday even achieve a co-operative commonwealth. Social insurance, Frances Perkins declared, was "a fundamental part of another great forward step in that liberation of humanity which began with the Renaissance."

Franklin Roosevelt did not always have this sense as keenly as some of the men around him, but his greatness as a President lies in the remarkable degree to which he shared the vision. "The new deal business to me is very much bigger than anyone yet has expressed it," observed Senator Elbert Thomas. Roosevelt "seems to really have caught the spirit of what one of the Hebrew prophets called the desire of the nations. If he were in India today they would probably decide that he had become Mahatma—that is, one in tune with the infinite." Both foes and friends made much of Roosevelt's skill as a political manipulator, and there is no doubt that up to a point he delighted in schemes and strategems. As Donald Richberg later observed: "There would be times when he seemed to be a Chevalier Bayard, *sans peur et sans reproche,* and times in which he would seem to be the apotheosis of a prince who had absorbed and practiced all the teachings of Machiavelli." Yet essentially he was a moralist who wanted to achieve certain humane reforms and instruct the nation in the principles of government. On one occasion, he remarked: "I want to be a *preaching President*—like my cousin." His courtiers gleefully recounted his adroitness in trading and dealing for votes, his effectiveness on the stump, his wicked skill in cutting corners to win a point. But Roosevelt's importance lay not in his talents as a campaigner or a manipulator. It lay rather in his ability to arouse the country and, more specifically, the men who served under him, by his breezy encouragement of experimentation, by his hopefulness, and—a word that would have embarrassed some of his lieutenants—by his idealism.

The New Deal left many problems unsolved and even created some perplexing new ones. It never demonstrated that it could achieve prosperity in peacetime. As late as 1941, the unemployed still numbered six million, and not until the war year of 1943 did the army of the jobless finally disappear. It enhanced the power of interest groups who claimed to speak for millions, but sometimes represented only a small minority. It did not evolve a way to protect people who had no such spokesmen, nor an acceptable method for disciplining the interest groups. In 1946, President Truman would resort to a threat to draft railway workers into the Army to avert a strike. The New Deal achieved a more just society by recognizing groups which had been largely unrepresented—staple farmers, industrial workers, particular ethnic groups, and the new intellectual-administrative class. Yet this was still a halfway revolution; it swelled the ranks of the bourgeoisie but left many Americans—share-croppers, slum dwellers, most Negroes—outside of the new equilibrium.

Some of these omissions were to be promptly remedied. Subsequent Congresses extended social security, authorized slum clearance projects, and raised minimum-wage standards to keep step with the rising price level. Other shortcomings are understandable. The havoc that had been done before Roosevelt took office was so great that even the unprecedented measures of the New Deal did not suffice to repair the damage. Moreover, much was still to be learned, and it was in the Roosevelt years that the country was schooled in how to avert another major depression. Although it was war which freed the government from the taboos of a balanced budget and revealed the potentialities of spending, it is conceivable that New Deal measures would have led the country into a new cycle of prosperity even if there had been no war. Marked gains had been made before the war spending had any appreciable effect. When recovery did come, it was much more soundly based because of the adoption of the New Deal program.

Roosevelt and the New Dealers understood, perhaps better than their critics, that they had come only part of the way. Henry Wallace remarked: "We are children of the transition—we have left Egypt but we have not yet arrived at the Promised Land." Only five years separated Roosevelt's inauguration in 1933 and the adoption of the last of the New Deal measures, the Fair Labor Standards Act, in 1938. The New Dealers perceived that they had done more in those years than had been done in any comparable period in American history, but they also saw that there was much still to be done, much, too, that continued to baffle them. "I believe in the things that have been done," Mrs. Roosevelt told the American Youth Congress in February, 1939. "They helped but they did not solve the fundamental problems. . . . I never believed the Federal government could solve the whole problem. It bought us time to think." She closed not with a solution but with a challenge: "Is it going to be worth while?"

"This generation of Americans is living in a tremendous moment of history," President Roosevelt stated in his final national address of the 1940 campaign.

"The surge of events abroad has made some few doubters among us ask: Is this the end of a story that has been told? Is the book of democracy now to be closed and placed away upon the dusty shelves of time?

"My answer is this: All we have known of the glories of democracy—its freedom, its efficiency as a mode of living, its ability to meet the aspirations of the common man—all these are merely an introduction to the greater story of a more glorious future.

"We Americans of today—all of us—we are characters in the living book of democracy.

"But we are also its author. It falls upon us now to say whether the chapters that are to come will tell a story of retreat or a story of continued advance."

Barton J. Bernstein

The Conservative Achievement of New Deal Reform

From the 1940s to the 1960s, most historians who wrote about the New Deal saw it as a major burst of reform that had modernized American government, strengthened the economy, and democratized society. In the 1960s, however, historians dissatisfied with what they saw as the hollow promises of postwar liberalism began to subject the New Deal to more critical analysis.

The essay that follows is perhaps the best known and most influential of what became known as the New Left critique of the New Deal. Taking issue with the basic assumptions of earlier scholarship, Barton Bernstein contends that Roosevelt and the New Dealers were fundamentally conservative—"doctrinaires of the center"—who acted to stymie the public's desire for bolder changes in the economic and political systems. The New Deal, he argues, achieved no recovery, thwarted truly radical ideas, bowed to racism, and won a popular following with seductive rhetoric, not substantial change. Far from a "halfway revolution"—let alone a "third American Revolution"—its "achievement" was to conserve undemocratic and unequal class relations and systems of corporate power.

Barton J. Bernstein is professor of history at Stanford University. He has written many articles and essays on twentieth century American his-

From *Towards a New Past* by Barton J. Bernstein, editor. Copyright © 1968 by Random House, Inc. Reprinted by permission of Pantheon Books, a division of Random House, Inc.

tory and edited *Towards a New Past: Dissenting Essays in American History* (1968) and *The Atomic Bomb: The Critical Issues* (1976).

Writing from a liberal democratic consensus, many American historians in the past two decades have praised the Roosevelt administration for its nonideological flexibility and for its far-ranging reforms. To many historians, particularly those who reached intellectual maturity during the depression, the government's accomplishments, as well as the drama and passion, marked the decade as a watershed, as a dividing line in the American past.

Enamored of Franklin D. Roosevelt and recalling the bitter opposition to welfare measures and restraints upon business, many liberal historians have emphasized the New Deal's discontinuity with the immediate past. For them there was a "Roosevelt Revolution," or at the very least a dramatic achievement of a beneficent liberalism which had developed in fits and spurts during the preceding three decades. Rejecting earlier interpretations which viewed the New Deal as socialism or state capitalism, they have also disregarded theories of syndicalism or of corporate liberalism. The New Deal has generally commanded their approval for such laws or institutions as minimum wages, public housing, farm assistance, the Tennessee Valley Authority, the Wagner Act, more progressive taxation, and social security. For most liberal historians the New Deal meant the replenishment of democracy, the rescuing of the federal government from the clutches of big business, the significant redistribution of political power. Breaking with laissez faire, the new administration, according to these interpretations, marked the end of the passive or impartial state and the beginning of positive government, of the interventionist state acting to offset concentrations of private power, and affirming the rights and responding to the needs of the unprivileged.

From the perspective of the late 1960s these themes no longer seem adequate to characterize the New Deal. The liberal reforms of the New Deal did not transform the American system; they conserved and protected American corporate capitalism, occasionally by absorbing parts of threatening programs. There was no significant redistribution of power in American society, only limited recognition of other organized groups, seldom of unorganized peoples. Neither the bolder programs advanced by New

Dealers nor the final legislation greatly extended the beneficence of government beyond the middle classes or drew upon the wealth of the few for the needs of the many. Designed to maintain the American system, liberal activity was directed toward essentially conservative goals. Experimentalism was most frequently limited to means; seldom did it extend to ends. Never questioning private enterprise, it operated within safe channels, far short of Marxism or even of native American radicalisms that offered structural critiques and structural solutions.

All of this is not to deny the changes wrought by the New Deal—the extension of welfare programs, the growth of federal power, the strengthening of the executive, even the narrowing of property rights. But it is to assert that the elements of continuity are stronger, that the magnitude of change has been exaggerated. The New Deal failed to solve the problem of depression, it failed to raise the impoverished, it failed to redistribute income, it failed to extend equality and generally countenanced racial discrimination and segregation. It failed generally to make business more responsible to the social welfare or to threaten business's pre-eminent political power. In this sense, the New Deal, despite the shifts in tone and spirit from the earlier decade, was profoundly conservative and continuous with the 1920s.

I

Rather than understanding the 1920s as a "return to normalcy," the period is more properly interpreted by focusing on the continuation of progressive impulses, demands often frustrated by the rivalry of interest groups, sometimes blocked by the resistance of Harding and Coolidge, and occasionally by Hoover. Through these years while agriculture and labor struggled to secure advantages from the federal government, big business flourished. Praised for creating American prosperity, business leaders easily convinced the nation that they were socially responsible, that they were fulfilling the needs of the public. Benefitting from earlier legislation that had promoted economic rationalization and stability, they were opponents of federal benefits to other groups but seldom proponents of laissez faire.

In no way did the election of Herbert Hoover in 1928 seem to challenge the New Era. An heir of Wilson, Hoover promised an even closer relationship with big business and moved beyond Harding and Coolidge by affirming federal responsibility for prosperity. As Secretary of Commerce, Hoover had opposed unbridled competition and had transformed his department into a vigorous friend of business. Sponsoring trade associations, he promoted industrial self-regulation and the increased rationalization of business. He had also expanded foreign trade, endorsed the regulation of new forms of communications, encouraged relief in disasters, and recommended public works to offset economic declines.

By training and experience, few men in American political life seemed better prepared than Hoover to cope with the depression. Responding promptly to the crisis, he acted to stabilize the economy and secured the agreement of businessmen to maintain production and wage rates. Unwilling to let the economy "go through the wringer," the President requested easier money, self-liquidating public works, lower personal and corporate income taxes, and stronger commodity stabilization corporations. In reviewing these unprecedented actions, Walter Lippmann wrote, "The national government undertook to make the whole economic order operate prosperously."

But these efforts proved inadequate. The tax cut benefitted the wealthy and failed to raise effective demand. The public works were insufficient. The commodity stabilization corporations soon ran out of funds, and agricultural prices kept plummeting. Businessmen cut back production, dismissed employees, and finally cut wages. As unemployment grew, Hoover struggled to inspire confidence, but his words seemed hollow and his understanding of the depression limited. Blaming the collapse on European failures, he could not admit that American capitalism had failed. When prodded by Congress to increase public works, to provide direct relief, and to further unbalance the budget, he doggedly resisted. Additional deficits would destroy business confidence, he feared, and relief would erode the principles of individual and local responsibility. Clinging to faith in voluntarism, Hoover also briefly rebuffed the efforts by financiers to secure the Reconstruction Finance Corporation (RFC). Finally endorsing the RFC, he also supported expanded lending by Federal Land Banks, recommended home-loan banks, and even approved small federal loans (usually inadequate) to states needing funds for relief. In this burst of activity, the President had moved to the very limits of his ideology.

Restricted by his progressive background and insensitive to politics and public opinion, he stopped far short of the state corporatism urged by some businessmen and politicians. With capitalism crumbling he had acted vigorously to save it, but he would not yield to the representatives of business or disadvantaged groups who wished to alter the government. He was reluctant to use the federal power to achieve through compulsion what could not be realized through voluntary means. Proclaiming a false independence, he did not understand that his government already represented business interests; hence, he rejected policies that would openly place the power of the state in the hands of business or that would permit the formation of a syndicalist state. . . .

Even though constitutional scruples restricted his efforts, Hoover did more than any previous American president to combat depression. He "abandoned the principles of laissez faire in relation to the business cycle, established the conviction that prosperity and depression can be publicly controlled by political action, and drove out of the public consciousness the old idea that depressions must be overcome by private adjustment," wrote Walter Lippmann. Rather than the last of the old presidents, Herbert Hoover was the first of the new.

II

A charismatic leader and a brilliant politician, his successor expanded federal activities on the basis of Hoover's efforts. Using the federal government to stabilize the economy and advance the interests of the groups, Franklin D. Roosevelt directed the campaign to save large-scale corporate capitalism. Though recognizing new political interests and extending benefits to them, his New Deal never effectively challenged big business or the organization of the economy. In providing assistance to the needy and by rescuing them from starvation, Roosevelt's humane efforts also protected the established system: he sapped organized radicalism of its waning strength and of its potential constituency among the unorganized and discontented. Sensitive to public opinion and fearful of radicalism, Roosevelt acted from a mixture of motives that rendered his liberalism cautious and limited, his experimentalism narrow. Despite the flurry of activity, his government was more vigorous and flexible about means than goals, and the goals were more conservative than historians usually acknowledge.

Roosevelt's response to the banking crisis emphasizes the conservatism of his administration and its self-conscious avoidance of more radical means that might have transformed American capitalism. Entering the White House when banks were failing and Americans had lost faith in the financial system, the President could have nationalized it—"without a word of protest," judged Senator Bronson Cutting. "If ever there was a moment when things hung in the balance," later wrote Raymond Moley, a member of the original "brain trust," "it was on March 5, 1933—when unorthodoxy would have drained the last remaining strength of the capitalistic system." To save the system, Roosevelt relied upon collaboration between bankers and Hoover's Treasury officials to prepare legislation extending federal assistance to banking. So great was the demand for action that House members, voting even without copies, passed it unanimously, and the Senate, despite objections by a few Progressives, approved it the same evening. "The President," remarked a cynical congressman, "drove the money-changers out of the Capitol on March 4th—and they were all back on the 9th."

Undoubtedly the most dramatic example of Roosevelt's early conservative approach to recovery was the National Recovery Administration (NRA). It was based on the War Industries Board (WIB) which had provided the model for the campaign of Bernard Baruch, General Hugh Johnson, and other former WIB officials during the twenties to limit competition through industrial self-regulation under federal sanction. As trade associations flourished during the decade, the FTC encouraged "codes of fair competition" and some industries even tried to set prices and restrict production. Operating without the force of law, these agreements broke down. When the depression struck, industrial pleas for regulation increased. After the Great Crash, important business leaders including Henry I. Harriman of the Chamber of Commerce and Gerard Swope of General Electric called for suspension of antitrust laws and federal organization of business collaboration. Joining them were labor leaders, particularly those in "sick" industries—John L. Lewis of the United Mine Workers and Sidney Hillman of Amalgamated Clothing Workers.

Designed largely for industrial recovery, the NRA legislation provided for minimum wages and maximum hours. It also made concessions to pro-labor congressmen and labor leaders who demanded some specific benefits for unions—recognition of the worker's right to organization and to collective bargaining. In practice, though, the much-heralded Section 7a was a disappointment to most friends of labor. (For the shrewd Lewis, however, it became a mandate to organize: "The President wants you to join a union.") To many frustrated workers and their disgusted leaders, NRA became "National Run Around." The clause, unionists found (in the words of Brookings economists), "had the practical effect of placing NRA on the side of anti-union employers in their struggle against trade unions. . . . [It] thus threw its weight against labor in the balance of bargaining power." And while some far-sighted industrialists feared radicalism and hoped to forestall it by incorporating unions into the economic system, most preferred to leave their workers unorganized or in company unions. To many businessmen, large and independent unions as such seemed a radical threat to the system of business control.

Not only did the NRA provide fewer advantages than unionists had anticipated, but it also failed as a recovery measure. It probably even retarded recovery by supporting restrictionism and price increases. . . . Placing effective power for code-writing in big business, NRA injured small businesses and contributed to the concentration of American industry. It was not the government-business partnership as envisaged by Adolf A. Berle, Jr., nor government managed as Rexford Tugwell had hoped, but rather, business managed, as Raymond Moley had desired. Calling NRA "industrial self-government," its director, General Hugh Johnson, had explained that "NRA is exactly what industry organized in trade associations makes it." Despite the annoyance of some big businessmen with Section 7a, the NRA reaffirmed and consolidated their power at a time when the public was critical of industrialists and financiers.

III

Viewing the economy as a "concert of organized interests," the New Deal also provided benefits for farmers—the Agricultural Adjustment Act. Reflecting the political power of larger commercial farmers and accepting restrictionist economics, the measure assumed that the agricultural problem was overproduction, not underconsumption. Financed by a processing tax designed to raise prices to parity, payments encouraged restricted production and cutbacks in farm labor. With benefits accruing chiefly to the larger owners, they frequently removed from production the lands of share-croppers and tenant farmers, and "tractored" them and hired hands off the land. In assisting agriculture, the AAA, like the NRA, sacrificed the interests of the marginal and the unrecognized to the welfare of those with greater political and economic power.

In large measure, the early New Deal of the NRA and AAA was a "broker state." Though the government served as a mediator of interests and sometimes imposed its will in divisive situations, it was generally the servant of powerful groups. . . . But it was some improvement over the 1920s when business was the only interest capable of imposing its will on the government. While extending to other groups the benefits of the state, the New Deal, however, continued to recognize the pre-eminence of business interests.

The politics of the broker state also heralded the way of the future—of continued corporate dominance in a political structure where other groups agreed generally on corporate capitalism and squabbled only about the size of the shares. Delighted by this increased participation and the absorption of dissident groups, many liberals did not understand the dangers in the emerging organization of politics. They had too much faith in representative institutions and in associations to foresee the perils—of leaders not representing their constituents, of bureaucracy diffusing responsibility, of officials serving their own interests. Failing to perceive the dangers in the emerging structure, most liberals agreed with Senator Robert Wagner of New York: "In order that the strong may not take advantage of the weak, every group must be equally strong." His advice then seemed appropriate for organizing labor, but it neglected the problems of unrepresentative leadership and of the many millions to be left beyond organization.

In dealing with the organized interests, the President acted frequently as a broker, but his government did not simply express the vectors of external forces. The New Deal state was too complex, too loose, and some of Roosevelt's subordinates were following their own inclinations and pushing the government in directions of their own design. The President would also depart from his role as a broker and act to secure programs he desired. As a skilled politician, he could split coalitions, divert the interests of groups, or place the prestige of his office on the side of desired legislation.

In seeking to protect the stock market, for example, Roosevelt endorsed the Securities and Exchange measure (of 1934), despite the opposition of many in the New York financial community. His advisers split the opposition. Rallying to support the administration were the out-of-town exchanges, representatives of the large commission houses, including James Forrestal of Dillon, Read, and Robert Lovett of Brown Brothers, Harriman, and such commission brokers as E. A. Pierce and Paul Shields. Opposed to the Wall Street "old guard" and their companies, this group included those who wished to avoid more radical legislation, as well as others who had wanted earlier to place trading practices under federal legislation which they could influence.

Though the law restored confidence in the securities market and protected capitalism, it alarmed some businessmen and contributed to the false belief that the New Deal was threatening business. But it was not the disaffection of a portion of the business community, nor the creation of the Liberty League, that menaced the broker state. Rather it was the threat of the Left—expressed, for example, in such overwrought statements as Minnesota Governor Floyd Olson's: "I am not a liberal . . . I am a radical. . . . I am not satisfied with hanging a laurel wreath on burglars and thieves . . . and calling them code authorities or something else." While Olson, along with some others who succumbed to the rhetoric of militancy, would back down and soften their meaning, their words dramatized real grievances: the failure of the early New Deal to end misery, to re-create prosperity. The New Deal excluded too many. Its programs were inadequate. While Roosevelt reluctantly endorsed relief and went beyond Hoover in support of public works, he too preferred self-liquidating projects, desired a balanced budget, and resisted spending the huge sums required to lift the nation out of depression.

IV

For millions suffering in a nation wracked by poverty, the promises of the Left seemed attractive. Capitalizing on the misery, Huey Long offered Americans a "Share Our Wealth" program—a welfare state with prosperity, not subsistence, for the disadvantaged, those neglected by most politicians. "Every Man a King": pensions for the elderly, college for the deserving, homes and cars for families—that was the promise of American life. Also proposing minimum wages, increased public works, shorter work weeks, and a generous farm program, he demanded a "soak-the-rich" tax program. Despite the economic defects of his plan, Long was no hayseed, and his forays into the East revealed support far beyond the bayous and hamlets of his native South. In California discontent was so great that Upton Sinclair, food faddist and former socialist, captured the Democratic nomination for governor on a platform of "production-for-use"— factories and farms for the unemployed. "In a cooperative society," promised Sinclair, "every man, woman, and child would have the equivalent of $5,000 a year income from labor of the able-bodied young men for three or four hours per day." More challenging to Roosevelt was Francis Townsend's plan— monthly payments of $200 to those past sixty who retired and promised to spend the stipend within thirty days. Another enemy of the New Deal was Father Coughlin, the popular radio priest, who had broken with Roosevelt and formed a National Union for Social Justice to lead the way to a corporate society beyond capitalism.

To a troubled nation offered "redemption" by the Left, there was also painful evidence that the social fabric was tearing— law was breaking down. When the truckers in Minneapolis struck, the police provoked an incident and shot sixty-seven people, some in the back. Covering the tragedy, Eric Sevareid, then a young reporter, wrote, "I understood deep in my bones and blood what fascism was." In San Francisco union leaders embittered by police brutality led a general strike and aroused national fears of class warfare. Elsewhere, in textile mills from Rhode Island to Georgia, in cities like Des Moines and Toledo, New York and Philadelphia, there were brutality and violence, sometimes bayonets and tear gas.

Challenged by the Left, and with the new Congress more liberal and more willing to spend, Roosevelt turned to disarm the discontent. "Boys—this is our hour," confided Harry Hopkins.

"We've got to get everything we want—a works program, social security, wages and hours, everything—now or never. Get your minds to work on developing a complete ticket to provide security for all the folks of this country up and down and across the board." Hopkins and the associates he addressed were not radicals: they did not seek to transform the system, only to make it more humane. They, too, wished to preserve large-scale corporate capitalism, but unlike Roosevelt or Moley, they were prepared for more vigorous action. Their commitment to reform was greater, their tolerance for injustice far less. Joining them in pushing the New Deal left were the leaders of industrial unions, who, while also not wishing to transform the system, sought for workingmen higher wages, better conditions, stronger and larger unions, and for themselves a place closer to the fulcrum of power.

The problems of organized labor, however, neither aroused Roosevelt's humanitarianism nor suggested possibilities of reshaping the political coalition. When asked during the NRA about employee representation, he had replied that workers could select anyone they wished—the Ahkoond of Swat, a union, even the Royal Geographical Society. As a paternalist, viewing himself . . . as a "partisan and benefactor" of workers, he would not understand the objections to company unions or to multiple unionism under NRA. Nor did he foresee the political dividends that support of independent unions could yield to his party. Though presiding over the reshaping of politics (which would extend the channels of power to some of the discontented and redirect their efforts to competition within a limited framework), he was not its architect, and he was unable clearly to see or understand the unfolding design.

When Senator Wagner submitted his labor relations bill, he received no assistance from the President and even struggled to prevent Roosevelt from joining the opposition. The President "never lifted a finger," recalls Miss Perkins. ("I, myself, had very little sympathy with the bill," she wrote.) But after the measure easily passed the Senate and seemed likely to win the House's endorsement, Roosevelt reversed himself. Three days before the Supreme Court invalidated the NRA, including the legal support for unionization, Roosevelt came out for the bill. Placing it on his "must" list, he may have hoped to influence the final provisions and turn an administration defeat into victory.

Responding to the threat from the left, Roosevelt also moved during the Second Hundred Days to secure laws regulating banking, raising taxes, dissolving utility-holding companies, and creating social security. Building on the efforts of states during the Progressive Era, the Social Security Act marked the movement toward the welfare state, but the core of the measure, the old-age provision, was more important as a landmark than for its substance. While establishing a federal-state system of unemployment compensation, the government, by making workers contribute to their old-age insurance, denied its financial responsibility for the elderly. The act excluded more than a fifth of the labor force leaving, among others, more than five million farm laborers and domestics without coverage.

Though Roosevelt criticized the tax laws for not preventing "an unjust concentration of wealth and economic power," his own tax measure would not have significantly redistributed wealth. Yet his message provoked an "amen" from Huey Long and protests from businessmen. Retreating from his promises, Roosevelt failed to support the bill, and it succumbed to conservative forces. They removed the inheritance tax and greatly reduced the proposed corporate and individual levies. The final law did not "soak the rich." But it did engender deep resentment among the wealthy for increasing taxes on gifts and estates, imposing an excess-profits tax (which Roosevelt had not requested), and raising surtaxes. When combined with such regressive levies as social security and local taxes, however, the Wealth Tax of 1935 did not drain wealth from higher-income groups, and the top one percent even increased their shares during the New Deal years.

V

Those historians who have characterized the events of 1935 as the beginning of a second New Deal have imposed a pattern on those years which most participants did not then discern. In moving to social security, guarantees of collective bargaining, utility regulation, and progressive taxation, the government did advance the nation toward greater liberalism, but the shift was exaggerated and most of the measures accomplished far less than either friends or foes suggested. Certainly, despite a mild bill authorizing destruction of utilities-holding companies, there was no effort to atomize business, no real threat to concentration.

Nor were so many powerful businessmen disaffected by the New Deal. Though the smaller businessmen who filled the ranks of the Chamber of Commerce resented the federal bureaucracy and the benefits to labor and thus criticized NRA, representatives of big business found the agency useful, and opposed a return to unrestricted competition. In 1935, members of the Business Advisory Council—including Henry Harriman, outgoing president of the Chamber, Thomas Watson of International Business Machines, Walter Gifford of American Telephone and Telegraph, Gerard Swope of General Electric, Winthrop Aldrich of the Chase National Bank, and W. Averell Harriman of Union Pacific—vigorously endorsed a two-year renewal of NRA.

When the Supreme Court in 1935 declared the "hot" oil clause and then NRA unconstitutional, the administration moved to measures known as the "little NRA." Reestablishing regulations in bituminous coal and oil, the New Deal also checked wholesale price discrimination and legalized "fair trade" practices. . . . In the so-called second New Deal, as in the "first," government remained largely the benefactor of big business, and some more advanced businessmen realized this.

Roosevelt could attack the "economic royalists" and endorse the TNEC investigation of economic concentration, but he was unprepared to resist the basic demands of big business. While there was ambiguity in his treatment of oligopoly, it was more the confusion of means than of ends, for his tactics were never likely to impair concentration. Even the antitrust program under Thurman Arnold, concludes Frank Freidel, was "intended less to bust the trusts than to forestall too drastic legislation." Operating through consent decrees and designed to reduce prices to the consumer, the program frequently "allowed industries to function much as they had in NRA days." In effect, then, throughout its variations, the New Deal had sought to cooperate with business.

Though vigorous in rhetoric and experimental in tone, the New Deal was narrow in its goals and wary of bold economic reform. Roosevelt's sense of what was politically desirable was frequently more restricted than others' views of what was possible and necessary. Roosevelt's limits were those of ideology; they were not inherent in experimentalism. For while the President explored the narrow center, and some New Dealers considered bolder possibilities, John Dewey, the philosopher of experimentalism, moved far beyond the New Deal and sought to reshape the system. Liberalism, he warned, "must now become radical. . . . For the gulf between what the actual situation makes possible and the actual state itself is so great that it cannot be bridged by piecemeal policies undertaken *ad hoc*." The boundaries of New Deal experimentalism, as Howard Zinn has emphasized, could extend far beyond Roosevelt's cautious ventures. Operating within very safe channels, Roosevelt not only avoided Marxism and the socialization of property, but he also stopped far short of other possibilities—communal direction of production or the organized distribution of surplus. The President and many of his associates were doctrinaires of the center, and their maneuvers in social reform were limited to cautious excursions.

VI

Usually opportunistic and frequently shifting, the New Deal was restricted by its ideology. It ran out of fuel not because of the conservative opposition, but because it ran out of ideas. Acknowledging the end in 1939, Roosevelt proclaimed, "We have now passed the period of internal conflict in the launching of our program of social reform. Our full energies may now be released to invigorate the processes of recovery in order to preserve our reforms. . . ."

The sad truth was that the heralded reforms were severely limited, that inequality continued, that efforts at recovery had failed. Millions had come to accept the depression as a way of life. A decade after the Great Crash, when millions were still unemployed, Fiorello LaGuardia recommended that "we accept the inevitable, that we are now in a new normal." "It was reasonable to expect a probable minimum of 4,000,000 to 5,000,000 unemployed," Harry Hopkins had concluded. Even that level was never reached, for business would not spend and Roosevelt refused to countenance the necessary expenditures. "It was in economics that our troubles lay," Tugwell wrote. "For their solution his [Roosevelt's] progressivism, his new deal was pathetically insufficient. . . .

Clinging to faith in fiscal orthodoxy even when engaged in deficit spending, Roosevelt had been unwilling to greatly unbalance the budget. Having pledged in his first campaign to cut expenditures and to restore the balanced budget, the President had at first adopted recovery programs that would not drain government finances. Despite a burst of activity under the Civil Works Administration during the first winter, public works expenditures were frequently slow and cautious. Shifting from direct relief, which Roosevelt (like Hoover) considered "a narcotic, a subtle destroyer of the human spirit," the government moved to work relief. ("It saves his skill. It gives him a chance to do something socially useful," said Hopkins.) By 1937 the government had poured enough money into the economy to spur production to within 10 percent of 1929 levels, but unemployment still hovered over seven million. Yet so eager was the President to balance the budget that he cut expenditures for public works and relief, and plunged the economy into a greater depression. While renewing expenditures, Roosevelt remained cautious in his fiscal policy, and the nation still had almost nine million unemployed in 1939. After nearly six years of struggling with the depression, the Roosevelt administration could not lead the nation to recovery, but it had relieved suffering. In most of America, starvation was no longer possible. Perhaps that was the most humane achievement of the New Deal.

Its efforts on behalf of humane *reform* were generally faltering and shallow, of more value to the middle classes, of less value to organized workers, of even less to the marginal men. In conception and in practice, seemingly humane efforts revealed the shortcomings of American liberalism. For example, public housing, praised as evidence of the federal government's concern for the poor, was limited in scope (to 180,000 units) and unfortunate in results. It usually meant the consolidation of ghettos, the robbing of men of their dignity, the treatment of men as wards with few rights. And slum clearance came to mean "Negro clearance" and removal of the other poor. Of much of this liberal reformers were unaware, and some of the problems can be traced to the structure of bureaucracy and to the selection of government personnel and social workers who disliked the poor. But the liberal conceptions, it can be argued, were also flawed for there was no willingness to consult the poor, nor to encourage their participation. Liberalism was elitist. Seeking to build America in their own image, liberals wanted to create an environment which they thought would restructure character and personality more appropriate to white, middle-class America.

While slum dwellers received little besides relief from the New Deal, and their needs were frequently misunderstood, Negroes as a group received even less assistance—less than they needed and sometimes even less than their proportion in the population would have justified. Under the NRA they were frequently dismissed and their wages were sometimes below the legal minimum. The Civilian Conservation Corps left them "forgotten" men—excluded, discriminated against, segregated. In general, what the Negroes gained—relief, WPA jobs, equal pay on some federal projects—was granted them as poor people, not as Negroes. To many black men the distinction was unimportant, for no government had ever given them so much. "My friends, go home and turn Lincoln's picture to the wall," a Negro publisher told his race. "That debt has been payed in full."

Bestowing recognition on some Negro leaders, the New Deal appointed them to agencies as advisers—the "black cabinet." Probably more dramatic was the advocacy of Negro rights by Eleanor Roosevelt. Some whites like Harold Ickes and Aubrey Williams even struggled cautiously to break down segregation. But segregation did not yield, and Washington itself remained a segregated city. The white South was never challenged, the Fourteenth Amendment never used to assist Negroes. Never would Roosevelt expend political capital in an assault upon the American caste system. Despite the efforts of the NAACP to dramatize the Negroes' plight as second-class citizens, subject to brutality and often without legal protection, Roosevelt would not endorse the anti-lynching bill. ("No government pretending to be civilized can go on condoning such atrocities," H. L. Mencken testified. "Either it must make every possible effort to put them down or it must suffer the scorn and contempt of Christendom.") Unwilling to risk schism with Southerners ruling committees, Roosevelt capitulated to the forces of racism.

Even less bold than in economic reform, the New Deal left intact the race relations of America. Yet its belated and cautious recognition of the black man was great enough to woo Negro leaders and even to court the masses. One of the bitter ironies of these years is that a New Dealer could tell the NAACP in 1936:

"Under our new conception of democracy, the Negro will be given the chance to which he is entitled. . . ." But it was true, Ickes emphasized, that "The greatest advance [since Reconstruction] toward assuring the Negro that degree of justice to which he is entitled and that equality of opportunity under the law which is implicit in his American citizenship, has been made since Franklin D. Roosevelt was sworn in as President. . . ."

It was not in the cities and not among the Negroes but in rural America that Roosevelt administration made its (philosophically) boldest efforts: creation of the Tennessee Valley Authority and the later attempt to construct seven little valley authorities. Though conservation was not a new federal policy and government-owned utilities were sanctioned by municipal experience, federal activity in this area constituted a challenge to corporate enterprise and an expression of concern about the poor. A valuable example of regional planning and a contribution to regional prosperity, TVA still fell far short of expectations. The agency soon retreated from social planning. ("From 1936 on," wrote Tugwell, "the TVA should have been called the Tennessee Valley Power Production and Food Control Corporation.") Fearful of antagonizing the powerful interests, its agricultural program neglected the tenants and the sharecroppers.

To urban workingmen the New Deal offered some, but limited, material benefits. Though the government had instituted contributory social security and unemployment insurance, its much-heralded Fair Labor Standards Act, while prohibiting child labor, was a greater disappointment. It exempted millions from its wages-and-hours provisions. So unsatisfactory was the measure that one congressman cynically suggested, "Within 90 days after appointment of the administrator, she should report to Congress whether anyone is subject to this bill." Requiring a minimum of twenty-five cents an hour ($11 a week for 44 hours), it raised the wages of only about a half-million at a time when nearly twelve million workers in interstate commerce were earning less than forty cents an hour.

More important than these limited measures was the administration's support, albeit belated, of the organization of labor and the right of collective bargaining. Slightly increasing organized workers' share of the national income, the new industrial unions extended job security to millions who were previously subject to the whim of management. Unionization freed them from the perils of a free market.

By assisting labor, as well as agriculture, the New Deal started the institutionalization of larger interest groups into a new political economy. Joining business as tentative junior partners, they shared the consensus on the value of large-scale corporate capitalism, and were permitted to participate in the competition for the division of shares. While failing to redistribute income, the New Deal modified the political structure at the price of excluding many from the process of decision making. To many what was offered in fact was symbolic representation, formal representation. It was not the industrial workers necessarily who were recognized, but their unions and leaders; it was not even the farmers, but their organizations and leaders. While this was not a conscious design, it was the predictable result of conscious policies. It could not have been easily avoided, for it was part of the price paid by a large society unwilling to consider radical new designs for the distribution of power and wealth.

VII

In the deepest sense, this new form of representation was rooted in the liberal's failure to endorse a meaningful egalitarianism which would provide actual equality of opportunity. It was also the limited concern with equality and justice that accounted for the shallow efforts of the New Deal and left so many Americans behind. The New Deal was neither a "third American Revolution," as Carl Degler suggests, nor even a "half-way revolution," as William Leuchtenburg concludes. Not only was the extension of representation to new groups less than full-fledged partnership, but the New Deal neglected many Americans—sharecroppers, tenant farmers, migratory workers and farm laborers, slum dwellers, unskilled workers, and the unemployed Negroes. They were left outside the new order. As Roosevelt asserted in 1937 (in a classic understatement), one third of the nation was "ill-nourished, ill-clad, ill-housed."

Yet, by the power of rhetoric and through the appeals of political organization, the Roosevelt government managed to win or retain the allegiance of these peoples. Perhaps this is one of the crueller ironies of liberal politics, that the marginal men trapped in hopelessness were seduced by rhetoric, by the style and movement, by the symbolism of efforts seldom reaching beyond words. In acting to protect the institution of private property and in advancing the interests of corporate capitalism, the New Deal assisted the middle and upper sectors of society. It protected them, sometimes, even at the cost of injuring the lower sectors. Seldom did it bestow much of substance upon the lower classes. Never did the New Deal seek to organize these groups into independent political forces. Seldom did it risk antagonizing established interests. For some this would constitute a puzzling defect of liberalism; for some, the failure to achieve true liberalism. To others it would emphasize the inherent shortcomings of American liberal democracy. As the nation prepared for war, liberalism, by accepting private property and federal assistance to corporate capitalism, was not prepared effectively to reduce inequities, to redistribute political power, or to extend equality from promise to reality.

Anthony J. Badger

The Unanticipated Consequences of New Deal Reform

Writing two decades after Barton Bernstein, Anthony Badger took issue with both the New Deal's liberal sympathizers and its leftist critics. In his comprehensive survey *The New Deal: The Depression Years, 1933–1940* (1989), Badger concluded with a perceptive analysis of the New Deal's shortcomings and accomplishments. Bernstein and other adherents of the "corporate liberal" critique of the New Deal, Badger argues, failed to realize that much of what they disparaged about the New Dealers—their conservative achievement—was the product of unanticipated consequences of New Deal actions. Although he acknowledges that the vision of the New Dealers was often limited, Badger stresses the formidable external constraints to greater changes in the economic and political systems. These constraints included opposition from Congress, the reliance on the ill-fated models of World War I, the uncertain consti-

tutional precedents, and the fragmented and limited capacities of the federal government in 1933. The "ultimate constraint" on more far-reaching action, however, was the conservative response of the American people to the New Deal. Traditions of self-help, localism, and individual liberty, Badger argues, severely circumscribed the New Deal's achievement. The New Deal, he concludes, was basically a "holding operation." It was the dramatic changes of World War II that created the "political economy of modern America."

Anthony Badger is Mellon Professor of History at Sidney Sussex College, Cambridge University.

The deficiencies of the New Deal were glaring. As the 9,000,000 unemployed in 1939 testified, the policies for industrial recovery did not work. The NRA failed to inject additional purchasing power into the economy. The commitment to deficit spending was belated and half-hearted. Neither through taxation nor through anti-trust prosecution was the Roosevelt administration able to break up the economic power of large corporations or to redistribute wealth. The New Deal's support for the countervailing power of trades unions was ambivalent. Roosevelt was a late convert to the Wagner Act and the Act itself was less responsible for the great organisational breakthrough in the mass-production industries than was the militancy of the rank-and-file workers.

In agriculture, crop reduction and price-support loans could not eliminate surplus production. The New Deal was unable to stimulate urban demand and absorb farm overproduction, nor did it solve the problem of too many people living on the land. Recovery programmes offered little to marginal farmers, sharecroppers, and farm labourers. The ambitious plans to solve the problems of rural poverty were largely still-born.

Spending on direct relief was always inadequate both under the FERA and later by the states. Too often relief perpetuated traditional and degrading attitudes towards welfare recipients. Work relief never reached more than 40 per cent of the unemployed. Spending constraints meant that WPA jobs were never invested with the legitimacy and dignity that New Dealers had hoped to impart. The social security system excluded many who needed help most, paid for benefits from the earnings of the beneficiaries, penalised the old and dependent in poorer states, and made no provision for health insurance. For the urban poor, the failure to develop a significant low-cost government housing programme left the worst problems of the inner city untouched. For the poor who were black, the New Deal did little. It enacted no civil rights measures and sanctioned continued discrimination and segregation in its programmes.

It is equally easy to replace this bleak catalogue of New Deal failure with a positive assessment of its success—the more so when New Deal activism is contrasted to the inaction of the federal government under Hoover.

In contrast to Hoover's vain exhortations to keep wages up, the NRA put a statutory floor under wages, checked the downwards deflationary spiral, and halted the relentless erosion of labour standards. Together with direct federal public works expenditure, the NRA seemed to prevent matters from getting worse and, through 1936, government intervention in the economy paralleled, if it did not cause, modest but definite recovery. A stabilised banking and securities system, eventual deficit spending, and protected labour standards gave hope for ultimate orderly recovery. The New Deal's acceptance of organised labour may have been halting but the attitude of the state to labour was effectively reversed. No longer were the forces of government automatically arraigned against trades unions. Rank-and-file militancy could not succeed without government protection. The Wagner Act and the change in government stance disciplined the most anti-union employers and protected the great gains of 1936–37 against economic downturn and employer backlash.

In contrast to Hoover's vain exhortations to reduce acreage, the voluntary domestic allotment plan gave farmers positive incentives to cut production. The benefit payments, farm credit, and debt adjustment all provided farmers with the tangible assistance that the Federal Farm Board had failed to give. The votes of farmers both in crop control and the 1936 elections were striking testimony to their perception that the New Deal had rescued commercial farmers both large and small, and almost all farmers were commercial farmers. In the 1980s, as American farmers once more face drought and foreclosure, the New Deal's achievement for agriculture recaptures some of its lustre. While the resettlement projects and tenant purchase loans of the Farm Security Administration may have "skimmed the cream" of the rural poor, rehabilitation loans and grants did reach many of the "submerged third" of the rural population. For all its defects, the FSA nevertheless was effective enough to arouse the fear of conservative politicians in the South.

The Depression had exhausted private, local, and state resources for relief before 1933. Hoover had bitterly resisted the remedy of direct federal grants. New Deal welfare programmes gave the unemployed money and jobs. The lasting loyalty of lower-income voters to Roosevelt expressed their appreciation of the very real and essential benefits they received. The Social Security Act created insurance for the old and unemployed which had existed nowhere in the public sector before and only minimally in the private sector. The Act initiated a quantum leap in the provision of assistance to the old, the blind, and dependent children. The Act might not have been rounded out in the way New Dealers hoped, but the interlocking and contributory system launched in 1935 did ensure that Congress would not lightly abolish it. The New Deal welfare programmes provided direct assistance to perhaps as many as 35 per cent of the population. It bequeathed a commitment to a minimum level of social welfare from which successive governments have never been entirely able to escape.

The political realignment that these welfare measures helped shape ensured that the measures needed to tackle urban poverty would in the future be a part of the liberal Democratic agenda. Similarly, the demands of blacks would now be pushed on the national Democratic Party by the developing civil rights coalition which included New Deal liberals. The shift in political allegiance by blacks in the 1930s bore witness to the genuine assistance they had received in the northern cities from relief and WPA programmes. Despite continued discrimination and segregation, southern blacks received assistance on a scale that surpassed anything they had been granted by any state or private sources. Farm programmes lessened the bonds of dependency of tenants and sharecroppers on white landlords, and the ferment of activity in Washington gave southern black leaders new hope that the federal government might eventually be the source of their salvation.

To lament the New Deal's deficiencies or to celebrate its achievements has only limited utility. Instead, what is needed is an examination of the relationship between reforms instituted by the New Deal and the longer-term developments of American society.

What needs to be explained therefore is why New Deal reforms had such unanticipated consequences. The business-warfare-welfare state that America eventually became was not the intentional construct of New Dealers. Much New Deal policy had been designed to curb the power of the key corporations that became so firmly entrenched after 1945. The advocates of social security had envisaged the withering away of assistance programmes not the mushrooming of welfare rolls. Those advocates expected to enact national health insurance in the future: they live instead to see the explosion of private medical insurance plans.

In the 1940s and 1950s Americans fled from the land. Yet in the 1930s rural planners had aimed to keep people on the land. New Dealers aimed to eradicate slums, regenerate the inner cities, and revitalise small towns. Yet their housing policies fostered suburban sprawl.

These unexpected developments were not the result of a plot in the 1930s by a corporate capitalist élite. New Deal reforms were not corporate liberal reforms designed to extend the hegemony of large-scale business over the economy and to defuse the threat of radical protest.

Banking and securities reforms may have stabilised credit and the stock exchange but they were opposed by the very businessmen who ultimately benefited from them. The NRA may have been the brain-child of trade association spokesmen, but few members of the corporate élite positively supported it: most regarded the NRA as a reform to be endured. When the NRA did not bring recovery, a few businessmen saw the virtue of working with it to limit the damage it could do but most fervently hoped for its demise.

Nor did corporate élites support New Deal labour reforms. These reforms did not represent a sophisticated strategy of containment of trades unions by the business community. The Wagner Act may have led to conservative and responsible unionism, but businessmen in the 1930s did not foresee the benefits of such a stabilised industrial relations system. On the contrary, many went to great lengths to try to forestall independent unions. At best, some grudgingly accepted the inevitable, but even they were determined to make no substantive concessions.

Nor does the evidence support the argument that the New Deal welfare measures were designed to ward off the threat of disorder by the unemployed and the poor. Perceived need identified by welfare workers and the political opportunity to act, not the threat of violence, explains the genesis and development of welfare policies. New Dealers did predict increased radicalism in due course if no steps were taken to improve the lot of the poor. The threat of disorder was also a useful spectre to raise before the eyes of conservative politicians. But, if anything, the New Deal stimulated rather than defused disorder. Demonstrations by the unemployed were mostly unavailing efforts to prevent cuts in New Deal benefits.

Some limitations of the New Deal were nevertheless self-imposed; some of its wounds self-inflicted. Roosevelt never pretended that his aim was anything other than to save and preserve capitalism. The consequences of banking and securities reform were conservative precisely because Roosevelt wanted to restore conservative investment practices. His anger at the business community sprang not from an anti-business philosophy, but from his irritation at the ingratitude of the group for whom the New Deal had done so much. This commitment to basic capitalist values made it all the more damaging that he failed to embrace early enough a compensatory fiscal policy. Such a policy might have brought the recovery he sought without disturbing the basic structure and value system of capitalism. The policy was intellectually available and the spending alternative was clearly presented to the president, particularly at the end of 1936. Instead, Roosevelt opted for policies that, first, starved many of his agencies of the funds needed to attain their social justice goals and, then, hastened recession in 1937–38, thereby immensely strengthening the conservative opposition that thwarted so many of the wider-ranging purposes of New Deal reform.

Roosevelt and the New Dealers were also handicapped by the contradictory or ambiguous vision of the America that they were seeking to create. Ultimately most of them believed that economic recovery would come from the revival of private enterprise, yet their convictions and political sensitivities inhibited them from wooing the business community wholeheartedly. There was no unanimity on the future industrial structure of the country. Some New Dealers continued to regard large corporations as efficient and inevitable businesses which should accordingly be regulated; others believed they should be broken up.

The New Deal consolidated an urban liberalism that frankly recognised the desirability of an increasingly urbanised America.

Yet Roosevelt himself was reluctant fully to accept that vision, and his lack of sympathy for urban dilemmas in part accounts for the inadequacy of the 1937 Housing Act. Roosevelt and others yearned to move people back on to the land yet the Department of Agriculture knew that there were actually too many people on the land. Planners in Agriculture were never entirely certain of their goals: were they to hasten the modernisation and rationalisation of farming, or were they to try to increase the numbers of small owners and enable them to stay on the land?

The fear of social security administrators that generous assistance programmes might undermine social insurance prevented the development of an adequate and comprehensive welfare programme.

Many New Dealers were fully conscious of these inconsistencies and acknowledged their reform limitations. Frances Perkins was once described by a friend as "a half-loaf girl: take what you can get now and try for more later." New Dealers were not blind to the failures of their own programmes: they had a practical appreciation of political constraints and hoped to refine and improve programmes in due course. Perkins herself was under no illusions about the weaknesses and gaps in the social security system. The Bureau of Agricultural Economics was fully aware of the long-term limitations of planned scarcity and of the need to stimulate urban consumption. No one had a shrewder perception of the damage spending constraints imposed on work relief than Harry Hopkins.

They were remarkably accessible to their critics. In part, accessibility reflected the still manageable size of the federal government. Sharecroppers from Arkansas could travel through the night to Washington, sit down in the early morning outside the Secretary of Agriculture's office, and actually talk to Henry Wallace when he came in to work. In part, accessibility reflected the lack of dogmatic certainty amongst New Dealers. Even the arbitrary Hugh Johnson responded to a shouting match with Leon Henderson by inviting him in to head the Research and Planning Division. When Will Alexander and Frank Tannenbaum exposed the consequences of the collapse of cotton tenancy, they were brought in to draft the Bankhead-Jones bill and to work in the Resettlement Administration. Even when the experience of critics was less happy—when for example Jerome Frank and the liberal reformers were purged from the AAA after the reinterpretation of the cotton contract—they were not cast aside. They went on to work in more congenial parts of the New Deal experiment—in Justice, the Labor Department, at the NLRB, or at the SEC.

Many of the problems that the New Deal found intractable were problems first uncovered by the New Dealers themselves. The existence of a permanently poor rural population in the South was not a problem much recognised by agricultural economists or farm policy-makers in 1933. It was a problem exposed by FERA workers who found an unexpected demand for relief in rural as well as urban areas. Their initiatives led to the assault on rural poverty through rehabilitation loans and resettlement communities. The full dimensions of the needs of the cities and the possibilities of federal action were first laid out by the National Resources Committee in their 1937 report *Our Cities: Their Role in the National Economy*. The TNEC identified in 1938 the needs of the South. The Great Plains Committee partially mapped the problems of the West in *The Future of the Great Plains*. Field studies for the relief agencies first highlighted the health and educational deficiencies of both rural and urban America and the particular plight of the young and women.

The New Deal was not static, it improved over time as deficiencies in existing programmes were exposed and new problems identified. Nowhere was this clearer than in its treatment of blacks. The ignorance of even sympathetic liberals like Eleanor Roosevelt mirrored at first the indifference with which the NRA and the AAA regarded blacks. Slowly she and others became aware that black problems could not be eradicated by generally targeting poverty. As a result of their perception of the special needs of blacks, agencies like the PWA, the WPA, and the Farm Security Administration pursued racial policies that had changed significantly from the white preoccupations of 1933.

Nevertheless, the first steps the reformers took too often turned out to be last steps. Their hopes of a more suitable distribution of wealth, of permanent emergency employment agencies, of a comprehensive welfare state, of coordinated planning and control of the nation's physical resources, and of a full-scale assault on rural poverty were dashed. Sometimes this failure was the result of missed opportunities. The New Dealers' pragmatism may have been self-limiting. As R. Alan Lawson noted, "Practicality can be treacherous. It urges compromise but may be used against compromise by deeming some evils too firmly rooted for practical reform to touch." It was undoubtedly prudent not to challenge the American Medical Association, for example, over national health insurance in 1935 in order to safeguard the Social Security Act itself. But in the future, the times were even less opportune to take on the AMA. For so many New Deal reforms, if the opportunity was not grasped in 1935, it would never present itself again.

Liberals were impatient with Roosevelt's lack of a thorough-going vision of reform and the administration's lack of valour, but the New Deal was more often restricted by external constraints imposed by the political and economic environment: the lack of a sufficient state apparatus, the strong forces of localism, the great difficulty of policy-making in an economic emergency, and entrenched conservative leadership in Congress.

The structure of the federal government of the early 1930s was inappropriate to centrally-directed radical reform. There was simply not the "state capacity" in Washington to manage central planning of the economy. Even if the political mandate for coercive overhead planning had existed in 1933, the government had neither the information with which to devise planning policies nor the bureaucracy with which to implement them. By the time the government had acquired the necessary information, the political opportunity to impose such plans had long gone, if it had ever existed. Nor was there a disinterested welfare bureaucracy capable of administering a national relief scheme or launching a purely federal social security system. The Department of Agriculture possessed a federal bureaucracy which had acquired considerable information about American farms. But even there neither crop control nor long-term planning could have been implemented without vesting crucial power in local committees of the farmers themselves.

The political constraints on centralised planning or purely federal programmes were formidable. Hostility to big government was not the preserve simply of conservative reactionary opponents of the New Deal. Suspicion of centralised federal authority governed the attitude of midwestern progressives, dissident demagogues, decentralist intellectuals like the Southern Agrarians, and many New Dealers themselves.

The forces of localism were in themselves a powerful check on New Deal aspirations. Not only were many New Deal programmes operated by state government agencies, but everywhere New Deal programmes were run by local officials who might defer more to local community sentiment than to directives emanating from Washington. Local administration of the farm programme put power in the hands of the local rural power structure and discriminated against the rural poor. Even the FSA found it difficult to overcome the tendency of its local officials to defer to local custom. Local administration of relief often allowed free play to the miserly and conservative prejudices and self-interest of local businessmen and farmers. Everywhere, local administration tended to countenance and perpetuate racial discrimination. The local role in the social security system gave rise to vast discrepancies in coverage and benefits. The intentions of the 1937 Housing Act were often defeated by local real estate interests that prevented the creation of local housing authorities. The formation of local REA cooperatives was thwarted by the ability of power companies to build "spite lines" to cream off the best business. Everywhere the pressure in Congress was to increase, not decrease, local involvement in the administration of New Deal programmes and to assert wherever possible state, not federal, control in order to safeguard entrenched local interests.

In any case some New Dealers saw positive virtues in such localism. They wanted to resurrect grass-roots democracy, to foster citizen participation. Local committees of farmers ran the AAA programmes, guided the TVA, advised on farm debt adjustment, land-use planning, and farm credit loans. The inhabitants were meant to govern Subsistence Homestead projects and Greenbelt towns. The REA operated through local cooperatives, the Soil Conservation programme through self-governing soil conservation districts. The aim of Indian reorganisation was to give self-government to the tribal councils. But this democratic vision was only partially successful. In the first place New Deal experiments in community building and participatory democracy were almost entirely rural in orientation. New Deal relief and welfare programmes made no attempt to draw on the tradition of urban community organisation that came from the settlement houses or the social unit experiment in Cincinnati. This social unit experiment in 1917 was an urban variant of the rural land-use planning committees—local community residents formed representative committees that met with a parallel committee of representatives from social service agencies. This was not a route taken in the 1930s. It would be the 1960s before urban welfare policy with Community Action Programs took up that approach again.

Post-war social scientists were quick to point to the drawbacks of participatory democracy in the rural areas. Sometimes grassroots democracy meant capitulation to local interest groups. At other times, interest groups destroyed democratic institutions that threatened them. Time and again it was also clear that the grass roots did not want to participate in the way New Deal planners wanted them to. Grass-roots democracy gave local sectional interests a veto over policy designed for the national interest. It is not surprising, given the constraints of localism, that many liberal New Dealers in the 1930s put their faith in enlightened national bureaucracy. Only in the 1960s and 1970s did this faith in federal bureaucracy seem misplaced.

The constraints of localism were compounded by the circumstances of policy-making and implementation in 1933. The economic emergency gave the New Deal vast opportunities to exercise powers that had not been used since World War I. Yet the spectacular exercise of that power for coherent planning required special circumstances, like the power vacuum in the Tennessee Valley in 1933. For the most part in 1933 the emergency, by contrast, severely restricted New Deal options. First, the emphasis was of necessity on recovery, rather than reform. Second, action had to be taken quickly. The banks had to be reopened in a week. NRA codes had to be drafted very quickly to provide an immediate boost to purchasing power. Relief money had to be distributed and spent at once. Millions of farmers had to be signed to contracts in weeks, not months.

Given both the lack of existing "state capacity" in Washington and the constitutional doubts on coercive government regulation, the New Deal had to rely on the consent of those being regulated to put recovery programmes into operation quickly. To reopen the banks required the cooperation of local bank officials and reliance on their information and good faith. The cooperation of businessmen who possessed a monopoly on information about their industries was essential if codes were to be drafted and administered. There was no alternative to the administration of the AAA by the Extension Service and local committees of farmers. Relief programmes had to be run by state government agencies. So it was that the New Deal fostered interest groups that in the long run obstructed its reforming designs. Thus, businessmen distorted the intent of the NRA and severely limited its ability to raise mass-purchasing power. Grass-roots democracy in agriculture facilitated the creation of commodity interest groups that pressed for ever more generous price supports in their own particular interest. The AAA also promoted the revival of a farm pressure group like the Farm Bureau Federation which ultimately turned against the New Deal's efforts to help the rural and the urban poor.

The circumstances of 1933 contributed to another major constraint on the New Deal: the power of the conservative opposition in Congress. The New Deal had to work with the existing congressional Democratic leadership in 1933 to secure the speedy passage of its essential recovery legislation. The recognition that the New Deal gave and the patronage it distributed undoubtedly bolstered the position of southern congressional leaders. Loyal congressional support for the New Deal was replaced by scepticism and mounting hostility about the direction of the non-emergency New Deal. As Roosevelt moved to complete the unfinished business of the New Deal in attacking urban and rural poverty, so he found it increasingly difficult to take Congress with him.

It is difficult to see how Roosevelt could have avoided this opposition from southern conservative Democrats and Republicans. He had achieved a partial political realignment. But the elimination of the southern conservative wing of his party would have required a much more systematic commitment that would have to have started in 1933 when his first priority was on immediate recovery. Even a more systematic commitment to realignment would probably have foundered on the unreliability of progressive non-Democrats, the refusal of conservatives to allow themselves to be portrayed as opponents of the New Deal, the difficulty of identifying from Washington genuine liberals with local political strength, and the difficulty of fighting local elections on national issues.

Congressional conservatives had effectively checked the expansion of the New Deal by 1940. What created, however, the political economy of modern America was the impact of the dramatic social changes unleashed by World War II on the "broker state" unwittingly created by the New Deal.

World War II was the juggernaut that ran over American society. The war opened up for the first time for the majority of

Americans the possibility of affluence rather than subsistence. For city dwellers, full employment and high wages offered the chance that, once private construction resumed after the war, they might be able to own their own homes and move to the suburbs. For farmers, war-time prosperity suggested that at the end of the war they might be able to enjoy the consumer goods—refrigerators, radios, and air conditioning—that rural electrification was making available to them. During the war 75 per cent of the population paid federal income tax: testimony to their affluence, not to legislative intent.

For businessmen, the war opened up undreamt-of profitability, restored leaders of large corporations to public esteem and respectability, and removed most threats of government regulation. For trades unions, the war forced management for the first time to sit down with them and bargain meaningfully. It established the parameters of post-war industrial relations. The war, not the New Deal, transformed rural America. High prices made possible mechanisation, investments in fertiliser and scientific farming, and consolidation into larger farms. Full employment gave the excess agricultural labour force the chance to dash gratefully to the new industrial jobs.

For blacks, the labour shortages in the defence industries and the armed services eventually broke down some discriminatory barriers and had some belated impact on the levels of their unemployment. As they flocked to the southern and northern cities, their political leverage increased. Urban migration in the South was an essential precondition for the development of the modern civil rights movement. The war similarly created new jobs for women, although it took longer for women than for blacks to translate new economic opportunity into increased consciousness and political gains. For the South, military spending during the war and Cold War, first on defence then later on space also, was the catalyst that sparked the region's take-off into self-sustaining economic growth. This growth would eventually draw most of the remaining rural population away from the cotton fields, reverse the traditional migration out of the region, and help facilitate the breakdown of traditional patterns of race relations. In the West, the defence industries on the coast once again attracted the migration that had been such a feature of the 1920s. The Depression, despite the extensive migration of the Arkies and Okies, had curtailed that population shift. From 1940 that expansion westwards would never again be slowed.

Seen through the lens of the war, the New Deal's overall function appears as a holding operation for American society: a series of measures that enabled the people to survive the Depression and to hold on until World War II opened up new opportunities. Industrial recovery programmes checked the deflationary spiral and yielded modest recovery that enabled businessmen to survive to enjoy dramatic war-time profits. Relief and welfare measures allowed the unemployed to struggle through until the war brought them jobs. Farm programmes enabled an underemployed labour force to stay on the land until the war created the urban demand which would absorb the surplus farm production and the industrial jobs which would absorb the surplus population. The plight of the poorest one third of the nation largely remained the New Deal's unfinished business.

The Office of War Information told Roosevelt that the American people's post-war aspirations were "compounded largely of 1929 values and the economics of the 1920s, leavened with a hangover from the makeshift controls of the war." This survey highlighted the ultimate constraint that circumscribed the New Deal's achievement: the underlying conservative response of the people themselves to the Depression. Middle-income Americans may have had more sympathy with the poor and the jobless in the 1930s than before or after. Workers may have exhibited greater class solidarity in those years. But more striking is the pervasive and persistent commitment to self-help, individual liberty, localism, and business-oriented individualism.

Businessmen, who had extracted many concessions from government, worked to end government regulation. Farmers, who had been rescued by massive government subsidies and price supports, argued that they wanted a fair price in the market place. Dust Bowl farmers, whose plight had been caused in part by their passion to plant wheat, wanted to grow more wheat. Submarginal farmers and tenant farmers wanted to own their own land, despite chronic rural overpopulation. The unemployed, having suffered from the collapse of the economic system, wanted another job, not a change in the system. Industrial workers, despite the unprecedented economic disaster, wanted a union contract and some rights on the shop floor, not control of the means of production. Mississippians, who had been rescued by unprecedented federal aid, stressed their steadfast commitment to states' rights. Westerners, who received more largesse than anyone else, proceeded again to elect conservative Republicans. Traditional values survived the Depression and the New Deal with great resilience. In the end, the New Deal was essentially a holding operation for American society because in the democratic, capitalist United States that was what most Americans wanted it to be.

II

The New Deal State and American Antistatism

About six weeks before Roosevelt was inaugurated as president, he traveled to Washington to meet with Herbert Hoover. On such trips Roosevelt was invariably joined by advisers and political leaders urging some kind of action to meet the worsening depression crisis. Pictured with Roosevelt on this occasion are (left to right): Admiral Cary T. Grayson, the head of the inauguration committee; Norman H. Davis, an American diplomat; Raymond Moley and Rexford G. Tugwell, both Columbia University professors and members of Roosevelt's "brains trust"; and William H. Woodin, Roosevelt's first secretary of the treasury. (AP/Wide World Photos. Photograph provided by the Franklin D. Roosevelt Library.)

Alan Brinkley

New Deal Liberalism and the New Deal State

In this essay Alan Brinkley argues that liberal New Deal thought regarding the functions of the national government underwent important changes during the late 1930s and the 1940s. During the New Deal's first years, Brinkley argues, the New Dealers had sought to reshape American capitalism. Some hoped to do this through antitrust, some through business-government cooperation, and some by strengthening the government's ability to regulate the private economy. These hopes, however, did not survive Roosevelt's presidency. Influenced by the ideas of the English economist John Maynard Keynes and the experiences of the 1937–1938 recession and World War II, American liberals gradually abandoned the idea of reorganizing industrial capitalism in favor of encouraging and sustaining economic growth.

Alan Brinkley is professor of history at Columbia University. He has written *Voices of Protest: Huey Long, Father Coughlin & the Great Depression* (1982) and *The End of Reform: New Deal Liberalism in Recession and War* (1995).

Alvin Hansen had been one of the principal economic advisers to the New Deal for nearly three years when he traveled to Cincinnati in March 1940 to speak to a group of businessmen. After his address, someone in the audience asked him what must have seemed a perfectly reasonable question: "In your opinion is the basic principle of the New Deal economically sound?" Hansen could not answer it. "I really do not know what the basic principle of the New Deal is," he replied. "I know from my experience in the government that there are as many conflicting opinions among the people in Washington under this administration as we have in the country at large."

Hansen's confusion was not uncommon in the cluttered, at times incoherent, political atmosphere of the late New Deal. The Roosevelt administration had moved in so many directions at once that no one could make sense of it all. Everyone was aware, of course,

From Fraser, Steve, and Gary Gerstle, *The Rise and Fall of the New Deal Order: 1930–1980.* Copyright © 1989 by Princeton University Press. Reprinted by permission of Princeton University Press.

of what the New Deal had done—of the laws it had helped pass, of the programs it had created, of the institutions it had launched or reshaped. But as Hansen suggested, few could discern in all this any "basic principle," any clear prescription for the future.

Only a few years later, however, most American liberals had come to view the New Deal as something more than an eclectic group of policies and programs. By the end of World War II, it had emerged as an idea: a reasonably coherent creed around which liberals could coalesce, a concept of the state that would dominate their thought and action for at least a generation. To some extent, battered and reviled as it has become, it remains at the center of American political life still.

This essay attempts to explain how and why liberal ideas of what the federal government should do evolved in response first to the recession of the late 1930s and then to the experience of World War II. The liberal concept of the state was not, of course, the only, or even the most important, factor in determining the form American government would assume. Nor was liberal ideology ever a uniform or static creed. But the broad outlines of what came to be known as "New Deal liberalism" remained fairly consistent for several decades after World War II; and those ideas played a major role at times in shaping the major expansions of federal responsibility that have transformed American government and, in more recent years, American politics.

I

The United States was one of the slowest of the advanced industrial nations to define an important social and economic role for its national government. The American state did not remain static, certainly, in the last decades of the nineteenth century and the first decades of the twentieth; but it grew slowly, haltingly, incompletely. The Great Depression, which would have been a difficult challenge for any state, was doubly intimidating in the United States because Americans had as yet made few decisions about what their government should do and how it should do it. As a result, the New Deal was not only an effort to deal with the particular problems of the 1930s; it was also a process of building government institutions where none existed, of choosing among various prescriptions for an expanded American state.

Through the first four years of the Roosevelt administration, however, making choices seemed to be nearly the last thing New Dealers were interested in doing. Instead, they moved unashamedly, even boastfully, in innumerable directions, proud of their experimentalism, generally unconcerned about the eclecticism of their efforts. Richard Hofstadter may have exaggerated when he described it as a program bereft of ideologies, "a chaos of experimentation." The New Deal was, in fact, awash in ideologies. What it lacked, however, was any single principle to bind its many diverse initiatives together. There were occasional cries, both in and out of the administration, for greater ideological coherence; predictions that without it, the New Deal would ultimately collapse in terminal confusion. But as long as the administration seemed politically unassailable and as long as the economy seemed on the road to recovery, it was easy to ignore such warnings.

In 1937, however, both the political and economic landscape changed. The president's ill-advised plan for "packing" the Supreme Court, first proposed a few weeks after his second inauguration, sparked a long-festering revolt among conservatives within his own party and caused an erosion of both his congressional and popular strength from which he was never fully to recover. An even greater blow to the administration's fortunes, and to its confidence, was the dismaying and almost wholly unanticipated recession that began in October 1937—an economic collapse more rapid and in some ways more severe than the crash of 1929. The new recession quickly destroyed the illusion that the Great Depression was over. And it forced a serious reevaluation among American liberals of the policies and philosophy of the New Deal. Out of the tangle of ideas and achievements of the early New Deal, many came now to believe, had to come a coherent vision that could guide future efforts. It was necessary, in short, to define the concept of New Deal liberalism.

II

There were in the late 1930s a number of potential definitions available to those engaged in this effort, and there seemed little reason at the time to assume that any one of them would soon prevail. Two broad patterns of governance, in particular, competed for

favor. Each had roots in the first years of the New Deal and in earlier periods of reform; each had important defenders.

For a time, at least, it seemed that the principal impact of the
1937 recession on American liberalism would be an enhanced belief in the value of an "administrative" or "regulatory" state, a government that would exercise some level of authority over the
structure and behavior of private capitalist institutions. Efforts to
reshape or "tame" capitalism had been central to American reform
ideology since the late nineteenth century and had been particularly prominent in the first years of the New Deal. Indeed, believing that something was wrong with capitalism and that it was the
responsibility of government to fix it was one of the most important ways in which progressives and liberals had defined themselves
through the first decades of the twentieth century.

In the immediate aftermath of the 1937 collapse, a powerful
group of younger New Dealers embraced this tradition again and,
without fully realizing it, began to transform it. They were something of a fresh force within the New Deal, a new generation of
liberals moving into the places vacated by the original "brain
trusters," most of whom had by then departed from public life.
Some occupied important positions of influence in the administration itself: Thomas Corcoran (often considered their unofficial
leader), Benjamin Cohen, Thurman Arnold, Leon Henderson,
James Landis, and Robert Jackson, among others. Some made
their influence felt as writers for the *New Republic*, the *Nation*, and
other magazines and journals. Felix Frankfurter (who had once
taught some of them at Harvard Law School and who had served
as a one-man employment agency for New Deal agencies) maintained his links from Cambridge. Henry Wallace and Harold Ickes
served at times as their allies in the cabinet. They were known as
the "New Dealers," a term that had once referred to the administration and its supporters as a whole but that now usually described
a particular group within that larger orbit.

Several things distinguished them from other members of the
administration and other advocates of reform. One was their hostility
to an idea that had entranced progressives for decades and had played
a major role in the early years of the New Deal—the idea of an associational economy, in which government would promote and regulate
the cartelization of private industries so as to reduce destructive com-

petition and maintain prices. The associational vision had shaped the first and most celebrated of the New Deal's reform experiments, the National Recovery Administration of 1933–1935. And the concept continued to evoke a vague, romantic affection in some corners of the administration. Donald Richberg and others continued to lobby in the late 1930s for a revival of NRA-like policies, and the president showed an occasional inclination to agree with them. But to the younger liberals of the late 1930s, the failure of the NRA was proof of the bankruptcy of the associational vision. They referred repeatedly to the "NRA of unhappy memory," the "NRA disaster," the "ill-conceived NRA experiment." The attempt to create a cartelistic "business commonwealth" capable of ordering its own affairs had, they claimed, produced only increased concentrations of power and artificially inflated prices. "The NRA idea is merely the trust sugarcoated," the *Nation* argued, "and the sugar coating soon wears off."

A second, related characteristic of these younger liberals was their rhetoric. Most rejected the conciliatory tone of the early New Deal, which had sought to draw the corporate world into a productive partnership with government. They favored, instead, the combative language of Franklin Roosevelt's 1936 campaign, with its sharp denunciation of "economic royalists." To much of the press and the public, what typified the "New Dealers" was a strong antipathy toward the corporate world and a fervent commitment to using government to punish and tame it.

In fact, attitudes toward businessmen varied greatly among the "New Dealers," and almost none were as hostile to corporate capitalism as their rhetoric at times suggested. Some did indeed believe that the new recession was a result of a corporate conspiracy: a deliberate "strike" by capital, designed to frustrate and weaken the administration. But even many of those who articulated this theory were careful to draw distinctions between "tyrannical" capitalists and those more "enlightened" business leaders who were already embracing some elements of the New Deal.

Whatever their opinions of corporate capitalism, however, virtually all the New Dealers agreed that a solution of the nation's greatest problems required the federal government to step into the marketplace to protect the interests of the public. The events of 1937 and 1938 had proved, they believed, that the corporate world, when left to its own devices, naturally frustrated the spontaneous workings of the market; that business leaders often conspired with one another to impose high "administered prices" on their customers; that the result was an artificial constriction of purchasing power and hence an unnecessarily low level of production. Only through a vigorous campaign against monopoly, therefore, could the economy be made to operate at full capacity.

Thus, on the surface at least, the most powerful impulse within the New Deal beginning early in 1938 was the revival of the old crusade against "monopoly." Rhetorical assaults on economic concentration echoed throughout the administration as New Dealers tried to forge an explanation for the setbacks of the year before. The president made the issue the centerpiece of an important 1938 message to Congress, in which he called for the creation of what became the Temporary National Economic Committee to examine "the concentration of economic power in American industry and the effect of that concentration upon the decline of competition." At about the same time, Roosevelt appointed Thurman Arnold, a professor at Yale Law School and a prolific political theorist, to succeed Robert Jackson as head of the Antitrust Division of the Justice Department. Arnold quickly made his office one of the most active and conspicuous in the federal government.

In fact, however, it was not the "atomizers," the believers in the Brandeisian concept of the decentralized, small-scale economy, who were moving to the fore. While the antitrust activists of the late New Deal used familiar antimonopoly rhetoric, their efforts had very little to do with actually decentralizing the economy. They were committed, instead, to defending the consumer and to promoting full production by expanding the regulatory functions of the state.

The record of Thurman Arnold was one indication of the form the "antimonopoly" impulse was now assuming. Arnold well deserved his reputation as the most active and effective director in the history of the Antitrust Division. By the time he left the Justice Department in 1943, he had radically expanded both the budget and the staff of his division; and he had filed (and won) more antitrust cases than the Justice Department had initiated in its entire previous history.

But Arnold was not using the antitrust laws to promote anything remotely resembling the Brandeisian concept of decentralization. On the contrary, he had been arguing for years, in his books, articles, and speeches, that the idea of "atomizing" the economy was nostalgic folly; that large-scale institutions were an inevitable, perhaps even desirable, consequence of industrialism; and that any effort to dismantle them would be not only futile but dangerous. In *The Folklore of Capitalism,* his celebrated 1937 book chronicling the meaningless ideological "rituals" Americans used to disguise political and economic realities, he gave special attention to what he considered one of the most vacuous of such rituals—the antitrust laws. They were, he wrote, "the answer of a society which unconsciously felt the need of great organizations, and at the same time had to deny them a place in the moral and logical ideology of the social structure. They were part of the struggle of a creed of rugged individualism to adapt itself to what was becoming a highly organized society."

The role of the Antitrust Division, Arnold believed, was not to defend "smallness" or to break up combinations, but to supervise the behavior of corporations. Size by itself was irrelevant. "I recognize the necessity of large organizations in order to attain efficient mass production," he wrote in 1939, shortly after assuming office. "I recognize that trust-busting for the mere sake of breaking up large units is futile." Three years later, as he neared the end of his tenure, he was saying the same thing, even more emphatically: "Big Business is not an economic danger so long as it devotes itself to efficiency in production and distribution. . . . There can be no greater nonsense than the idea that a mechanized age can get along without big business."

How was government to measure "efficiency in production and distribution"? Arnold's answer was simple: by the price to the consumer. Whatever artificially inflated consumer prices (and thus reduced economic activity)—whether it was the anti-competitive practices of a giant monopoly, the collusive activities of smaller producers acting to stabilize their markets, or (and here he raised the ire of some of his fellow liberals) the excessive demands of such powerful labor organizations as the building trades unions—was a proper target of antitrust prosecution. Any organization that did not harm the consumer, regardless of its size, had nothing to fear. Hence the antitrust laws became in Arnold's hands vehicles for expanding the regulatory scope of the state, not tools for altering the scale of economic organizations. Enforcement, he claimed, "is the problem of continuous direction of economic traffic. . . . The competitive struggle without effective antitrust enforcement is like a fight without a referee."

In this, of course, Arnold was saying little that was inconsistent with the actual history of antitrust law enforcement, and certainly nothing that was inconsistent with the previous record of the New Deal in confronting economic concentration. It was, however, a statement sharply at odds with the long-standing ideology of anti-monopoly. Arnold's views were more reminiscent of Theodore Roosevelt's nationalistic view of the economy (or Thorstein Veblen's concern with efficiency) than of the more truly antimonopolist views of the populists or Brandeis or the Wilson of 1912. No one recognized that more clearly than the old Midwestern progressives to whom antitrust still meant (as William Borah put it in a hostile exchange during Arnold's confirmation hearings) "breaking up monopolies." Suspicious of Arnold from the start, they viewed his tenure in the Justice Department as a disaster—which, by their standards, it turned out to be. His success in using the antitrust laws to police rather than forestall "bigness" was a serious, perhaps final, blow to the old concept of those laws as the route to genuine decentralization. That was precisely Arnold's intention.

The TNEC, similarly, was an antimonopoly inquiry more in name than in substance. It included among its members such inveterate congressional antimonopolists as Borah, Rep. Hatton Sumners of Texas, and Sen. Joseph O'Mahoney of Wyoming (the chairman). But most of the congressional members soon lost both interest and faith in the committee as the real work of the investigation fell increasingly under the control of the young New Dealers appointed to represent the administration: Arnold, Jerome Frank, William O. Douglas, Isador Lubin, and (directing the investigative staff) Leon Henderson, men far less concerned about the size of the institutions of the economy than about their effect on consumers and their accountability to the state. At times subtly, at times explicitly, the TNEC inquiry debunked old antimonopolist assumptions that small enterprises were inherently preferable to large ones; it cited time and again the value of efficiencies of scale; and it sought to find new ways for the government to intervene in the economy to protect the public from the adverse effects of a concentration of power that it seemed to concede was now inevitable.

The work of the TNEC dragged on for nearly three years. The committee examined 655 witnesses, generated eighty volumes and over twenty thousand pages of testimony, published forty-four monographs, and, as time passed and the inconclusiveness of the enterprise became clear, gradually lost the attention of both the public and the president. Its final report, issued in April 1941, attracted virtually no serious attention in a nation already preoccupied with war; and the entire episode was soon largely dismissed as a "colossal dud" or, more charitably, a "magnificent failure." "With all the ammunition the committee had stored up," *Time* magazine commented at the end, "a terrific broadside might have been expected. Instead, the committee rolled a rusty BB gun into place [and] pinged at the nation's economic problems."

The feeble conclusion of the TNEC inquiry illustrated the degree to which the antimonopoly enthusiasms of 1938 had faded by 1941. But the character of the inquiry during its three years of striving illustrated how the rhetoric of antimonopoly, even at its most intense, had ceased to reflect any real commitment to decentralization. If economic concentration was a problem, and most liberals continued to believe it was, the solution was not to destroy it, but to submit it to increased control by the state.

The New Dealers of the late 1930s used many different labels to describe their political ideas: "antimonopoly," "regulation," "planning." But while once those words had seemed to represent quite distinct concepts of reform, they described now a common vision of government—a vision of capable, committed administrators who would seize command of state institutions, invigorate them, expand their powers when necessary, and make them permanent forces in the workings of the marketplace. The task of liberals, William Douglas wrote in 1938, was "to battle for control of the present government so its various parts may be kept alive as vital forces of democracy." What Americans needed above all, Thurman Arnold argued, was a "religion of government which permits us to face frankly the psychological factors inherent in the development of organizations with public responsibility."

James Landis, chairman of the Securities and Exchange Commission from 1935 to 1937 and later dean of Harvard Law School, published in 1938 a meditation on his own experiences in government in which he expressed something of this new faith. "It is not without reason," he wrote in *The Administrative Process*, "that a nation which believes profoundly in the efficacy of the profit motive is at the same time doubtful as to the eugenic possibilities of breeding supermen to direct the inordinately complex affairs of the larger branches of private industry." But the impossibility of finding "supermen" to manage the economy (as some progressives had once dreamed) was, Landis believed, not a reason to retreat from state activism. It was a reason to enlarge the federal bureaucracy, to substitute for the unattainable "super manager" the massed expertise of hundreds of individual administrators. "A consequence of an expanding interest of government in various phases of the industrial scene," he insisted, "must be the creation of more administrative agencies. . . . Efficiency in the processes of governmental regulation is best served by the creation of more rather than less agencies."

Increasing the regulatory functions of the federal government was not, of course, an idea new to the 1930s. Curbing corporate power, attacking monopoly, imposing order on a disordered economic world—those had been the dreams of generations of reformers since the advent of large-scale industrialization. But the concept of an administrative state that was gaining favor in the late New Deal, while rhetorically familiar, was substantively different from the visions that had attracted reformers even five years earlier. Younger liberals continued to use the language of earlier reform impulses; but without ever quite saying so, they were rejecting one of the central features of those impulses.

For decades, American reformers had dreamed of creating a harmonious industrial economy, a system that could flourish without extensive state interference and produce enough wealth to solve the nation's most serious social problems. There had been widely varying ideas about how to create such an economy, from the associational visions of creating a smoothly functioning, organic whole out of the clashing parts of modern capitalism to the antimonopolist yearning for a small-scale decentralized economy freed of the nefarious influence of large combinations. But the larger dream—the dream of somehow actually "solving" the problems of modern capitalism—had been one of the most evocative of all reform hopes and the goal of most progressives and liberals who advocated an expanded state role in the economy.

By the end of the 1930s, faith in such broad solutions was in retreat. Liberal prescriptions for federal economic policy were becoming detached from the vision of a harmonious capitalist world. The state could not, liberals were coming to believe, in any fundamental way "solve" the problems of the economy. The industrial economy was too large, too complex, too diverse; no single economic plan could encompass it all. Americans would have to accept the inevitability of conflict and instability in their economic lives. And they would have to learn to rely on the state to regulate that conflict and instability.

This new vision of the state was in some ways more aggressive and assertive than the prescriptions it replaced. And it was the very limits of its ultimate ambitions that made it so. The new breed of administrators would operate from no "master plan." Nor would they ever reach a point where economic reforms obviated the need for their own services. They would, rather, be constantly active, ever vigilant referees (or, as Arnold liked to put it, "traffic managers"), always ready to step into the market to remove "bottlenecks," to protect efficiency and competition, and to defend the interests of consumers, who were replacing producers as the ultimate focus of liberal concern. The regulators would not, could not, create lasting harmony and order. They would simply commit the state to the difficult task of making the best of an imperfect economic world.

The aggressively statist ideas of the new liberals aroused intense and constant controversy—controversy that revealed how untenable their position really was. The idea of perpetual intrusive government involvement in the workings of the economy, with no hope of ever setting things right in a way that would permit the government to withdraw, was a rebuke both to the anti-statist impulses deeply embedded in American political culture and to the natural yearning for simple, complete solutions to important problems. Even most liberals were never fully comfortable with the idea that there was no real "answer" to the economic question. So it is perhaps unsurprising that when an alternative "solution," with an appealing, almost dazzling simplicity, began to emerge, it found a ready, even eager, following.

III

While some New Dealers were expressing enthusiasm for an expanded regulatory state, others within the administration were promoting a different course of action that would ultimately become more important in shaping the future of liberalism. They proposed that the government make more energetic use of its fiscal powers—its capacity to tax and spend—to stimulate economic growth and solve social problems. Advocates of the fiscal approach, like advocates of regulation, were principally interested in aiding consumers and increasing mass purchasing power. But they seized on different tools. Theirs was a vision of an essentially compensatory government, which would redress weaknesses and imbalances in the private economy without directly confronting the internal workings of capitalism. Such a state could manage the economy without managing the institutions of the economy.

There were few signs early in 1937 that new, more ambitious fiscal policies were on the horizon. Instead, the administration began the year in a confident mood and seemed prepared to return to the still appealing orthodoxies of balanced budgets and reduced spending. The depression, it appeared, was finally over. Unemployment remained disturbingly high, to be sure, but other signs—factory production, capital investment, stock prices—were encouraging. Inspired by these apparent successes, fiscal conservatives pressed their case with an almost gleeful vigor.

Leading the campaign for "fiscal responsibility" was Secretary of the Treasury Henry Morgenthau, Jr., whose relentless private efforts to win Roosevelt's support for a balanced budget belied his public image as a passive sycophant with no strong ideas of his own. Morgenthau and his allies admitted that deficit spending had been necessary during the economic emergency, but they had never credited the concept with any real legitimacy. And now that the New Deal had "licked the Great Depression," as a treasury official wrote in 1937, it was time to put the nation's finances back in order. The president, who had never been fully reconciled to the budget deficits he had so consistently accumulated, was receptive to such arguments. In the spring of 1937 he agreed to a series of substantial cuts in federal spending that would, he believed, balance the budget in 1938.

The idea of a balanced budget was appealing for reasons beyond inherited dogma. Morgenthau managed to persuade the president that only by eliminating deficits could the New Deal truly prove its success; federal spending, he argued, had become a crutch, propping up an economy that—because of the administration's achievements—could now stand on its own. Roosevelt, moreover, recalled the charges of fiscal irresponsibility he had leveled against Hoover in 1932 and saw a balanced budget as a way to vindicate his earlier attacks. Economists in the Treasury Department argued further that there was a danger now of inflation and that trimming the federal deficit would contribute to price stability. There were dissenters. Chief among them was Marriner Eccles, chairman of the Federal Reserve Board, who called efforts to balance the budget "dangerously premature" and defended deficits as "a necessary, compensatory form of investment which gave life to an economy operating below capacity." But nothing could prevail against the sunny optimism and strenuous bureaucratic infighting of Morgenthau and his allies. "The President gave me . . . everything that I asked for," Morgenthau gloated in the spring of 1937. "It was a long hard trying fight but certainly at some time during the weeks that I argued with him he must have come to the conclusion that if he wants his Administration to go forward with his reform program he must have a sound financial foundation."

The economic collapse of the fall of 1937 destroyed hopes for a balanced budget in 1938. More significantly, it discredited many of the arguments supporting those hopes. "No one can doubt," the *New Republic* wrote, "that the sudden withdrawal of hundreds of millions of dollars of federal relief funds, the smashing of thousands of projects all over the country, did contribute materially to the creation of our present misery." Within a few months, even many erstwhile defenders of fiscal orthodoxy had come to believe that the spending cuts of the previous spring had been an important, perhaps even a decisive, cause of the recession. The center of power in the debate over fiscal policy suddenly shifted.

Morgenthau and his allies in the Treasury Department continued to argue strenuously for fiscal conservatism even in the face of the new disasters. But they were now arguing almost alone. Throughout the early months of 1938, Eccles arranged meetings with sympathetic administration officials to press the case for spending and quickly mobilized influential supporters—Henry Wallace, Harold Ickes, Harry Hopkins, Aubrey Williams, Leon Henderson, Lauchlin Currie, Mordecai Ezekiel, Beardsley Ruml, Isidor Lubin—committed to a vigorous new anti-recession program. In March, a group of spending advocates assembled in Warm Springs, where the president was vacationing. And while Williams, Ruml, and Henderson huddled at a nearby inn preparing ammunition, Hopkins sat with the president in the "Little White House," spread the evidence out on the rickety card table Roosevelt liked to use as a desk, and persuaded him to shift his course. A few weeks later, the president sent a message to Congress proposing a substantial new spending program: an additional $1.5 billion for work relief, another $1.5 billion for public works, and an expansion of credit of approximately $2 billion. It was not enough, some critics maintained. But at a time when the nation's peacetime budget had never exceeded $10 billion, most considered $5 billion substantial indeed.

What was particularly significant was the way Roosevelt explained the new proposals. In his first term, he had generally justified spending programs as ways to deal with particular targeted problems: helping the unemployed, subsidizing farmers or homeowners or troubled industries, redeveloping the Tennessee Valley. Now he justified spending as a way to bring the economy as a whole back to health. "We suffer primarily from a lack of buying power," he explained in a fireside chat early in 1938 (its text drawn in part from a Beardsley Ruml memo). It was time for the government "to make definite additions to the purchasing power of the nation." He accompanied his announcement (as he was fond of doing) with references to the historical precedents for his decision:

> In the first century of our republic we were short of capital, short of workers and short of industrial production; but we were rich in free land, free timber and free mineral wealth. The Federal Government rightly assumed the duty of promoting business and relieving depression by giving subsidies of land and other resources.
>
> Thus, from our earliest days we have had a tradition of substantial government help to our system of private enterprise. But today the government no longer has vast tracts of rich land to give away. . . . [N]ow we have plenty of capital, banks and insurance companies loaded with idle money; plenty of industrial productive capacity and several millions of workers looking for jobs. It is following tradition as well as necessity, if Government strives to put idle money and idle men to work, to increase our public wealth and to build up the health and strength of the people—to help our system of private enterprise to function.

Roosevelt's comfortable references to the past failed to mask the genuinely unprecedented nature of his statement. Government spending, the president now implied, was no longer a necessary evil, to be used sparingly to solve specific problems. It was a positive good, to be used lavishly at times to stimulate economic growth and social progress. Without fully realizing it, he was embracing the essence of what would soon be known as Keynesian economics. He was ushering in a new era of government fiscal policy.

In many respects, fiscal activism was no newer to the 1930s than the regulatory innovations with which it coexisted. Federal subsidization of private interests was as old as the federal government itself. But the kind of spending New Dealers supported throughout the 1930s, and the rationale they were gradually developing to justify it, suggested an important departure. In the past, government subsidies had almost always promoted the productive capacities of the nation. They had been designed to assist the builders of roads, bridges, dams, railroads, and other essential elements of the economic infrastructure. They had encouraged settlement of the West and the development of new agricultural frontiers. More recently, they had assisted banks and other financial institutions to weather the storms of the depression.

But ideas about government spending changed significantly in the late New Deal. Instead of advocating federal fiscal policies that would contribute directly to production and economic development, liberals pressed for policies that would promote mass consumption. Alvin Hansen, one of the first important American economists to grasp and promote the teachings of Keynes, took note of this important shift in outlook. The best way to ensure a prosperous future, he was arguing in the late 1930s, was "to work toward a higher consumption economy," to make consumer demand the force driving production and investment instead of the other way around. And the most efficient way to create such demand was for the government to pump more spending power into the economy—through public works, social security, federal credit mechanisms, and other methods. "Consumption," he argued, "is the frontier of the future."

IV

These two broad approaches to the problems of the economy—increased state regulation and increased use of fiscal policy—coexisted relatively easily in the late 1930s. Indeed, most New Dealers considered them two halves of a single strategy and seldom thought very much about the differences between them.

What bound these two strategies together most closely was an assumption about the American economy that suffused liberal thought in the late 1930s and helped drive efforts to discover a new role for the state. Even before the 1937 recession, doubts had been growing within the New Deal about the nation's capacity ever again to enjoy the kind of economic growth it had experienced in the half-century before the Great Depression. The setbacks of 1937 only reinforced those concerns. The economy had been dragging for nearly a decade; sluggish growth and high unemployment were beginning to seem part of the natural order of things. Out of those fears emerged the concept of the "mature economy."

The idea that economic expansion was not (and could not become) limitless drew from a long tradition of such predictions in America, stretching back at least to the nineteenth century. . . .

It was not simply the exhaustion of land and other natural resources that presented problems. Nor was it the slackening population growth of the 1930s, which had led many analysts to predict very slow future increases and a leveling off at 175 million around the year 2000. The most important source of "economic maturity," defenders of the concept claimed, was the end of "capital accumulation." The great age of industrial growth was finally over. The basic industries were now built. No new sectors capable of matching railroads, steel, and automobiles as engines of expansion were likely to emerge. And since economic growth alone would no longer be sufficient to meet the needs of society, new forms of management were now essential if the nation's limited resources were to be sensibly and fairly allocated. . . .

The mature-economy idea provided powerful support to arguments for increasing the regulatory functions of the state. An economy in which dynamic growth was no longer possible placed nearly unbearable pressures on those in the marketplace to avoid risks and thus to collude to raise (or "administer") prices. Only a strong administrative state could combat this dangerous trend. But the same concept added strength to arguments for greater government spending as well. In the absence of large-scale private investment, only the government had the resources (and the broad "national" view of the economic problem) necessary to keep even modest economic growth alive.

The writings of Alvin Hansen illustrate how the belief in economic maturation was helping to fuse regulatory and spending ideas. Hansen agreed that "the age of capital investment is past"; and he explained the result with the idea of what he called "secular stagnation"—a concept that became one of his principal contributions to Keynesian theory (and one that Keynes himself never fully accepted). Private institutions, Hansen argued, had lost the ability to create large-scale economic growth; indeed, they were now likely actually to retard such growth through anti-competitive practices as they struggled to survive in a more difficult world. One solution, therefore, was vigorous antitrust efforts to restore fluidity to the marketplace. Like Keynes, however, Hansen believed that fluidity alone would not be enough. Government also had a responsibility to sustain and, when necessary, increase purchasing power to keep alive the higher levels of consumption upon which the mature economy would now have to rely. Regulatory and fiscal mechanisms would work together to produce economic growth.

But the partnership of the regulatory and compensatory visions, which for a time had seemed so natural and untroubled, did not last, at least not on equal terms. By 1945, the idea of the administrative state, which had seemed so powerful in the late 1930s, was in decline; and the faith in fiscal policy, so tentatively embraced in 1938, had moved to the center of liberal hopes. The reason for that change was not simply that the spending initiatives of the late 1930s seemed to work; even when they did, many liberals continued to consider spending little more than a temporary stopgap and continued to believe that more lasting statist solutions were necessary. The change was also a result of the American experience in World War II.

V

World War I spawned two decades of bitter recriminations among Americans who believed the nation had intervened in the conflict for no useful purpose. But it also helped shape bright dreams among progressives of a more harmonious economic world at home, dreams of a vaguely corporatist economy in which private institutions would learn to cooperate on behalf of the public interest and in which the state would preside benignly over a new era of growth and progress.

Those dreams, however untrue to the realities of the wartime experience, fueled a generation of reform efforts and helped shape the early New Deal.

In the 1940s, by contrast, the war itself—the reasons for it, the necessity of it—produced little controversy and few recriminations. But neither did it evoke among liberals anything comparable to the World War I enthusiasm for a reformed and reordered economy. On the contrary, the war helped reduce enthusiasm for a powerful regulatory state and helped legitimize the idea of a primarily compensatory government.

Many factors contributed to this wartime evolution of opinion. The political climate was changing rapidly: The Republicans had rebounded in the 1938 and 1940 elections; conservatives had gained strength in Congress; the public was displaying a growing antipathy toward the more aggressive features of the New Deal and a declining animus toward big business. Liberals responded by lowering their sights and modifying their goals. The labor movement, similarly, encountered during the war intense popular hostility, along with strong pressure from the government to abandon its more ambitious political goals. Its accommodation with the state, and its alliance with the Democratic party, limited its capacity to act as an independent political force and to press for structural economic reforms. Liberals who had once admired the collective character of some European governments looked with horror at the totalitarian states America was now fighting and saw in them a warning about what an excessively powerful state could become. And the emergence of an important American role in the world, which virtually all liberals came to believe must extend indefinitely beyond the end of the war, directed attention and energy away from domestic reform ideas.

But the war had two more direct effects on liberal hopes for the state. It forced American government actually to attempt many of the aggressive managerial tasks that reformers had long advocated. The results of those efforts not only failed to increase faith in the ability of the state to administer a rationalized economy but actually diminished it. At the same time, the war spurred a revival of the economy that dispelled some of the doubts liberals had once harbored about the capacity of capitalism to expand and the ability of private institutions to govern themselves.

In the beginning, at least, many liberals expected otherwise. The war, they hoped, would strengthen the case for a government role in administering the economy and would enhance the influence and prestige of state bureaucracies and administrators. . . .

By 1945, however, the wartime experience had led most [liberals] to conclude otherwise: that neither a new economic order nor active state management of the present one were necessary, possible, or desirable; that the existing structure of capitalism (including its relative independence from state control) represented the best hope for social progress; and that the government's most important task was less to regulate the private economy than to help it expand and to compensate for its occasional failures.

Even at the start, the government approached the task of organizing the economy for war in a way that suggested a degree of anti-statism. For two years before Pearl Harbor, the president and most of his principal advisers resisted the idea of creating a single, centralized locus of authority for mobilization and preferred instead to disperse power widely among an array of ad hoc committees, boards, and agencies. A series of production crises ultimately forced Roosevelt early in 1942 to create a single agency with a single director charged with supervising the war economy. But the shift was more apparent than real. Genuine authority remained divided, and the only ultimate arbiter of the chaos— Roosevelt himself—was always too preoccupied with other issues (or too incapacitated by his declining health) to resolve the confusion. World War II never produced a bureaucratic mechanism comparable to the War Industries Board of 1918, nor did it produce a production manager comparable to Bernard Baruch. There was, therefore, no comparable model of economic planning to fuel liberal hopes.

The administration similarly resisted the idea of placing control of the wartime economy in the hands of professional civil servants or others from the permanent state bureaucracy. This was not, of course, entirely a matter of choice. The federal government, despite its considerable expansion during the 1930s, still lacked anything approaching sufficient bureaucratic capacity for managing a mobilization effort. The civil service and the professional political community had little experience or expertise in supervising the institutions of the industrial economy. The one major effort to "modernize" the federal bureaucracy and equip it to perform more advanced administrative tasks—Roosevelt's executive reorganization plan of 1938—had encountered substantial political opposition and had ultimately produced only modest reforms. And so it was inevitable, perhaps, that the state would turn to the private sector for its administrative talent. But there was also an element of conscious preference to that choice. In the more conservative climate of the 1940s, Roosevelt preferred a conciliatory approach to war mobilization, an approach that liberal critics sometimes charged was an abdication of power to corporate figures but that the president believed was simply prudent politics.

The central agency of mobilization was the War Production Board, whose four-year existence was an almost endless bureaucratic ordeal. Roosevelt created the WPB in January 1942, only weeks after America's formal entry into the war, as the successor to a long string of failed organizational efforts. It was, he promised, to be the single production agency with a single manager for which many critics had been clamoring all along. But the WPB failed on several levels to fulfill hopes for effective government supervision of the economy. It was, in the first place, not in any real sense a state institution at all. It was, rather, a collection of corporate executives and corporate lawyers, most of them still drawing salaries from their peacetime employers and working temporarily for the government for token payments (hence the label "dollar-a-year men," by which, like their World War I counterparts, they were generally known). Many of the leading WPB officials were implacably hostile to anything that smacked of centralized planning and considered it their mission not only to expedite war mobilization but to resist any attempt to make the war an occasion for the permanent expansion of the state. "The arsenal of democracy . . . is still being operated with one eye on the war and the other on the convenience of big business," the always skeptical I. F. Stone wrote only months after the WPB began operations. "The progress made on production so far is the fruit of necessity and improvisation rather than of foresight and planning, and the men running the program are not willing to fight business interests on behalf of good will and good intentions.". . .

For many liberals, then, the WPB served not as an inspiration but as an alarming indication of what government management of the economy would become: a mechanism by which members of the corporate world could take over the regulatory process and turn it to their own advantage. What made the WPB experience particularly disturbing, moreover, was that it was not an aberration. Corporate "capture" of state institutions had been a lament of many liberals for years; that the war not only failed to reverse that tendency, but seemed to advance it, raised questions about whether traditional forms of regulation were workable at all.

The actual performance of the WPB did little more to encourage hopes for state planning than its structure. Although it managed to avoid any genuine catastrophes, the agency was in continual administrative disarray. It was crippled from the start by its lack of adequate authority to resist other centers of power (most notably the military) in the battle for control of production decisions. It failed miserably to protect the interests of small business, despite strenuous efforts from both within the agency and without to force it to do so. It suffered continually from the unwillingness of the president to support its decisions unreservedly; Franklin Roosevelt preferred to keep all potential power centers (and thus all possible rivals) in his administration relatively weak. . . .

Even some of the strongest supporters of federal regulatory efforts in the late 1930s found the experience of the war years discouraging. In 1937, Thurman Arnold had called on Americans to develop a "religion of government." By 1943, he was disillusioned and impatient with what he had seen of state control of the economy. "The economic planners are always too complicated for me," he wrote his friend William Allen White. "They were bound to get in power during a period of frustration"; but their time, he implied, had passed. The dreams of an extensive regulatory state were coming to seem unrealistic, perhaps even dangerous. And that realization encouraged a search for other, less intrusive, vehicles of economic management.

VI

Declining faith in the managerial capacities of the state coincided with another development that had profound effects on liberal assumptions about the future: the revival of American capitalism. After a decade of depression, a decade of declining confidence in the economy and despair about the prospects for future growth, the industrial economy restored itself and, perhaps more important for the future of national politics, redeemed itself in a single stroke.

In the process, it helped erode one of the mainstays of late-depression liberalism. The wartime economic experience—the booming expansion, the virtual end of unemployment, the creation of new industries, new "frontiers"—served as a rebuke to the "mature economy" idea and placed the concept of growth at the center of liberal hopes. The capitalist economy, liberals suddenly discovered, was not irretrievably stagnant. Economic expansion could achieve, in fact had achieved, dimensions beyond the wildest dreams of the 1930s. Social and economic advancement could proceed, therefore, without structural changes in capitalism and without continuing, intrusive state management of the economy. It could proceed by virtue of growth.

Assaults on the concept of "economic maturity" began to emerge as early as 1940 and gathered force throughout the war. Alvin Hansen himself partially repudiated the theory in 1941 ("All of us had our sights too low," he admitted). The *New Republic* and the *Nation,* both of which had embraced the idea in 1938 and 1939, openly rejected it in the 1940s—not only rejected it, but celebrated its demise. The country had achieved a "break," the *Nation* insisted, "from the defeatist thinking that held us in economic thraldom through the thirties, when it was assumed that we could not afford full employment or full production in this country."

But to believe that growth was feasible was not necessarily to believe that it was inevitable. "Enough for all is now possible for the first time in history," a 1943 administration study reported. "But the mere existence of plenty of labor, raw materials, capital, and organizing skill is no guarantee that all reasonable wants will be supplied—or that wealth will actually be produced." Except perhaps for the prospect of military defeat (a prospect seldom contemplated by most Americans), nothing inspired more fear during the war years than the specter of a peacetime economic collapse and a return to the high levels of unemployment that had been the most troubling and intractable problem of the 1930s. How to prevent that collapse now became the central element on the national political agenda; and for liberals, as for others, that meant a basic change in outlook. Instead of debating how best to distribute limited output and how most efficiently to manage a stagnant economy, reformers began to discuss how to keep the wartime economic boom—and the high levels of income and employment it had produced—alive in the postwar years. "Full employment" was the new rallying cry of liberal economists; all other goals gradually came to seem secondary. And the route to full employment, the war seemed to demonstrate, was not state management of capitalist institutions, but fiscal policies that would promote consumption and thus stimulate economic growth.

The new approach was particularly clear in the deliberations of those committed to the idea of "planning," above all, perhaps, in the work of the National Resources Planning Board. In the first years of the war (before its demise in 1943 at the hands of hostile congressional conservatives), the NRPB produced a series of reports outlining an ambitious program for postwar economic growth and security. It showed in the process how the "planning" ideal was shifting away from the vision of a rationally ordered economy (prominent in the early 1930s) and away from the idea of the activist, regulatory state (a central feature of late 1930s reform) and toward the concept of compensatory action. Planning would enable government to stimulate economic growth through fiscal policies. It would allow the state to make up for the omissions and failings of capitalism through the expansion of welfare programs. It need not involve increased state management of capitalist institutions.

The NRPB had begun its life in 1933 under Harold Ickes in the Interior Department. And during its first half-dozen years of existence (under four different names and several different structures), it had generally reflected a view of planning derived from the city planning backgrounds of many of its members and from the regional planning experience of the Tennessee Valley Authority and other, smaller, New Deal projects. City planning and regional planning— the coordination of government programs in particular localities to reshape the social, physical, and economic environment—served for a time as microcosmic models for a larger concept of a planned society. The federal government, through a combination of public investment, public welfare, and extensive regulation, could become a major actor in the workings of the national economy, could direct its course, shape its future.

The concept of planning to which the NRPB became principally committed in the first years of the war was subtly yet significantly different. The board continued to outline public works projects and to insist on their importance; but it usually portrayed such projects now less as vehicles for remaking the environment than as opportunities for countercyclic government spending. Its mission was to create a "shelf" of potential public undertakings, from which the government could draw projects "as insurance against industrial collapse and unemployment"; the intrinsic value of the projects as vehicles for urban or regional planning had become secondary. Welfare programs (and, above all, an expansion of the Social Security system) had, in the meantime, moved to the center of the NRPB prescription for federal social activism—both because such programs now appeared affordable (given the new abundance apparently within the nation's grasp) and because they could themselves serve the cause of growth by increasing and redistributing purchasing power.

The board's 1942 report, *Security, Work, and Relief Policies* (released by the president early in 1943), outlined a program of "social security" of such breadth and ambition that it was widely dubbed the "American Beveridge Report," after the nearly simultaneous study that led to the creation of a new British welfare state. But the NRPB proposals were, in fact, significantly different from, and in some ways more extensive than, their British counterparts. The Beveridge Report restricted itself largely to a discussion of social welfare and insurance mechanisms; the NRPB proposed such mechanisms in the context of what it considered a larger goal: the maintenance of full employment. The board's 1943 "National Resources Development Report" called explicitly for government programs to maintain a "dynamic expanding economy on the order of 100 to 125 billions of national income." Only a few years before, such a figure would have seemed preposterously high. "We must plan for full employment," members of the board wrote in a 1942 article explaining their proposals. "We shall plan to balance our national production-consumption budget at a high level with full employment, not at a low level with mass unemployment."

The board did not altogether abandon its concern about state management of economic institutions. Even very late in its existence, it continued to include in its reports recommendations for expanded antitrust efforts, for new regulatory mechanisms, and for other extensions of the government's administrative role. One of its

1943 documents, in fact, spoke so explicitly about a drastic expansion of state control of the economy that it evoked rare applause from I. F. Stone, who generally decried the administration's "timidity," but who saw in the NRPB proposals "large and historic aims."

But this lingering interest in what Franklin Roosevelt once dismissed as "grandiose schemes" was by now secondary—both to the members of the board themselves and, to an even greater extent, to other liberals interpreting its work—to the larger, simpler task of maintaining economic growth. "We know," the authors of the 1943 "Resources Development Report" wrote,

> that the road to the new democracy runs along the highway of a dynamic economy, to the full use of our national resources, to full employment, and increasingly higher standards of living. . . . We stand on the threshold of an economy of abundance. This generation has it within its power not only to produce in plenty but to distribute that plenty.

As columnist Ernest K. Lindley noted, "The most striking characteristic of the two [1943 NRPB] reports is their essential conservatism. The postwar is keyed to the restoration of the free enterprise system and its encouragement and stimulation."

Central to this new emphasis on growth was the increasing influence of the ideas of John Maynard Keynes and of the growing number of American economists who were becoming committed to his theories. By the late 1930s, Keynes himself was already personally friendly with some of the leading figures of the New Deal. At the same time, leading American economists were becoming proponents of Keynesian ideas. Alvin Hansen, Mordecai Ezekiel, and Gardiner Means, for example, all of whom were active on the NRPB and all of whom reached broader audiences through their essays in economic journals and liberal magazines, had by the early years of the war become converted to at least a portion of Keynes's general theory. . . .

The wartime expansion had proved to liberals that given sufficient stimuli, the economy could grow at an impressive rate. Keynes's economic doctrines (and the larger constellation of ideas derived from them) suggested ways to introduce in peacetime the kinds of stimuli that had created the impressive wartime expansion.

They offered, in fact, an escape from one of liberalism's most troubling dilemmas and a mechanism for which reformers had long been groping. They provided a way to manage the economy without directly challenging the prerogatives of capitalists. Growth did not necessarily require constant involvement in the affairs of private institutions, which (as the experience of wartime mobilization helped demonstrate) was both endlessly complex and politically difficult; it did not require a drastic expansion of the regulatory functions of the state. "To produce in plenty" required only the indirect manipulation of the economy through the use of fiscal and monetary "levers"; and to "distribute that plenty" required the creation of an efficient welfare system. Such measures were not (as some liberals had once believed) simply temporary stopgaps, keeping things going until some more basic solution could be found; they were themselves the solution.

The renewed wartime faith in economic growth led, in short, to several ideological conclusions of considerable importance to the future of liberalism. It helped relegitimize American capitalism among a circle of men and women who had developed serious doubts about its viability in an advanced economy. It robbed the "regulatory" reform ideas of the late 1930s of their urgency and gave credence instead to Keynesian ideas of indirect management of the economy. And it fused the idea of the welfare state to the larger vision of sustained economic growth by defining social security mechanisms as ways to distribute income and enhance purchasing power. No other single factor was as central to the redefinition of liberal goals as the simple reality of abundance and the rebirth of faith in capitalism abundance helped to inspire.

VII

By the end of World War II, the concept of New Deal liberalism had assumed a new form; and in its assumptions could be seen the outlines of a transformed political world. Those who were taking the lead in defining a liberal agenda in the aftermath of the war still called themselves New Dealers, but they showed relatively little interest in the corporatist and regulatory ideas that had once played so large a role in shaping the New Deal. They largely ignored the New Deal's abortive experiments in economic planning, its failed efforts to create harmonious associational arrangements, its vigorous if short-lived antimonopoly and regulatory crusades, its open skepticism toward capitalism and its captains, its overt celebration of the state. Instead, they emphasized those New Deal accomplishments that could be reconciled more easily with the vision of an essentially compensatory government. They lauded the New Deal's innovations in social welfare and social insurance; a decade earlier many had considered such initiatives of secondary importance. They credited the New Deal with legitimizing government fiscal policy as a way of dealing with fluctuations in the business cycle and guaranteeing full employment; few liberals in the 1930s had understood, let alone supported, such policies. Above all, perhaps, postwar liberals celebrated the New Deal for having discovered solutions to the problems of capitalism that required no alteration in the structure of capitalism; for having defined a role for the state that did not intrude it too far into the economy. In earlier years, many liberals had considered the absence of significant institutional reform one of the New Deal's failures.

This transformation had proceeded slowly, at times almost imperceptibly, so much so that for a time many liberals were unaware that it had even occurred. But for those who cared to look, signs of the change were abundant. It was visible, for example, in the character of the postwar liberal community. The "planners," "regulators," and "antimonopolists" who had dominated liberal circles eight years earlier were now largely in eclipse, without much influence on public discourse. Thurman Arnold, Robert Jackson, and William Douglas were sitting on federal courts. Thomas Corcoran was practicing law. Benjamin Cohen was accepting occasional assignments as a delegate to international conferences. Leon Henderson, one of the last of the true "New Dealers" to hold a major administrative post during the war, had resigned as head of the Office of Price Administration in December 1942 and had become an embittered critic of the government's failures, convinced that without more assertive state planning and regulation the nation faced an economic disaster after the war.

No comparably powerful network could be said to have emerged by 1945 to take their place; indeed, many liberals were now so preoccupied with international questions and with the emerging schism within their ranks over the Soviet Union that they paid less attention to domestic issues. But those who did attempt to define a domestic agenda were largely people fired with enthusiasm for the vision of a full-employment economy, people who considered the New Deal's principal legacy the idea of effective use of fiscal policy and the expansion of social welfare and insurance programs. In place of the "statist" liberals who had helped define public discourse in the 1930s were such people as Alvin Hansen, one of the architects of the principal liberal initiative of 1945, the Full Employment bill; or Chester Bowles, the last director of the Office of Price Administration, whose 1946 book *Tomorrow Without Fear* called not for an expansion, or even a continuation, of the regulatory experiments with which he had been involved during the war but for an increased reliance on fiscal policy.

The Democratic platform in 1944 was another sign of the changing political landscape. Four years earlier, the party had filled its platform with calls for attacks on "unbridled concentration of economic power and the exploitation of the consumer and the investor." It had boasted of the New Deal's regulatory innovations, its aggressive antitrust policies, its war on "the extortionate methods of monopoly." The 1944 platform also praised the administration's antimonopoly and regulatory efforts—in a perfunctory sentence near the end. But most of its limited discussion of domestic issues centered on how the New Deal had "found the road to prosperity" through aggressive compensatory measures: fiscal policies and social welfare innovations.

The changing landscape of liberalism was visible as well in some of the first retrospective celebrations of the New Deal, in the way early defenders of its legacy attempted to define its accomplishments. In 1948, Arthur M. Schlesinger, Jr., published an essay entitled "The Broad Accomplishments of the New Deal." The New Deal, he admitted, "made no fundamental attempt to grapple with the problem of the economies of concentration or of the decline in outlets for real investment." But that, he claimed, was not really the point. The New Deal's most significant accomplishments were much simpler and more important: "The New Deal took a broken and despairing land and gave it new confidence in itself. . . . All [Roosevelt's] solutions were incomplete. But then all great problems are insoluble."

VIII

The importance of the New Deal lies in large part, of course, in its actual legislative and institutional achievements. But it lies as well in its ideological impact on subsequent generations of liberals and in its effects on two decades of postwar government activism. And in that light, the New Deal appears not just as a bright moment in which reform energies briefly prevailed but as part of a long process of ideological adaptation.

For more than half a century, Americans concerned about the impact of industrialization on their society—about the economic instability, the social dislocations, the manifest injustices—had harbored deep and continuing doubts about the institutions of capitalism. Relatively few had wanted to destroy those institutions, but many had wanted to use the powers of government to reshape or at least to tame them. And that desire had been a central element of "progressive" and "liberal" hopes from the late nineteenth century through the late 1930s.

The ideological history of the late New Deal, from the troubled years after 1937 through the conclusion of the war, is the story of a slow repudiation of such commitments and the elevation of other hopes to replace them. By 1945, American liberals, as the result of countless small adaptations to a broad range of experiences, had reached an accommodation with capitalism that served, in effect, to settle many of the most divisive conflicts of the first decades of the century. They had done so by convincing themselves that the achievements of the New Deal had already eliminated the most dangerous features of the capitalist system; by committing themselves to the belief that economic growth was the surest route to social progress; and by defining a role for the state that would, they believed, permit it to compensate for capitalism's inevitable flaws and omissions without interfering with its internal workings. Thus reconciled to the structure of their economy, liberals of the postwar world could move forward into new crusades—fighting for civil rights, eliminating poverty, saving the environment, protecting consumers, opposing communism, reshaping the world—crusades that would produce their own achievements and their own frustrations, and that would one day lead to another, still unfinished, ideological transformation.

Ellis W. Hawley

State-Building in an Antibureaucratic Culture

For almost half a century one of the unchallenged assumptions of the New Deal was that it had established a "modern state" of regulatory and social-welfare systems comparable to those of other industrial nations. The New Deal was synonymous with "big government." No one disputes that the New Deal substantially enlarged the size and functions of the national government. Scholars such as Otis Graham and Barry Karl, however, have argued that what the New Deal created was a government that was weak and fragmented and possessing only a limited capacity to plan and manage the national economy. In this insightful essay, Ellis Hawley accepts this view and argues that what emerged from the New Deal was a national government with a "hollow core" at its center. But why was this the case? Hawley's answer questions much of what has been written about the New Deal for he argues that the New Dealers were divided over whether to build powerful national bureaucracies through which to govern. Much of the New Deal reflected America's deeply rooted "antibureaucratic" impulses that sought to maintain limited, restrained, and fragmented government. These impulses shaped the New Deal state-building process in critical ways, and the result was a national government that grew out of a mix of bureaucratic and antibureaucratic values.

Ellis W. Hawley is professor of history emeritus at the University of Iowa and has written *The New Deal and the Problem of Monopoly: A Study in Economic Ambivalence* (1966) and *The Great War and the Search for a Modern Order* (1979).

As we reconsider the New Deal from the perspective of more than fifty years, we need to look anew at the New Deal state as it took shape in the years between 1933 and 1939. Indeed, the time seems particularly ripe for this. For not only have we come to realize that we know too little about it. We are also learning again about the value of state-centered studies; or, as the current movement in his-

The *New Deal and Its Legacy: Critique and Reappraisal,* Robert Eden, ed. Copyright © 1989 by Robert Eden. Reproduced with permission of Greenwood Publishing Group, Inc., Westport, CT., pp. 77–90.

tory and the social sciences puts it, about the necessity of "bringing the state back in."

For a time, studies of the state—that is, of governmental structure, apparatus, and workings—had fallen into disrepute. The state, it was said, was only a tool, or a register of the forces in society. For the Marxists, it was a tool of the ruling class; for pluralists, a register of the contending interests in society; for others, a register of the impact of social movements. The explanation for what the state did lay elsewhere, and therefore it did not really deserve much study. Recently, however, this view of the matter has been changing. The structure of the state does demonstrably make a difference; government officials are not simply tools or registers. They can, and do, act independently to alter governmental outputs. Hence it behooves us to understand a nation's polity as well as its society if we are to understand its historical behavior. . . .

In American popular thought the state that came out of the New Deal has usually been seen as a result of bureaucratization reaching the national level and establishing itself there as a central feature of modern American life. The assumption underlying this view . . . is that the growth of government in the 1930s moved us toward the kind of bureaucratization characteristic of the "welfare state" elsewhere, and that the consequences lie at the heart of current political cleavages. Yet we have also had a considerable body of scholarship in recent years that directly challenges this assumption and stresses the failure of the New Deal to construct a true administrative state of the type that emerged elsewhere. The emphasis in this scholarship is on the divergence between the path that America has followed since the New Deal, and the path taken by statebuilders in other industrialized democracies. We have had a line of thought, in other words, that would favor undoing the New Deal, not because it led us into the errors being committed abroad, but because it erected obstructions in the path of needed institutional development.

Can these two approaches be reconciled? Can the New Deal state be represented both as a product of bureaucratic formation at the national level and as a result of anti-bureaucratic traditions seeking to prevent and find substitutes for bureaucratic development? I believe that it can; and my thesis in what follows is that seeing it in this way can add important dimensions to our understanding of the New Deal. More exactly, I shall look first at the heritages of state-building and opposition to bureaucracy that existed at the beginning of the New Deal; second, at the continuing interplay between the search for an administrative state and the quest for ways to do without one, during this period; and third, at the results as they became parts of the government. Understanding these matters will help us to reach a better understanding not only of the history of state-building in the 1930s, but also of the legacy from the period.

Roots of the Administrative State

We may begin by noting that the United States in 1933 did not yet have an administrative state, at least not in the European sense. We did, however, have a considerable history of efforts to build . . . one. As a nation, we never had the monarchical or military bureaucracies that elsewhere became the foundation for administrative states. Our revolution had been directed against them, and in the nineteenth century we developed our own peculiar form of the modern state. It lodged power not in a bureaucratic elite, but in patronage-based political parties, local governmental units, and a strong judicial system. Modern bureaucracy here had emerged primarily in the private sector, largely in connection with the rise of big business, rather than in the public. And those who had seen bureaucratic expansion as the answer to our national problems had not been able to put much of what they advocated into practice before 1933. True, they had established bridgeheads in the public sector, notably in new forms of municipal government, in the creation of various regulatory commissions, in some public support for data production, and in measures aimed at bringing business methods into governmental work. But the administrative apparatus created was not a large one, and it remained highly fragmented, narrowly constrained, and linked to or dependent on the forms of governmental power that had been established earlier. The nation lacked the kind of autonomous administrative establishment to be found elsewhere, and it retained much that was hostile to the acquisition of one.

This is not to say, however, that the United States of 1933 had escaped the influences that contributed elsewhere to the rise of administrative states. To a degree, it had shared in the revulsion against laissez-faire policies, against partisan politics, and against legalistic constitutionalism, revulsions that had helped bureaucratic elites to acquire power in other nations. And the result was the emergence here—particularly in portions of the business community, the new technocratic professions, and segments of the intellectual community engaged in discourse with their counterparts abroad—of reform policies that deplored America's lack of an administrative establishment and looked to developing one as the path to greater efficiency, harmony, and rationality. Such prescriptions had been part of the agitation for reform during the so-called "Progressive era" preceding World War I. They had continued to find advocates in the postwar period, some of whom invoked the war experience to support their arguments. And they were available in 1933 as prescriptions the New Deal might adopt.

Developments from 1930 to 1933, moreover, had created wider openings for such policies. The persistence and deepening of the Depression lent credence to those who blamed market failure. They also created greater impatience with government as it existed; and they had discredited President Hoover's notion that correctives could be coaxed from the nation's private sector. By 1932 there was much discussion of the need for national economic planning and a national welfare system; and in a number of the schemes for meeting this perceived need, a central role was assigned to a new administrative state. In theory, in other words, the new duties could and should be performed by a special group of officials, who were to rise above the bickering of special interests, construct new institutions to serve the public or national interest, and thus become the enlightened controllers and guardians that were needed in a modern industrial society. America's liberal creed and institutional structure, it was argued, had once served it well. But the time had now come to join other democratic nations in developing a "new liberalism," one that recognized the realities of industrial urban life and capitalist development and that made a national administrative establishment a prime tool in securing further national progress.

The New Dealers had at hand, then, a heritage of efforts to implement bureaucratic government, a set of proposals that were the product of this history, and a political crisis that provided a greater opportunity to set them in motion. . . . And among the

New Dealers were a number of people already inclined toward administrative statism. They were to be found in the Brains Trust that provided Roosevelt with ideas during the 1932 campaign; among the reformers now converging on Washington; and among the "experts" being summoned there, especially experts with credentials in such disciplines as public administration and institutional economics.

Yet, while these resources were at hand, the New Deal did not turn out to be a straightforward push to create a new administrative state. Also at hand were opposed public policy traditions, a heritage combining the promise of social rescue and renewed progress with appeals to anti-bureaucratic values—formulations, in other words, that were supposed to save us not only from the anti-social workings of the market, but also from bureaucratic tyranny. . . . [F]our such formulations stand out; and each of these proved to have important implications for what followed.

One such formulation, clearly evident in 1933, was the notion of a "business commonwealth," meeting the needs for planning and welfare through business-led corporative (as opposed to government-run bureaucratic) institutions. This is sometimes seen as an importation from the fascist, social Catholic, and neo-capitalist movements in Europe; and it did, of course, bear certain resemblances to them. But it also had firm roots in the American past. It was the latest in a line of similar formulations reaching back to the crisis of the 1890s—formulations that would make temporary use of government to coax needed social machinery from the new organizations that had formed in the private sector. And like its antecedents, it could and did appeal not only to private sector elites of various sorts, but also to the anti-bureaucratic symbols deeply embedded in American political discourse. The institutions envisioned, so the argument ran, would make possible new forms of "self-government," "community action," "responsible individualism," and "modern democracy." And these would then allow us to have continuing order and progress, while retaining our safeguards against bureaucracy.

A second formulation, also clearly apparent in 1933, although in different circles, was what we might call the "populist commonwealth." This, in theory, could make planning and welfare unnecessary by returning power to the "people" and their "communities" and conclaves. Envisioned here was a reformist state that would use its power to establish a "people's" money, a "people's" tax system, a "people's" antimonopoly law, and other "people's" instruments— all working to destroy the corporate power that had allegedly put the people in chains and robbed them of their capacity to prosper. But at least as the rhetoric had it, none of this would mean power for a new administrative class. On the contrary, as in a line of similar formulations reaching back beyond the 1890s to the early days of the republic, it would save us from the anti-democratic designs of pretentious "experts" who had helped to forge the chains in the first place.

A third formulation, even more in evidence than the two already noted, called for a temporary or emergency form of the administrative state. The underlying assumption in this case was that unusual circumstances had created a "crisis," which required a temporary departure from our normal methods of governance and decision-making. In part, the analogies drawn here were to the temporary structures of management that had arisen to keep order and provide relief in the wake of natural disasters. But in larger part, they were to the administrative apparatus that had been established and used during World War I, in the national emergency of 1917 and 1918. Most of the wartime machinery had been set up outside the regular agencies of government; it had amounted in effect to borrowing private sector administrative resources for public purposes; and it had then been abolished once the emergency had passed. Its construction and usage had been such (or so the argument ran) that it had not brought the evils and dangers inherent in bureaucratic government. And the argument was now that we could be rescued by a similar apparatus, which again would be so constructed and used as to be anti-bureaucratic in its larger effects. As in the case of the other formulations, this was, in theory, a way to have one's cake and eat it too.

Finally, entering the picture as a fourth formulation was a conception of expanded government in which public administrators would be used to implement the designs of deserving interest groups but would not be given the kind of power that would enable them to become a bureaucratic establishment running an administrative state. They would, in other words, remain tied to and take their identities from the groups that they served, would be constrained by a continuing division of powers, and would be coordinated by political brokers as opposed to master administrators.

Envisioned was a kind of "interest group commonwealth" or what some writers later called the "broker state." We would be rescued from the intolerable features of the market economy through a politically brokered administrative expansion, which would allow groups in need of protection or enhanced economic power to acquire them. But the expansion would be such that power would remain in the hands of politicians and interest-group leaders. We would be saved from bureaucratic statism.

What the New Deal really had at hand, then, was not only a set of prescriptions for giving America an administrative state, but also formulations for using government in ways that were supposed to allow us to continue without such a state. It could seize on the latter without ranging itself against the anti-bureaucratic tradition. And in practice, much of the New Deal state grew out of efforts to apply these formulas. . . . By examining [the details of this practice], we can begin to understand how the New Deal state arose within a political culture that retained strong strains of anti-statism and why some now regard it as having erected obstacles to modern state-building, rather than advancing that process.

Early New Deal Policies

During the first phase of the New Deal, what historians usually call the First New Deal, running from the Hundred Days of 1933 to early 1935, these notions that salvation and renewed progress could come without resorting to administrative statism were clearly evident. There were, as we look back on the period, opportunities for building a genuine administrative establishment or at least for laying the groundwork on which one might subsequently have been erected. The Economy Act of 1933 gave the President extensive powers to reorganize the executive branch. The new agency for public works and resource planning had some potential for becoming the national planning board envisioned in schemes for administrative direction. And the support for bureaucratic regulation that led to measures like the Securities Exchange Act had at least some potential for producing a much larger and more coherent regulatory complex. If Roosevelt, in particular, had conceived of the New Deal as administrative state-building, or if he had been very receptive to those who did, more of this potential might have been realized. But neither was the case, and the extraordinary presidential power that might have been used for such ends was not. The grant of power under the Economy Act was turned to what one scholar has called "picayune purposes." And for the Roosevelt of this period, the formulations that would allow us to continue without an administrative state proved far more attractive than the prescriptions for giving us one.

More specifically, the administrative complex that emerged during this initial period was largely shaped and justified by a mixture of the "emergency management" and "business commonwealth" ideas. One component in the mix was Roosevelt's invocation of the war analogy to call for an emergency government capable of waging a "war on the depression," a government that, as authorized and established, did resemble the one that Roosevelt had been part of (as assistant secretary of the navy) in 1917 and 1918. Once again we had an array of new agencies, theoretically established for emergency purposes; and as in the earlier case, these were set up outside the regular agencies of government, were reliant on a temporary "nationalization" of private sector administrative resources rather than on a regular civil service, and were supposed to pass out of existence after this war had been won.

The other component in the mix was Roosevelt's embracing of the idea that corporative institutions could combine self-government with a capacity for national management and that such institutions could become established through a temporary use of governmental power to promote the process. The early New Deal agencies, in other words, were to function not only as emergency managers, but also as institutional "midwives," leaving us with new societal formations capable of channeling market forces into constructive paths and keeping them out of destructive ones. And Roosevelt, whose earlier work with business associations had involved attempts at such promotion, was now to serve as general supervisor of these institutional midwives.

The heart of the early New Deal state, to be still more specific, was the administrative apparatus to carry into effect the National Industrial Recovery Act, the Agricultural Adjustment Act, and the Federal Emergency Relief Act. These were the key measures intended to alter social outputs; and in the machinery for their implementation, we have the clearest examples of this mixture of the emergency and midwife states, both supposed to save us from the kind of bureaucracy that we had always been reluctant to establish. The National Recovery Administration (NRA) was in large measure modeled on the War Industries Board of 1918, but was also thought of as a midwife helping an organizational society give birth to new planning, regulatory, and welfare institutions. The Agricultural Adjustment Administration (AAA) was thought of in much the same way, although in its case the administrative resources temporarily "nationalized" were primarily those of the farm organizations and agricultural colleges, not those of the food processors, as had been the case during World War I. And the Federal Emergency Relief Administration was conceived of not as the nucleus of a new social service state, but as a provider of temporary aid to community-centered welfare institutions and as an agency that might in the process help new institutions of this sort to be born. In all three cases one finds an overlay of anti-statist rhetoric attuned to the anti-bureaucratic symbols and traditions long embedded in our political culture.

If these structures were the heart of the early New Deal state, however, they were not the whole of it. Also helping to shape and justify some portions of it was the neo-populist thinking to be found in a variety of protest groups and congressional initiatives. Some of this was embraced by New Deal policymakers, mostly, it seems, with the idea of containing or co-opting its supporters. And what resulted were tools that, in theory, could be used to alter social outcomes by loosening the grip of the "money power" on "the people" or by protecting virtuous competitors from the continuing machinations of "corporate power." To be more specific, we got legislation empowering the president and the treasury to implement populist monetary remedies, legislation under which the district courts might act as agents of social rescue from the "money lenders," legislation divorcing investment from commercial banking, and a combination of legislation and executive action that added neo-populist enclaves and sounding boards to the structures being created by the NRA and AAA. The early New Deal state was hardly the "people's state" envisioned in neo-populist thinking. But it contained a number of concessions to such thinking, and these concessions brought into it another variation of the nation's anti-bureaucratic tradition.

From the beginning, moreover, Roosevelt's experience as a politician made him receptive to the fourth formulation allegedly capable of improving on market performance while retaining safe-guards against bureaucratic statism—to the idea, in other words, of a politically brokered administrative expansion driven by inter-est group desires, kept safe by constraints against its coalescence into a bureaucratic establishment, and harnessed to national pur-poses by political leadership and finesse. Even as he embraced the emergency and midwife concepts, and made concessions to neo-populism, Roosevelt found room in his program for an adminis-trative expansion geared to interest group initiatives. One thinks particularly of such new administrative units as the Railroad Re-tirement Board, the Federal Coordinator of Transportation, and the Federal Grazing Service. And as interest group and inter-agency conflict rose within the major structures created in 1933, generating in the process a variety of similar initiatives, the Presi-dent's role as manager and aggregator of these began to over-shadow his roles as emergency chieftain, supervisor of midwives, and "people's" tribune. The broker state, justified by conceptions of interest group liberalism and administration by conflict, was in the making.

Much of the early New Deal's administrative apparatus, then, was erected in the name of anti-bureaucracy; and when the expec-tations aroused were not fulfilled, two competing lines of explana-tion arose and by 1934 had become parts of an ongoing internal debate. One stressed the apparatus's lack of administrative capac-ity. . . . The needed capacity, it claimed, could come only through the lodging of more planning . . . power in the hands of qualified bureaucratic elites. The other line of explanation seized on the anti-bureaucratic components in the formulations and insisted that these were . . . being eroded. According to it, the problem lay with power-hungry bureaucratic aggrandizers who were seeking to turn economic self-government into government control, people's tools into bureaucratic ones, emergency administration into a bu-reaucratic establishment, and properly constrained administrative expansion into a power base for bureaucratic elitism. Such were the arguments now coming from the NRA code authorities and AAA committees, from neo-populist protest groups, and from defenders of interest group autonomy and vested institutional power. And given the resonance of these in our political culture, they helped to sustain institutional obstacles to the prescriptions for greater "ad-ministrative capacity."

Hence, as early as 1934, the administrative creations of the New Deal were being denounced not only for their interference with free-market forces and established ways, but also for the obstacles they had erected in the path of modern state-building and good national management. It was a situation that would continue and in time have its counterpart in scholarly discourse.

An Administrative State in the Making

During the New Deal's second phase, what historians usually call the Second New Deal of 1935 and 1936, the effort to accommodate the nation's anti-bureaucratic tradition would persist. But in this period the convergence of several developments did bring forth something closer to the administrative states operating elsewhere. One such development was adverse court decisions rejecting the legal basis of the emergency and midwife concepts and putting much of the First New Deal's administrative system out of business. Of particular importance here was the decision overturning the NRA, *Schechter v. U.S.,* 295 U.S. 495 (1935). Another development was the changing political configuration, marked especially by a loss of business power and prestige, the emergence of anti-New Dealism in the business community, and political gains for labor and other proponents of greater economic and social democracy. By 1935 this altered configuration had not only changed the makeup of Congress and the pattern of presidential policy advice, but also made reliance on private sector administrative resources increasingly difficult. And third, new links were being forged between would-be administrative state-builders and those making gains in the political arena. Key groups of industrial relations specialists, social work and social science professionals, legal technicians, and resource-usage experts were now having considerable success in selling bureaucratic prescriptions—with appropriate roles, of course, for their specialties—to the labor movement and to reform-minded politicians and legislators.

Essentially, it was the convergence of these three developments that gave us what most historians would regard as the heart of the New Deal state as it was operating by the end of 1936. From it came the Wagner Labor Relations Act and the new bureaucracy for regulating industrial relations and collective bargaining. From it came the Social Security Act and the new bureaucracy to administer programs of social insurance; and from it also came new powers for the bureaucracies associated with the Securities and Exchange Commission and the Federal Reserve Board, a new jobs program that brought federal officials as well as federal funds into local communities, and an altered farm program that assumed the need for a permanent bureaucracy as opposed to an emergency structure or a midwifing operation. Policy, as expressed in laws and administrative decisions, was, for a while, being made by people who believed that federal bureaucracies had—or could acquire—the competence to perform these new social duties and function as effective national tools. Those who had seen the United States as lagging behind in this regard now believed that it was catching up. And New Deal lawyers seemed convinced that the shaky legal basis for these new national tools could be solidified through skillful litigation leading to the acceptance of new constitutional doctrines.

During this period an American administrative state did appear to be in the making, and by 1937 the equation of this with progress was being asserted and celebrated in books like James M. Landis's *The Administrative Process* and Thurman Arnold's *The Folklore of Capitalism*. Yet, as we look back on the period, it is also apparent that the emergence of these new bureaucracies was neither the whole of New Deal state-making, nor a development that was giving us anything approaching the full-fledged administrative state. For one thing, remnants of the earlier formulas for letting us do without such a state persisted and continued to shape some laws and administrative instruments. And for another, the new bureaucracy was still highly fragmented and particularized and still subject to the constraints of other forms of institutional power. It had, as later critics would put it, a "hollow core," a void where there should be a national planning agency and machinery for harmonizing agency goals with national ones; and it had to operate in an environment in which much of America's nineteenth-century state had survived and a good deal of power was still lodged with judges, party politicians, legislative committees, and local governmental units.

The persistence of the earlier formulations can be readily noted in measures that were important, if not central, parts of the Second New Deal's measures. The continuing effort to contain and co-opt neo-populist initiatives left its mark in the Revenue

Acts of 1935 and 1936, in another farm bankruptcy law, in protective measures for "independent" merchants, and in portions of the new Banking Act and Public Utility Holding Company Act. All of these were supposed to create new people's tools for use against the money power and economic imperialism. The emergency concept continued to be evident in a reemployment apparatus that was supposed to disappear when the economic pump had been primed and relief was no longer needed—not become a continuing tool for macro economic and manpower planning. And a mixture of the midwife and empowered interest group solutions continued to be evident in measures that were supposed to improve the performance of "sick" industries by salvaging elements of the NRA apparatus and continuing to entrust private sector administrative resources with public duties. Action of this sort was taken for such industries as petroleum, forestry, trucking, bituminous coal, and some foodstuffs.

The other point about the New Deal state in this period— that the new bureaucracies did not add up to anything approaching a full-fledged administrative state—was not only a point stressed in continuing calls for administrative reform, but one evident in a variety of failed bureaucratic visions that ran afoul of persisting critiques and constraints. The bureaucracies of the Second New Deal were forced to function largely as a collection of political interest groups, not as a unified structure engaged in national management and recognized as an indispensable "fourth branch" of government. And those who would equip the government with a centrally placed mechanism for national planning, hopefully by strengthening and broadening the pioneering work of such agencies as the National Resources Committee and the Tennessee Valley Authority (TVA), found themselves repeatedly frustrated. New openings had appeared in 1935, openings through which bits and pieces of a "national bureaucracy" could be and were slipped. But these bits and pieces still had to accept narrowly constrained roles and accommodate themselves to a political framework and culture that, in many respects, were hostile to their presence.

Even in this second phase, then, the rise of the New Deal state was not accompanied by a repudiation of America's longstanding and deeply rooted antipathy toward governmental power exercised by a bureaucratic elite. The state assumed a number of new social duties and added bureaucratic machinery to assist in performing them. But the earlier formulas for securing a good society without entrusting power to bureaucrats persisted. And the new "national bureaucracy" had to accommodate itself to a milieu supportive of anti-bureaucratic values and to operate without the mechanisms it needed to begin functioning as a system of national management.

A Hollow Core

The third phase of the New Deal, from 1937 to 1939, has usually been seen as a time when the reformist expectations aroused by the electoral outcomes in 1936 were frustrated by revivals of conservative strength, and when the consequent stalemate pushed Roosevelt into such strategies to maintain the system as compensatory spending and lending, anti-trust action, and consolidation of previous gains. In most histories of the period the battle over administrative reform is mentioned but relegated to a decidedly peripheral place. There are scholars, however, who believe that it does not belong there. Historians like Barry Karl, in particular, would assign it a much more central place, and on the basis of their work, it does seem possible that the events of this period can be given a quite different reading. It can be seen as a time when serious efforts were made to fill the "hollow core" in the state's bureaucratic apparatus, when we might have developed—but did not—the managerial component characteristic of modern states elsewhere, and when our failure in this regard meant that subsequent American state-building would stay within the patterns discernible in the earlier New Deal period.

One thing distinguishing this period from its predecessors was Roosevelt's close relation for a time to people who would bring "top-level management" to what the New Deal had wrought and would create an "up-to-date, efficient, and effective instrument for carrying out the will of the nation." In 1936 Roosevelt had responded to proposals for the study of management problems by creating the President's Committee for Administrative Management, chaired by public administration expert Louis Brownlow. After the election he had embraced most of the committee's recommendations and made them the basis of a government reorganization bill sent to Congress in

January of 1937. The goal, according to the bill's drafters and proponents, was to "develop" the presidency "on the side of management and administrative supervision as well as on the political side." And to do that the bill proposed to create a number of new managerial tools and mechanisms, not just for a particular President, but for the office as an institution. Among these were to be a new managerial staff and stronger mechanisms of fiscal control; a national planning agency having both adviser and directive powers; and a greatly strengthened organizational capacity able to mold politicized semi-autonomous administrative units into a harmonious structure of national management.

This effort to fill the hollow core with professional managers and planners has usually been seen as an isolated initiative unconnected to other measures being pushed at the time. But again, some historians have begun to question this view by pointing out that three other attempted reforms during this period amounted to attacks on power structures that were seen as obstacles to the attainment of national management. One was the court reform sent to Congress some three weeks after the government reorganization bill. This, in essence, would restaff the courts with jurists who saw no constitutional barriers in the way of an expanding domain of administrative law and managerial power. The second was party reform, an initiative that finally led to the attempted "purge" of 1938. It was intended essentially to break the obstructive power of the Southern political organizations and the people they sent to Congress. And the third was the scheme to establish regional planning institutions, commonly referred to as the TVA's Seven Sisters. This was a scheme that, in its early versions, would have created a network of regional and local planning authorities responsive to central direction by a national planning board and posing a direct challenge to the whole structure of state and local influence on resource distribution. Had all these initiatives been successful, this period might have become a truly revolutionary one in establishing and legitimating the kind of institutions that our anti-bureaucratic traditions had long taught us to fear and shun.

These potentially revolutionary initiatives, however, were not successful. As one might expect, they aroused the ire of the power-holders under attack, proved vulnerable to new invocations of traditional anti-bureaucratic rhetoric and wisdom, and produced only minor changes in the polity that they were intended to transform. The expectation that Roosevelt's extraordinary success at the polls could be translated into an instrument of transformation, supported by the people and the experts alike, proved to be a faulty one; and with the coming of new economic setbacks in late 1937, Roosevelt found his capacity to win legislative victories further diminished. Under these circumstances, moreover, he had soon fallen back on the earlier formulas. During the first half of 1938 he lent sporadic encouragement to a new crop of corporative schemes for national management through private sector resources. Some of his advisers thought that he wanted to revive the NRA. During the same period he called for a new set of emergency tools and for more people's tools to cope with the machinations of corporate power. And, viewed in retrospect, his legislative successes in 1938 were essentially of the type that allowed other bits and pieces of a national bureaucracy to slip through and accommodate themselves to a political framework and culture that remained hostile to bureaucratic ideals. What was new, by the end of the period, was the rise of the notion that coordination could be achieved through the management of spending, taxing, and anti-trust decisions. But the thrust of this thinking and what it produced was toward helping to keep the hollow core hollow. It was not, and would not be, filled.

In this third period, then, the anti-bureaucratic tradition continued to play an important role in shaping the New Deal state. As of 1939, to be sure, a limited Reorganization Act had passed; a new executive office of the president had been established; and—of greatest importance a new majority on the Supreme Court was stretching the Constitution so as to make room legally for the New Deal's bits and pieces of a national bureaucracy. But none of this had superseded earlier formulas for doing without a bureaucratic state. Nor should it obscure the fact that efforts to realize the managerial vision embraced by Roosevelt in early 1937 had come off second best in the clash with traditional power-holders who invoked traditional anti-bureaucratic rhetoric and wisdom. America's bureaucratic creations on the national level, most of them products of New Deal action, could not be integrated into a larger structure responsive to state managers. And this meant, as Barry Karl notes, that they would continue to be "managed" by a political system responsive to the pressures and powers of party organizations, interest groups, and the local elites who ran the nation's cities and states.

The Anti-Bureaucratic Tradition vs. The Growth of Government

When we look more closely at just how the New Deal arose and survived, three conclusions are worth noting.

One is the degree to which reality does not correspond to the received picture—that an American version of the administrative or managerial state came into its own in the 1930s and has remained a central feature of the American polity ever since. There were elements in the New Deal trying to change the polity in this way, and at times Roosevelt was receptive to and supportive of them. This was especially true in the year 1937. But the anti-bureaucratic tradition and what it had produced in the past not only constrained such initiatives, but also became internalized in the New Deal constructions that were supposed to provide viable alternatives to bureaucratic statism. The state that emerged had a "hollow core" where the state managers were supposed to be; and along with its bits and pieces of a national bureaucracy, it had accumulated a variety of accretions that resulted from efforts to apply the corporative, neo-populist, empowered interest group, and emergency formulas.

Second, a closer look at the New Deal state provides us with a better understanding of how the use of governmental power can grow within a political framework and culture that retained much of its hostility to state managers and bureaucratic ideals. It can grow, as the workings of the New Deal demonstrated, by being lodged in or linked to emergency managers, private sector administrative resources, people's tools, deserving interest groups, or survivals of our nineteenth-century state, all of which claim to have an anti-bureaucratic function and have shown some capacity to make this claim credible. It can grow particularly at a time when much of the population is disillusioned with market-oriented economic policy and legalistic constitutionalism, as was the case from 1933 to 1939. We may need to rethink our views about the growth of government since the New Deal and our strategies for influencing the growth process by considering the circumstances of the New Deal period.

Finally, a better understanding of the New Deal state as it took shape between 1933 and 1939 can help us in our efforts to understand the polity we have today. There have, of course, been changes. We have had other bursts of governmental expansion, notably in the early 1950s when we added the national security state; in the mid–1960s when we added the minority rights and Great Society programs; and in the early 1970s when we added the new regulatory complex concerned with environmental protection. But the main contours of the American state that emerged during the 1930s and 1940s are still with us. We have not moved on to a managerial state in the sense of filling the hollow core with managerial institutions run by state managers and planners. The reforms along this line that have come out of a series of study commissions have been minimal. Nor have we departed from the strategies that allowed the New Deal to expand the usage of governmental power while accommodating anti-bureaucratic traditions. Not surprisingly, New Deal state-building has been and continues to be attacked both from a libertarian perspective and from a managerial one.

New Deal Policies and

Programs

The "Jane Addams Memorial" was painted by Mitchell Siporin for the WPA's Illinois Federal Art Project in 1936. It honors Addams's work as a humanitarian social reformer on behalf of Chicago's ethnic working classes and as head of the Women's Peace Party. Like many Federal Art Project painters, Siporin included workers, farmers, and immigrants in the painting in an effort to create a more democratic "people's" art. (Fine Arts Collection, Public Buildings Service, U.S. General Services Administration. Item #FA216. Photograph courtesy, National Archives and Records Administration.)

Mark H. Leff

Soaking the "Forgotten Man": Social Security, Taxation, and the New Deal's Fiscal Conservatism

The Social Security Act of 1935 was very likely the single most important piece of New Deal legislation. It established not just the old-age pension system—or Social Security—but also unemployment insurance and other social-welfare programs. Critics at the time, and historians ever since, have applauded Social Security as a badly overdue innovation but also lamented its many unusual features. The most important of these was the employee-employer payroll tax. Whereas established European old-age pension programs were financed out of "general" tax revenues, the New Deal's Social Security system was financed by a flat-rate "contributory" tax. Much like a private insurance or pension plan, then, only "contributors"—those who paid the payroll tax—were eligible for a Social Security pension upon retirement. One problem with this system was that it excluded married women who did not earn wages or a salary. Another was that this system of financing was a highly "regressive" system of taxation in which those with lower incomes bore the heaviest share of the tax burden, or tax incidence. For all of the 1930s rhetoric about "soak the rich" taxes, the burden of the most important new tax of the decade was borne by those least able to afford it.

Why was this the case? Why so conservative and regressive a tax? One popular explanation is that Roosevelt believed that a contributory system would protect Social Security from future political assaults should a more conservative Congress and president come to dominate American politics. In the essay that follows, however, Mark Leff questions this explanation. He claims that it was Roosevelt's commitment (and that of his treasury secretary, Henry Morgenthau) to fiscal conservatism that best explains the regressive tax. Roosevelt and Morgenthau wanted to avoid large deficits and find less expensive ways of financing the existing federal deficit. As a result, Leff explains, they opposed using general government revenues to pay for old-age pensions even though this would have worked to redistribute income more fairly.

Mark Leff, "Taxing the 'Forgotten Man': The Politics of Social Security Finance in the New Deal," *Journal of American History*, 70 (Sept. 1983), 359–381. Reprinted by permission.

What emerges from Leff's work of historical detection is an account of Social Security financing that illustrates both Roosevelt's conservatism *and* the external constraints on New Deal action. And as he suggests, the consequences of both continue to weigh heavily to this day.

Mark Leff specializes in the history of twentieth century America at the University of Illinois. He has written *The Limits of Symbolic Reform: The New Deal and Taxation, 1933–1939* (1984).

Franklin D. Roosevelt considered social security to be "the cornerstone of his administration." Today, in the midst of the widely bruited social security "crisis," he might be less quick to take credit. That the payroll tax in particular is Roosevelt's prime contribution to the modern tax system seems a terrible mistake, an affront to the progressive reputation of the New Deal. It is a classic regressive tax, letting the rich off more cheaply than wage earners. The prominence of this levy in our tax system—the payroll tax for old age insurance garners several times as much revenue as the corporate income tax—is not the New Deal's proudest legacy. But it is an appropriate one to explore if we are to understand either the New Deal or the nature of the modern social security crisis.

For New Deal historians, finding fault with the social security system—particularly its old age insurance component—has all the challenge of shooting fish in a barrel. William E. Leuchtenburg, though seeing the Social Security Act as landmark legislation that "established the proposition that the individual has clear-cut social rights," comes close to offering a consensus position in his critique of the statute. "In many respects," he writes, "the law was an astonishingly inept and conservative piece of legislation. In no other welfare system in the world did the state shirk all responsibility for old-age indigency and insist that funds be taken out of the current earnings of workers." The disparagement of the financing provisions of old age insurance does not stop there. No critical assessment of the New Deal is complete without parading payroll taxes as the clinching evidence against the progressivity of the New Deal tax system. To be sure, the initial payroll-tax rate for the old age insurance system was low; at the close of the 1930s its yield was only one-half that of the individual or corporate income tax. Even without the scheduled rate increases, however, the old age insurance tax still represented a not inconsiderable 10 percent of federal tax collections.

Surely this apparent paradox—that a New Deal so solicitous of its image as champion of the "forgotten man" should produce such a "conservative piece of legislation"—demands explanation. Why, in particular, did the New Deal rely exclusively on regressive payroll taxes to finance old-age annuities? . . . Many within the administration itself considered the incidence of the payroll tax to be a distinct drawback. The regressivity issue prompted Harry Hopkins to propose the use of general tax revenues drawing more upon upper incomes. Rexford G. Tugwell, the house radical, joined Hopkins in making the case against the payroll tax to Roosevelt. Although the president never gave an inch, Tugwell carried on a running battle with him during formulation of the administration's social security plan between June 1934 and January 1935. A payroll tax, Tugwell argued, "was very little different from the sales tax"; only the substitution of income taxes or a general tax subsidy could lift the burden from those least able to pay and reduce the tax drag on the economy. Even Morgenthau's Treasury Department, ultimately a strong backer of exclusive payroll-tax financing, found the issue of incidence disconcerting. A key Treasury memo warned of the unfortunate deflationary "effect of diverting funds from current consumption to savings" through the "regressive" payroll tax. Recognizing this problem, a department position paper looked to the future for redress, expressing the pious hope that "we may be able in the course of time to return to the mass of our population in the form of reduced taxes on consumption goods what we take from it in payroll taxes."

This malaise during the formulation process was only a preview of the eventual reaction to the payroll tax. Even the timing was unfortunate. At the very outset of the New Deal the atmosphere of urgency had made it easier to overlook regressive taxes. However, in the period bracketing the drafting and enactment of social security, from mid-1934 to mid-1935, the diminished fear of economic collapse thawed an undercurrent of dissent. The payroll-tax proposal thus emerged at the height of assertive, self-confident pressure from those favoring more rapid change, and it would be dogged by criticism throughout the decade. Central to this criticism was the demand for redistribution of income to achieve a more equitable society and a healthier economy. Thus, payroll-tax incidence was not a mere technical or esoteric issue. . . .

To a large extent, the "question of finance" boiled down to a question of the impact of taxes on the distribution of the nation's income. Given the plight of the depression's poor, this concern for equity seems natural enough, but it intertwined with a broader economic analysis prevalent across the political Left in the 1930s. The widely accepted "underconsumption" theory, which Roosevelt himself had repeatedly embraced in campaign speeches, warned of economic stagnation if buying power continued to be stifled by the concentration of wealth at the top. According to this analysis of the depression, the rich, who spent a smaller share of their income on consumer items than did the masses, had gotten too big a piece of the pie. The mass of consumers were thus unable to buy back the mounting volume of things they made. This created a downward spiral in which production was cut back, savings became a further drag on the economy as they piled up in the bank accounts of the rich for lack of investment opportunities, workers were fired, purchasing power declined further, and so on.

Thus, it became an economic imperative to expand consumer purchasing power by taking the "sterile," "petrified" savings of corporations and the rich and putting the money in the hands of people who would spend it. Taxation was a natural way of tapping these savings. No wonder that the incidence of the payroll tax could assume such importance. Not only would the tax have a direct impact on the shrunken incomes of the impoverished, but many felt it would siphon off the consumer demand needed to maintain production.

The administration's social security proposal thus faced vigorous attack for relying on payroll taxes instead of drawing more heavily on "exceptionally large incomes." The nation's leading social-insurance theorists—Isaac Rubinow, Abraham Epstein, and Paul Douglas—all urged a more progressive financing scheme. Epstein, in particular, was beside himself. He dismissed social security as "a system of compulsory payments by the poor for the impoverished" that relieved "the well-to-do from their share of the social burden."

The opposition to payroll taxes, of course, went beyond expert analyses. A broad spectrum of the American Left was mortified that the administration's social security plan had botched the opportunity to redistribute power and income. Highlighting the tax's burden on workers and its failure to extract a just share from the rich, the *New Republic* concluded in 1935 that "the law is almost a model of what legislation ought not to be." As late as 1941, the *Nation* still had not made its peace with the payroll tax, calling it "the most regressive levy on our statute books, surpassing, in that regard, even the sales tax.". . .

The congressional election in 1934 had assured that this critique would receive a hearing. Although the tremendous Democratic majorities resulting from the election (Democrats outnumbered Republicans by three to one) were in part a vote of public confidence in Roosevelt, this new Congress, Leuchtenburg observes, threatened to push the president "in a direction far more radical than any he had originally contemplated." Many new Democrats had been elected on platform pledges of recovery through income redistribution, and left-wing third parties now held ten seats in the House and two in the Senate. To some business leaders, Roosevelt became "the bulwark between the country and the 'wild men' of Congress."

In such a Congress the payroll tax would not have a free ride. In the House the tax received its most conspicuous condemnation during the consideration of a radical alternative to social security, the Lundeen workers' social-insurance bill. More a rallying point than a serious legislative proposal, the Lundeen bill, in under five hundred words, mandated an unemployment compensation plan that extended to jobs lost through anything from old age to ill health, but explicitly exempted workers from the enormous consequent financial burden. Yet it collected an impressive string of endorsements from radical, liberal, and labor groups, even squeaking through the House Labor Committee in March 1935.

The failure of Roosevelt's social security proposal to provide "for redistribution of the national income, as does the Workers' Bill," handed critics a readily exploitable issue, which goes a long way toward explaining why this unrealistic plan got as far as it did. The payroll tax, advocates of the Lundeen bill argued, would prolong the depression by sapping consumer purchasing power. Their plan, in contrast, would requisition income from "channels of surplus investment" to fuel the real motor of recovery: the depleted resources of the working class. The debate over the Lundeen bill can thus be understood as a conduit for protest of the social security financing scheme. . . .

The question of why social security finance bore so harshly on the "forgotten man" thus remains an enigma. The explanation obviously cannot lie in the failure of decision makers to recognize or to voice concern about the incidence of payroll taxes. It is also clear that neither foreign social-insurance precedents nor pressures for immediate aid to the impoverished dictated an exclusively contributory system.

Unfortunately, to discard inadequate explanations is easier than to provide convincing alternatives. That task is almost irretrievably confused by the complex decision-making process leading to the 1935 Social Security Act and the major amendments to it in 1939. Divining legislative intent is always a hazardous undertaking; by the time a bill has run the legislative gauntlet, its parentage is mixed and its support is diverse. These problems are magnified for the Social Security Act. Before it even reached Congress, it encountered a confusing array of draftees: a cabinet-level Committee on Economic Security (CES) and its staff of social-insurance specialists recruited from outside government, a Technical Board of in-house experts, and an Advisory Council of public, labor, and management representatives. Moreover, the program shifted direction only a few years after it took effect, in the Social Security Act Amendments of 1939. No wonder, then, that one of the hottest recent issues in social security—whether supplementing the social security reserve fund with general tax revenues represents a breach of faith with the historical intentions of the program—is susceptible to such differing interpretations. The result depends on where—the CES, the Advisory Council, the president, the Senate—and when—1935 or 1939—one searches for the answer. . . .

[T]he issue can be clarified by reviewing the chronology of decisions on social security finance. Roosevelt himself played a determining role. When he established the mechanism for formulating the social security proposal in June 1934, he set out some constricting ground rules. The funds for the program, he announced to Congress, "should be raised by contribution rather than by an increase in general taxation." During the formulation stage of his national social-insurance plan in 1934–1935 the president periodically reiterated his preference for exclusive payroll-tax financing. In his first meeting with the leading social security drafters he reminded them that old age insurance "must be self-supporting, without subsidies from general tax sources." Then, at the opening of an administration-sponsored conference of experts on economic security, Roosevelt again stressed that social security could not be allowed "to become a dole through the mingling of insurance and relief" and thus "must be financed by contributions, not taxes." At about the same time he made it clear to Tugwell that he was "inclined toward a wholly contributory scheme with the government not participating."

It is important to put these guidelines in context. On the one hand, many CES staff and Advisory Council members entered their assignments with developed positions on the federal role in social insurance that a few months' association with the administration could not be expected to efface. But the brevity of their tenure as social security drafters also cut the other way, making it difficult to develop and mount a campaign for an alternative to presidential directives. In addition, it was unwise to quarrel with a president whose enthusiastic support might be necessary to guide a coherent program through Congress. After all, social security was to be *his* proposal, and on the issue of social security financing, the president's intentions were clear. There was no more important influence on the drafting process.

This reasoning helps explain the basic form of the old age insurance program, with its employee-employer payroll taxes and its "contractual" tie between the "premiums" that an individual pays in and the benefits to which he is entitled. It is all the more curious, therefore, that the draft of the proposal that reached the president's desk was not fully "self-supporting"; it provided that in 1965 the old age insurance fund would begin paying out more than it took in, at which time the federal government would begin contributing to the social security reserve fund to prevent it from shrinking. What could account for this decision to buck the president's express wishes? The recommendation was certainly no casual afterthought; it carried a compounded endorsement received during consideration at each stage (Technical Board, Advisory Council, CES staff, and CES) of the drafting process.

On the surface, the explanation is simple. The various staff and CES reports placed primary emphasis on one main theme: the problem of workers who were on the verge of retirement. As little as five years of payroll-tax contributions would qualify these older workers for a social security annuity. But five years of taxes, according to strict contractual insurance standards, could purchase pensions of less than a dollar a month. As Edwin Witte, executive director of the CES staff, explained, a "psychological factor" needed to be taken into account: "A pension of such a small amount as people who are in the system only a short time can buy, will never be satisfactory to them. It will seem to them that they are being cheated." The CES therefore recommended that middle-aged and older workers receive reasonable "unearned" pensions (the floor was eventually set at ten dollars monthly) that would "ultimately be paid by the federal government."

There are reasons to believe that broader objectives than the protection of early annuitants were involved here, for the proposed eventual government contribution to cover these unearned annuities dovetailed too neatly with other CES staff concerns. Since the ratio of contributors to eligible retirees would be so high in the early years of the program, no government subsidy would be required to keep it afloat in the first decades. But later, that subsidy would be substantial. The projected government contribution would climb to a plateau of nearly $1.5 billion annually in 1980, more than either employees or employers would contribute in payroll taxes. This certainly would have eased the malaise over the regressive burden of social security finance. Moreover, early unearned benefits would draw down the reserve fund to a more manageable level. To let each contributor's payroll taxes sit idle in a mountainous reserve fund until he or she retired was considered "unthinkable" and "out of the question," particularly in light of the effect on an economy already plagued by depressed consumer buying power.

Thus, however carefully the drafters covered their tracks in moving away from the president's contractural private insurance model for social security, it is clear that their proposal fundamentally diverged from his guidelines. At base, the drafters were simply less drawn to that model than was Roosevelt. The CES staff, for example, was almost offhanded in its assertion that it might become necessary for the government to "increase its contributions to insure the lowest paid workers an adequate pension." Thomas H. Eliot, a key figure in the formulation and early implementation of the Social Security Act, even ventures the opinion that the "initial annuitants" rationale was the "convenient excuse" of those who did not want social security to be "self-supporting" and who "believed that our system, like those in Europe, should be financed equally by employers' contributions, employees' contributions, and general revenues."

At least at the drafting stage, then, the use of general tax revenues as a supplement to regressive payroll taxes had been sanctioned. Though the depth of Roosevelt's understanding of this fact is open to question, he must have been aware of it; Hopkins and Perkins spent several hours on December 24, 1934, orally presenting the CES report to him and gaining his endorsement of its recommendations. However, just after the president received the "final" written report—on January 16, 1935, one day before he was committed to sending the CES report to Congress as the framework of his social security proposal—he summoned Perkins to his office for an emergency meeting. The government subsidy, he told her, bordered on immorality. By loosening the tie between the amount contributed and the retirement benefits received, it foisted an accumulated deficit on future congresses and transformed the pension into "the same old dole under another name," he complained. Roosevelt accordingly ordered the financing provisions redrafted to make old age insurance entirely self-supporting, and CES members perforce fell in line. However, only hours remained before Roosevelt would forward the final CES report to Congress, not enough time to rework a financing formula that was so deeply embedded in the report's discussion of old age insurance. Instead, the report's commitment to a government contribution to old age insurance was clumsily watered down by excising tabular references to the eventual government subsidy and by conceding that the report's financing formula might well require revision (alternative higher rates were suggested), since "there may be valid objection to this plan, in that it involves too great a cost upon future generations."

Although the imperfectly dismantled original plan did resurface in congressional testimony, the government-subsidy idea was soon squelched for good. Treasury officials and CES staff members hammered out a revised financing scheme that met Roosevelt's approval. With CES acquiescence, Morgenthau presented this plan to the House Ways and Means Committee. The new scheme was designed to obviate the need for any government contribution to the reserve fund in the foreseeable future. It doubled the initial old age payroll-tax rates, stepped up rates every three years instead of every five, cut pensions for retirees in the first ten to thirty years of the program, and envisaged a reserve fund of $50 billion by 1980. This tightened, self-sustaining financing package, with certain benefit and coverage adjustments that held the maximum reserve fund down to $47 billion, was the one adopted into law by Congress.

This eleventh-hour rescue of the social security system from general-revenue financing was greeted unenthusiastically by the initial drafters. Barbara N. Armstrong, one of the leading technical advisers on old age insurance, captured this mood in writing rather bitterly that the new financing scheme was "a little bewildering to the staff." Even Secretary Perkins, ever a Roosevelt loyalist, greeted the withdrawal of presidential approval from the CES report with understandable disappointment and no little annoyance with the man she suspected as the true culprit. As far as she was concerned, the voice may have been the voice of Roosevelt, but the hand was the hand of his treasury secretary.

Morgenthau's role, in fact, was an open secret. His overriding concern for the financial integrity of social security, along with his sketchy understanding of that system, led many associated with the CES to view him as a bull in their china shop. Morgenthau's main impact on social security financing, however, came late in the drafting process. During late 1934 he was preoccupied with the administration's impending work-relief proposal; he thus left much of the social security work to assistants, one of whom—Josephine Roche, who had just joined the Treasury Department—gave approval to the financing-plan and government-subsidy components of the recommendations presented to Roosevelt in late December. However, when the December CES report was sent to Morgenthau for his final approval, he received an unnerving staff analysis of it. In a concise, easily understood memorandum, George Haas, the Treasury Department's director of research, tore into the financing provisions for old age insurance. The proposed financial scheme, he demonstrated, gave earlier retirees "far more than they pay for," provided "actuarially inadequate rates during the early years" to cover the annuities of earlier retirees, and would thus burden "future generations" through what would ultimately be "a very large Federal outlay." Haas therefore recommended that the "prudent" course would be to phase in higher payroll taxes more rapidly.

"Prudent," with its implications of fiscal irresponsibility on the part of the CES, was a loaded word in Treasury Department circles. Apparently for the first time, Morgenthau now grasped the large deficit built into the social security financial plan. A secretary of the treasury, particularly one on the defensive over current government deficits and recent gold manipulations, trades on an image of fiscal responsibility. That image would inevitably be tarnished by a proposal to make future generations responsible for social security deficits of over $1 billion annually. In a plaintive phone call to Hopkins, Morgenthau charged that the financing issue was a "bad curve" that had "never come up in any discussion I've ever had." "I don't think that anybody realizes how much it will run to over a period of years," he told Hopkins. "That's what scares me."

The CES met on January 7, 1935, to thrash out Morgenthau's objections to its report. But the committee's partial concessions did not pacify Morgenthau, whose concerns were more fundamental. Only a personal plea from CES chairman Perkins convinced him to sign the CES report without a disclaimer that he opposed its financing provisions. It is also all but certain, as was widely believed at the time, that Morgenthau laid his misgivings before the president. This was a battle Morgenthau ultimately won; the revised plan that his staff worked out with the CES was basically a capitulation to the Treasury Department position.

The fact that Roosevelt's concerns so closely paralleled those of his treasury secretary does not, of course, necessarily reflect Morgenthau's persuasive powers. The guidelines established by the president in 1934 and 1935 make it plain that he and Morgenthau were working with a set of similar assumptions. It seems more appropriate, then, to see Morgenthau as a catalyst to the president's own concerns. Roosevelt, in fact, continued to display his cautious, fiscally conservative approach to social security finance. In 1937, for example, he asserted that "as regards social insurance of all kinds, if I have anything to say about it, it will always be contributed, both on the part of the employer and the employee, on a sound actuarial basis. It means no money out of the Treasury."

From the vantage point of today's shriveled social security reserve fund, it is hard to believe that the position taken by Roosevelt and Morgenthau actually triumphed. In fact, it did not. Roosevelt's financing plan, with its scheduled incremental hikes in the payroll tax, barely got off the ground. An interesting dynamic was at work. Paradoxically, the very fiscal conservatism of the 1935 social security plan may have undermined the long-term fiscal soundness of social security. The inherent vulnerability of the original financing plan is sharply underlined by the almost immediate overhaul it underwent at the end of the 1930s. In the short period between 1935 and 1939 an irresistible consensus built up to topple the strict insurance model from its pedestal. That consensus ran the ideological gamut from Right to Left, encompassing businessmen who feared high taxes and orgies of deficit spending, Republicans in electoral alliance with a revivified Townsend movement, countercyclical economic theorists who saw the payroll tax as a massive drain on purchasing power, the labor forces of the American Federation of Labor and the Congress of Industrial Organizations, and left-wing voices preoccupied with the unmet promise of social security as a tool of income redistribution.

The punishing recession of 1937–1938, which in a matter of months had erased half of the economic advances achieved earlier in the New Deal, only enhanced the vulnerability of the payroll tax, since many economists and informed observers deemed the three-quarters of a billion dollars that old age insurance had siphoned out of the economy in 1937 partly responsible for the downturn. Moreover, the recession put the administration on the defensive, generating efforts to promote recovery through heightened attentiveness to business demands. The groundwork was laid for a fundamental revision of Roosevelt's conception of social security.

The mounting pressures put the administration and the social security hierarchy in an uncomfortable and even agonizing position. Necessarily amenable to concessions, both the Social Security Board and the new Advisory Council on Social Security adopted a number of recommendations that served to attenuate the connection between contributions and benefits: replacing the full reserve with a smaller "contingency reserve," offering certain annuity benefits to the family of the contributor, and accelerating and raising retirement payments in the first years of the program. Most importantly, both groups jettisoned the Roosevelt-Morgenthau decision to implement social insurance without any planned government subsidy.

While the Roosevelt administration had little trouble endorsing the new infusion of benefits, the question of how to respond to the clamor for a payroll-tax freeze was more painful. Haunted by two alternative formulas for disaster—that a tax freeze precedent might either starve out the social security program or cause runaway benefit expansion by removing fiscal discipline—the Social Security Board shared Morgenthau's fear that any cut in planned payroll taxes would "maybe be a device that will eventually kill [social security]." Ultimately, however, Morgenthau cast his lot with the opponents of the scheduled payroll-tax hike and carried Roosevelt along. The administration had made a full, though reluctant, capitulation. While Witte, a last-ditch defender of the reserve fund and the individualist principles it protected, greeted the administration's concessions with "a sinking feeling about the future of old age insurance," the Social Security Act Amendments of 1939 sailed through Congress, carrying the House 364 to 2 and the Senate by 57 to 8.

The revisions of 1939 thus underscored the inherent flaws in the original Roosevelt-Morgenthau financing formula. By coupling early benefits with a decline in planned taxes, the new law seriously eroded the contractual insurance principle. Congress refused to face up to the consequences. Then, and too often thereafter, it took the expedient course of blocking scheduled tax increases without establishing a clear framework for later generations to meet the benefit claims that would accumulate.

The balance sheet on New Deal social security finance is therefore highly discouraging. Exclusive reliance on payroll taxes, far from being a foregone conclusion, contravened international precedent, expert advice, and much of the political pressure for aid to the elderly. The resultant financing scheme took far less than a proportionate share from the rich, created a deflationary reserve fund that helped produce the recession of 1937, and was so fiscally overcautious that the administration itself was forced to renege on its implementation (and thus to threaten the program's future) by the end of the decade.

Why had Roosevelt, clearly the system's chief architect, not grasped at more flexible alternatives? Unfortunately, Roosevelt's calculations are notoriously difficult to pin down. Historical explanations often suffer from his care to avoid leaving a paper trail. But indications of his rationale are available, ones of considerable importance in appreciating his overall position on social policy.

On the principle that the president must be taken at his word—a principle that is not always fruitful in Roosevelt scholarship—Roosevelt's position is not hard to ascertain. If one concept pervades the social security debate and the commentaries on it, it is the importance of the insurance model. Roosevelt, in particular, in his public statements and private conversations, insisted that social security should operate on "insurance principles." This contractual private insurance model not only necessitated payroll taxes (the only analogue to insurance premiums); it also bolstered Roosevelt's position that the system should support itself without government funding. Even short-term political considerations seem to have been sacrificed to the insurance model. For a president to boost taxes (without expanding government services) beyond what his advisers suggest is rare enough, but for him to propose a system that levies its taxes five years before it pays out significant benefits is freakish.

Given the stigma attached to public relief, the insurance model had considerable allure. The punitive and demeaning conditions imposed on "reliefers" to reinforce the work ethic seemed inappropriate for people who had come to the end of their working lives. The insurance model, in contrast, protected the dignity of social security recipients, whose past payroll-tax contributions distanced them from government "charity cases."

The presumed effect of the insurance model on the individual recipient, then, helps account for its appeal. To an unparalleled extent, American social insurance was sold in terms of its contribution to thrift and self-reliance. A social security annuity, advocates repeatedly stated, was an "earned right." The individualist ethos was highlighted by giving each contributor his own social security card and account, on the basis of which his retirement benefits would be calculated. The key to this system, as Roosevelt had said as early as 1930, was that workers' benefits would "be a result of their own efforts and foresightedness." To protect incentive, each dollar contributed in payroll taxes would entitle the worker to a higher pension (in the enacted plan, maximum scheduled annuities exceeded the minimum by over eight to one). Thus, workers would "be receiving not charity, but the natural profits of their years of labor and insurance."

It was in this insurance context that the tax incidence argument discussed earlier could be most easily dismissed. For if the payroll tax was only an insurance premium to purchase future benefits, it actually offered the mass of lower-paid workers a very good return on their money. As Secretary Morgenthau put it, payroll taxes would "provide a substitute form of savings from which our workers will receive far greater and more assured benefits than from many other forms of savings now in existence." It is apparent that the insurance model and the market principle that higher wages should purchase higher retirement benefits were deeply embedded in the 1935 Social Security Act.

The inexorable logic of the insurance model and its cultural resonance might seem to reduce Roosevelt's responsibility for the shortcomings of social security finance. After all, the shibboleths of individualism, self-help, and incentive were not unique to him; the president was presumably responding to a set of *national* values also embraced by the public and Congress. As evidence for the public belief that an individual should earn his benefits, one could cite polls recording overwhelming majorities favoring work relief over the dole and opposing the transfer of the employee's share of the payroll tax to his employer. Just as important for the enactment of social security were strong indications that key members of Congress also held such attitudes. Members of the Senate Finance and House Ways and Means committees were acutely sensitive to questions of fiscal and moral integrity; they also tended to look askance at any proposal involving higher levies on the rich. Such attitudes were a formidable obstacle to less regressive levies. Congressional skepticism of this sort was one reason why alternatives to the payroll tax were deemed "impracticable . . . at the present time."

Such evidence, many have concluded, indicates that Roosevelt was politically savvy in making a firm and near-total distinction between poor relief and social security. Yet the popular and congressional constraints on the president should not be misinterpreted. Both in Congress and out, the major movements for retirement benefits eschewed payroll taxes. Even the apparent early popularity of social security does not appear to have been an endorsement of the insurance model; in fact, a large share of the public in the 1930s did not even know that their own payroll-tax payments would automatically entitle them to an old age pension. Moreover, the sentiments of certain congressmen, however strategically placed, should not obscure the portrait sketched earlier of the leftward pressure on Roosevelt after the 1934 election from a Congress more receptive to old age assistance than to old age insurance. The notion that a full-blown insurance model was essential to sell the newly elected Congress on old age security is a questionable one. In fact, a more conservative Congress at the end of the decade, in its deferment of scheduled tax increases and its acceleration of benefits, proved eager to depart from pure insurance principles.

Finally, the insurance model—at least in its commoner, less extreme version—did not require exclusive reliance on payroll taxes. One could argue that any significant employee payroll tax would establish an "earned right" to a pension. Roosevelt himself had endorsed supplementary government contributions to the insurance fund when he was governor of New York, and his social security experts in the middle and late 1930s also found it possible to espouse the insurance principle while proposing future government financial participation in the plan. What is crucial here is not the insurance model itself but the Rooseveltian priorities that led to such a rigorous application of that model.

One variant of the insurance model explanation, however, has been found particularly compelling by historians. The payroll tax, they argue, was the result of a sophisticated political calculation on Roosevelt's part. As evidence—virtually the only evidence that anyone offers—they cite the following response by Roosevelt to a critic of the payroll tax: "I guess you're right on the economics, but those taxes were never a problem of economics. They are politics all the way through. We put those payroll contributions there so as to give the contributors a legal, moral and political right to collect their pensions and their unemployment benefits. With those taxes in there, no damn politician can ever scrap my social security program."

It is no wonder that this statement is so frequently quoted. It puts the familiar concept of an earned right to a pension in a context that is marvelously Machiavellian, almost vintage private Roosevelt. Though the objection that partial payroll-tax financing might have achieved the same effects applies here too, one is still tempted to say that if this was not Roosevelt's logic, it should have been. Best of all, the analysis is stunningly prescient. Republicans soon found that social security was too popular a concept to be attacked head on. By the end of the 1930s, in fact, much of the pressure for pay-as-you-go social security came precisely from those who believed that future congresses would be forced to carry through on the payroll-tax commitment and to fund excessively generous annuities. Indeed, despite annuities worth many times the value of their contributions, social security recipients continue to see their pensions as a contractual right paid for by their payroll taxes, affording old age insurance a high degree of what one social security insider proudly calls "political insulation" from conflict. The notion that "no damn politician can scrap my social security program"—conceded on all sides by the end of the 1930s—seems a reasonable part of a defense of the payroll-tax-financed insurance program that Roosevelt put forward.

This emphasis on the future of old age pensions is certainly consistent with other concerns of the time. It squares with Roosevelt's well-recognized belief in a cyclical theory of politics, which lent a special urgency to bringing about reform before the climate for change disappeared and a conservative era returned. Much of the New Deal's relief and jobs legislation, Roosevelt recognized, would lapse once the economy revived. Thus, to safeguard old age insurance as "a fundamental in our future civilization," Roosevelt sought to distinguish it from emergency legislation. The payroll tax, along with the insurance model of which it was such a vital part, underlined this distinction. And given Roosevelt's concern for the durability of old age insurance, he may well have recognized that the tens of millions who were building up pension rights with their payroll-tax contributions would constitute a corps of defenders for the program. In fact, one rationale for the payroll tax that we know Roosevelt shared with other old age insurance advocates was that it would confirm each worker's sense of participation in the program and responsibility for it. Thus, while available evidence cannot corroborate Roosevelt's recollection that his concern for the future of social security *determined* his advocacy of payroll taxes, this type of concern was very much on his mind.

One should be cautious, however, in building too grand an explanatory edifice on this evidentiary foundation, particularly since Roosevelt's oft-quoted statement on the politics of the payroll tax derives from an associate's recollection of a conversation with the president in the summer of 1941, more than six years after Roosevelt had staked out his position on social security finance. Those six years would surely have driven home certain economic and political lessons regarding social security. Even had Roosevelt's own loosened commitment to budget balancing not dulled the gloss of fiscal responsibility associated with the payroll tax, any hope that the tax could assure the fiscal integrity of social security would have evaporated once Congress began rejecting scheduled increases in

1939. Thus, the payroll tax could no longer be defended on its own merits; the social security fiscal program had already come unhinged. But if it could be tied to the political popularity of social security, it was on firmer ground. Old age insurance had become one of the New Deal's most popular and entrenched programs during the few years between its enactment and the president's 1941 remarks. Roosevelt's defense of his financing scheme was thus a convenient one, bolstering the beleaguered payroll tax by linking it to social security's most visible success. And though there was some concern that financial revisions might bring about a fiscal crisis in the distant future, Roosevelt covered this too by emphasizing the role of payroll taxes in creating an irresistible expectation of a pension. Knowing how the system had come out, he was in an excellent position to claim foresightedness. Of such stuff, accurate historical memory is not made.

When successive explanations fall short, the problem may lie less in the intractability of the phenomenon to be explained than in the common assumptions used to derive those explanations. Generally, the regressivity of social security finance is seen as an aberration to be understood in terms of unique exigencies of social security itself, such as the desire to protect the dignity and self-reliance of the recipients and the special political calculations attending old age insurance. Upon deeper examination, however, it becomes clear that social security finance must also be understood not as an aberration but as a manifestation of the New Deal's approach to fiscal problems in its first two years.

The New Deal is loved, hated, and remembered for many things, but fiscal conservatism is not one of them. Roosevelt's rhetorical broadsides at "loose fiscal policy" and his effort to balance the government's "regular" budget while boosting "emergency" expenditures have been treated as curiosities. Such a stance seems more useful as quotation fodder for Ronald Reagan than as a perspective for understanding the New Deal, with its reputation for high deficits and lavish social spending. As many New Deal historians have pointed out, this dismissive approach is a mistake. Frank Freidel, who treats this theme with particular perception, stresses the "sincerity" of Roosevelt's fiscal conservatism, calling it a "first priority" and an "integral component" of "Roosevelt's overall recovery program." Though this "staunch belie[f] in a balanced budget," as Freidel concedes, was ultimately "overshadowed" by conflicting phases of that recovery program, it remains vital to understanding the New Deal in general and social security in particular. Old age insurance, after all, was a permanent, not an emergency program. That it be financially "sound" (a word used four times in one paragraph of Roosevelt's social security message) was thus a requirement; anything else would send out the wrong signals. We know that Morgenthau was aghast at the projected size of government subsidies for old age insurance. He informed the CES that "the proposed plan of avoiding a large reserve by keeping contributions too low (from an actuarial point of view) and paying out higher benefits than are earned in the early years of the scheme obscures what is really happening and is thus fundamentally unsound." More to the point, Roosevelt himself, presumably egged on by Morgenthau, reacted with the same kind of moralistic fiscal conservatism. "It is almost dishonest to build up an accumulated deficit for the Congress of the United States to meet in 1980. We can't do that. We can't sell the United States short in 1980 any more than in 1935." Moral questions here merged with ones of image, what Eliot calls the "political need to refrain from an unbalanced budget" or anything that would tend to create one.

Certainly Roosevelt's objection to more generous old age proposals such as the Townsend Plan emanated primarily from his concern that any old age program financed out of general tax revenues would be a budget-busting drain on the treasury. Particularly revealing is a late-night note to Felix Frankfurter, in which a frustrated Roosevelt reported a meeting with a dozen congressional spokesmen who favored old age pensions of fifty to two hundred dollars monthly. The president had warned that a failure to heed "the financial limitations" could lead to "either failure to borrow or starting the presses" and had expressed utter disgust with the congressional response that financial problems could wait until after enacting the pensions. It was precisely this sort of irresponsible giveaway that Roosevelt sought to sidetrack with a "financially safe" contributory social-insurance system coupling benefits to payroll-tax payments. Through old age insurance, Roosevelt believed, every worker who contributed a payroll tax would have a stake in the fiscal integrity of the system.

Sound social security financing not only demonstrated long-term fiscal responsibility; it also allayed the government's short-term financial problems by means of the reserve that accumulated in the early years when the ratio of payroll-tax payers to old age insurance recipients was so high. Contemporary critics of social security, while exaggerating the conspiratorial character of this consideration, had nevertheless pinpointed something that helped to sell the financial plan to the administration. As the man responsible for marketing the government's debt securities, Morgenthau was very much aware that payroll-tax receipts "could be invested in the public debt . . . thereby reducing the net demands upon the Treasury"—an argument with such appeal that Morgenthau was indiscreet enough to broach it in his congressional testimony. Roosevelt too could not have been unmoved by the fact that the old age trust fund would lessen the need to go out into the private market (to Wall Street, no less) to finance New Deal deficits; we know, for example, that he became enthusiastic about unemployment insurance when told that it could significantly reduce the borrowing needs of the government and that his enthusiasm waned when he determined that this estimate was exaggerated.

The central point here is that general revenue financing would have reduced what Roosevelt and Morgenthau deemed a fiscal advantage. An immediate government contribution to the reserve fund would have been merely a "bookkeeping entry," since the federal budget, already well in the red, had nothing to transfer to the trust fund. According to Perkins, this helped doom the idea as an empty gesture that would gratuitously raise the New Deal deficit. Even the more salable proposal to begin a federal subsidy in future years would have involved a much lower payroll-tax reserve in the early years, reducing social security's fiscal bonus to the New Deal.

Thus, social security finance was shaped by the administration's conservative financial inclinations and by its desire to mitigate deficit problems. While these considerations clarify the rejection of general revenue subsidies, it could be argued that they do not explain why the administration did not propose some other form of taxation besides payroll taxes. Why not seek a tax plan that showed sensitivity to the calls for a redistribution of income and placed less of a burden on "the forgotten man at the bottom of the economic pyramid"?

To answer this question, one must understand the constraints on New Deal tax policy, especially in its first two years. A citizenry whose wealth and income had been sapped by the depression was scarcely eager to shoulder additional burdens. It was therefore not easy to raise taxes in the 1930s. More important, though, it never had been. This difficulty went beyond the universal problems that any society experiences in revenue collection. Taxation has always lacked a certain legitimacy in this country; the government could not impel direct sacrifices without challenge. In effect, the government could not openly tax "the people." This injunction allowed for some substantial loopholes. The government could tax those whose surplus of income minimized their sacrifice (the rich and corporations); it could impose a charge for a received government service or privilege; or it could tax "nonessential" items like cigarettes or furs. Even these rules could be stretched during an emergency—such as war—or when money was raised as a part of a broader social or economic program—such as tariff protection for American products.

None of these loopholes, however, had advanced the income tax far beyond the original Populist-Progressive impulse to quell the abuses of the privileged super-rich. In the 1930s, more than 95 percent of the public were exempted, and most of the rest were taxed very lightly—an approach that continued until World War II forced the enactment of the modern broad-based income tax. The income tax thus had a tragic flaw: its revenue-collecting potential was quite limited. Even Roosevelt's famed income tax reforms of the mid-1930s touched so few people as to represent a drop in the bucket for social security finance; the payroll tax yielded as much each month as the notorious income tax provisions of the 1935 Wealth Tax did in a year. To be a productive tax capable of sustaining the revenue jolt of an old age insurance program, the personal income tax would have had to transcend its own history and dip deeper into the income stream. Thus, whatever its theoretical superiority, it was not then a reasonable alternative to the payroll tax, for, as the CES staff reported, "personal income taxes with the present exemptions could not be expected to yield sufficient additional revenues to meet the new charges even on the basis of sharply increased rates." Moreover, as one New Deal economist later noted, to lower those exemptions or to raise middle-bracket rates enough to support the social security system was politically impossible. The mere attempt to restructure the tax system in this manner would have legitimized opposition charges that the masses would have to pay for New Deal extravagance and might have placed the social security system itself in jeopardy.

But even disregarding the lean yield of the narrowly based income tax, the administration had another reason to reject the frequent calls to at least supplement payroll taxes with income or inheritance taxes on the rich. Until mid-1935 and 1936, when Roosevelt sought political gain by scapegoating "economic royalists," taxes on the rich would have contravened the administration's strategy for recovery from the depression. Despite the popularity of underconsumptionist explanations of the collapse, John Braeman notes, "Roosevelt's commitment to the preservation and perpetuation of capitalism . . . and his hostility to large scale deficit spending" helped leave "his administration dependent upon private enterprise to furnish the major stimulus for getting the country moving again." Thus, Braeman concludes, Roosevelt "shied from moves that might retard recovery by further undermining business confidence."

Social security finance, then, worked under extraordinary constraints: it could tax neither "the people" nor the "super-rich." At the same time, fiscal responsibility required that *somebody* be taxed to cover the government's new commitments. This was a dilemma that the Roosevelt administration faced repeatedly during the early New Deal. And, what is crucial for the purposes here, it unvaryingly resolved the dilemma by seeking revenue wherever it would encounter the least resistance. For the Roosevelt administration, questions of tax incidence were a dispensable priority. What emerged instead was a political system in search of an excuse, seeking a way to tax "the people" without seeming to do so and without exciting opposition. I have examined the resulting tax policy elsewhere, but even a brief overview should establish the nature of the solution to this problem. The Roosevelt administration renewed the Hoover administration's major "emergency" excise taxes on gas, cars, radios, refrigerators, and the like. Although these taxes explicitly targeted consumers, existing taxes were far less controversial than new levies. The administration also coupled its call for Prohibition repeal with taxes on beer and hard liquor. These too would siphon off a greater share of the incomes of the poor than of the rich, but few would object; the tax was levied on alcohol, not "the people," and taxation was a small price to pay for cheap legal booze. (By "taking this money," one senator explained, "we would be plucking the goose without making him squawk, so to speak.") The administration's third major revenue raiser was the agricultural processing tax, used to fund the New Deal's agricultural subsidy program. Though essentially a sales tax on the most basic necessities, it too could achieve passage as a lower-profile component of a high-priority program. As columnist Ernest K. Lindley observed in 1936, the Roosevelt administration had given little consideration to the "economic and social effects" of its taxes, finding it "easier to follow an opportunistic policy of getting a little here and there, whenever it could find an excuse for prodding Congress into action." This approach only intensified the effect of declining depression incomes and profits on the tax system. Under the Hoover administration, a substantial majority of the government's revenue collections came from individual and corporate income taxes. But under Roosevelt, even before the passage of the payroll tax, revenue from these taxes dropped to one-third of federal tax collections—less than the amount brought in by the new taxes on consumers and the poor. If a New Deal redistributive tax machine existed in those years, it operated only in reverse.

The payroll tax fits neatly into this pattern. Like the agricultural processing tax, it was legitimized by the program of which it was an integral part. Perhaps the New Deal could not tax "the people," but it could sell them a cut-rate insurance policy. The employer component of social security finance even had the kind of slippery incidence pattern that had protected other New Deal regressive taxes from the organized opposition of unsophisticated consumers. Since people do not readily think in terms of tax incidence, the employer payroll tax could easily be seen as one that exempted "the people," despite the expert consensus that the burden would be shifted to wage earners or consumers. Thus, in the 1936 campaign Roosevelt repeatedly attacked critics of social security for deceitfully concealing that employee taxes for old age insurance would be matched by employers—a point that seems a bit devious itself, given his later statement in a press conference that "obviously in 9,999 cases out of 10,000" the employer share of payroll taxes "will be passed on in the cost of goods sold."

Social security finance is only an enigma to the extent that one expects it to sustain the New Deal's reputation for commitment to "a wiser, more equitable distribution of the national income." This principle has little to do with old age insurance and less to do with New Deal tax policy. The forgotten man, cut adrift by other New Deal priorities, proved eminently forgettable. But the payroll tax is lasting proof that he had not escaped the notice of New Deal tax collectors.

Pete Daniel

The New Deal and Southern Agriculture

In 1938, Franklin Roosevelt described the American South as "the Nation's No. 1 economic problem." The South at the time was the poorest, most rural, and least developed part of the United States. No region was more in need of federal aid; yet wedded to the traditions of local and private paternalism, no region found it more difficult to accept assistance.

In this essay, Pete Daniel examines the impact of New Deal relief and agricultural programs on the South. This impact, he notes, was "complex, contradictory, and revolutionary." The AAA and other farm programs not only failed to reform southern agriculture and its huge inequalities but actually benefited landlords and property-holding farmers at the expense of tenants and sharecroppers. At the same time, the New Deal measures helped to fuel a technological revolution after the depression that transformed the South's farm economy and its rural society.

Pete Daniel is curator, National Museum of American History and author of *Breaking the Land: The Transformation of the Cotton, Tobacco, and Rice Cultures since 1880* (1985) and *Official Images: New Deal Photography* (1987).

Patrician newspaperman and author Virginius Dabney recalled that during Franklin D. Roosevelt's first term as president a friend of his "counted the number of separate Federal agencies which were trying to help the farmer in one Southern county, and reported finding no fewer than twenty-seven!" Dabney's exclamation point suggested a radical break with the past. Indeed, the South's tradition of opposition to federal intrusion dated at least to the debate over federal assumption of Revolutionary War debts and reemerged time and again—with the Old Republicans, the nullification crisis, the Civil War, and insistence that states could best handle race relations after Emancipation. To accept, indeed, welcome, dozens of

Daniel, Peter, from *The New Deal and the South*. Edited by James C. Cobb and Michael V. Namorato. University Press of Mississippi, 1984. Copyright © 1984 by The University Press of Mississippi. Reproduced by permission.

federal agencies signaled a shift in the relationship of southern states to the federal government. There was an apocalyptic aspect to this change. To a people who still tasted defeat, dimly recalled a promise of a yeoman's paradise, and believed in Biblical redemption, the New Deal appeared as the millennium; and its personification, Franklin D. Roosevelt, sent the twenty-seven federal agencies to revitalize the economy, punish the unrighteous, and usher in a reign of justice, or so it seemed. What at first appears as an inexplicable acceptance of federal agencies among a people who had been largely shielded from national aid can be better understood by examining briefly the nature of southern communities and some of the forces of change in the half-century before the New Deal.

I

Southern states not only repudiated federal intrusion but in many respects shunned government aid from any source. Southern counties, towns, and communities handled their problems informally. Until the second quarter of the twentieth century, state and local governments in the rural South had provided meager organized relief. Although there were people who lived on the edge of survival, southern communities informally looked after their own. In the largely agrarian southern society, even uneducated and unskilled people could find enough work to put food on the table. The work ethic permeated the South, and for those who did not work the community had pillorying terms—lazy, good for nothing, no account, trash. Even the most dismal tenant farmer took pride in working, and his wife likely took pride in her kitchen, children, and chores. The South measured its people by brawn and stoicism, although the ability to tell stories and church attendance, or the lack of it, also figured. Those who accepted the gospel of hard work received community support even if they failed, but the community scorned the idle. . . .

Southern rural and small town communities were a kaleidoscope of relationships among blacks and whites, men and women, rich and poor, old and young, farmers and merchants, lenders and borrowers. In the cracks between the crystals, there was room for nonconformity, but there also lingered the threat of ostracism or violence if the established patterns were threatened. The strength of communities had helped rural southerners to withstand the forces that since the Civil War had reconfigured the tenure system and driven many people into dependency upon landlords for the elements of survival.

As Civil War and Reconstruction memories retreated into the mists of fantasy, landownership concentrated into fewer hands, and a new set of owners—life insurance companies, banks, mortgage companies, or counterparts of the local Snopes family—took title to the land. Prolific southerners filled the countryside, and farmers increasingly found it difficult to find good land to till. At the same time, the position of the cotton-growing states east of the Mississippi River was weakened by the boll weevil infestation that began in Texas in the 1890s and by 1920 had reached the Atlantic Ocean. The weevil not only destroyed cotton and scattered farmers as it advanced but it also increased the cost of production due to the poison and intensive cultivation methods needed to halt its life-cycle. The pace of cotton's westward migration—its destiny—accelerated, and the Mississippi Delta, Oklahoma, Texas, and later New Mexico and California, which had less infestation and thus a lower cost of production, outproduced the old cotton growing states of the East. The disruption of World War I, especially the migration of blacks, the collapse of the agricultural market in 1920, the lack of any plan successfully to reduce the growing surplus of commodities, the 1927 Mississippi River flood, the drought three years later, and the depression came as successive jolts to rural southerners. To a people who read their Bibles, the hard times suggested some divine retribution. Such a combination of economic and climatic disasters had never coincided before, and the remedy was beyond the means of communities, a strain on state governments, and ideologically repugnant to the federal government dominated by Republicans.

II

In the context of these troubles, Roosevelt loomed as a prophetic figure, a Moses who could unseat the entrenched powers that held people in bondage. Farmers listened to his fireside chats, placed his photograph on the mantel, wrote him letters, cheered the unprecedented activity of Congress in translating his ideas into policy, and welcomed the host of agencies that suddenly materialized in every community. As so many letters and reports revealed, southern people were impressed with such agencies, because no one had ever shown any such interest in their welfare. For example, Sarah and John Easton lived in an abandoned filling station in rural Wilson County, North Carolina. "I'm a Democrat; I stand for the New Deal and Roosevelt," John Easton told two WPA interviewers. "I am for the WPA, the NYA, the NRA, the AAA, the FHA, and crop control. . . . We've got mighty little of the government money," he admitted, but "the government shore give us enough when it paid for Amy's leg operation." One of his twin daughters had been born with a deformity that had been corrected with the help of a federal agency. Such stories were replicated throughout the South as millions of people had been touched to a lesser or greater extent by some federal agency. Yet the impact upon people varied, and it depended on race, class, commodity culture, local and federal administrators, and many other factors.

When the federal government set up work and relief programs that substituted for sharecropping or community alms, most recipients were elated. . . . Government jobs in many cases paid more than rural people had ever earned. So long as federal relief policies did not disperse the seasonal work force or drive wages too high planters accepted them.

Historians who have studied the rural South of the 1930s have shown that some of the New Deal agencies were insensitive to the human disruption in cotton-growing areas, especially in Arkansas where the Southern Tenant Farmers Union emerged. These tenants basically wanted to preserve and reform the sharecropping system, as did their champions in the Cotton Section who were purged for defending them. While some early New Deal agencies offered innovative approaches to jobs and housing, others created after the initial mood of experimentation had passed represented the status quo or advocated reform of longstanding abuses in the tenant system. On the other hand, the AAA and the USDA in general epitomized the forces of change that insisted on clearing off surplus farmers and instituting a more businesslike system of farming. The government represented larger farmers who, like business interests thirty years earlier, were attempting to rationalize agriculture. To find the most revolutionary aspects of the New Deal in the South, one must look not to the welfare programs that pacified the dispossessed or the trickle of dollars that spilled into the pockets of sharecroppers and tenants but rather to the changing structure of agriculture fueled by the AAA.

In a larger sense, the twenty-seven federal agencies that Virginius Dabney's friend counted substituted for landlords and community relief. The federal government increasingly supplanted landlords and merchants with federal relief, and, at the same time, with acreage allotments and benefit payments assumed direction over agriculture that had once belonged to the planter class. Changes in such responsibilities altered the relationship between landlord and tenant and created a different attitude toward relief. After initial opposition and enduring ambivalence, landlords and merchants abdicated their paternalistic role. More thoroughly than Sherman's army, the New Deal troops marched through the southern countryside and reconfigured it; the old order declined, and in its place emerged a rural South modeled on the long-held dream of the United States Department of Agriculture of large farms, plentiful implements, and scientific farming.

In retrospect it is easy to regard the changes in southern rural life as inevitable, as part of some cosmic design. Was it inevitable that sharecropping disappear, that machines replace people, that surplus rural laborers migrate to become surplus urban laborers, or that farms expand and become more businesslike? If one looks at the Federal Emergency Relief Administration (FERA) program in Franklin County, North Carolina, the answer is no. This county was targeted as a rural problem area, one of the worst of southern counties in terms of unemployment and the need for federal relief. Indeed, four banks failed during the depression, and in 1934 only one remained open. Most rural people were tenants; two-thirds of the county's farmers had no stake in ownership. Although idle sawmills and textile plants contributed to the unemployment problem, the primary problem sprang from the agricultural depression and "the landlord-tenant system having proved inadequate to the task of carrying the labor supply over the present period of restricted production."

The FERA in Franklin County attacked problems with imagination and boldness. When the Civil Works Administration shut down in March 1934 after spending $52,000 and employing 253 people, 807 families faced unemployment. Because so few jobs existed outside agriculture even in good times, FERA administrator C. W. E. Pittman searched for farms. Four hundred relief families secured tenant positions, and one hundred village people sought work relief and odd jobs. Another hundred clients were unemployable and went on direct relief. The other two hundred families could work, but depression shut them out of the traditional farming culture. There was plenty of land available but not enough work stock or tobacco and cotton allotments. The State Emergency Relief Administration furnished the county seventeen mules, and more than any single factor this raised the hopes of people on relief.

The FERA staff called a meeting with an advisory group composed of the county farm agent, agriculture teachers, federal and private lending representatives, and the farm managers from two life insurance companies; each of these brought a landowner to the meeting. All sympathized with the program and offered suggestions. A sharecropping arrangement seemed familiar and promising, so the agency tried to place the two hundred families "on such terms as would permit them to produce more corn, vegetables, peas, and sorghum than they could consume" and barter the surplus "for items they could not produce, namely, meat, flour, and clothing." Pittman's plan turned back the clock to an older tradition of subsistence and barter that preceded commercial agriculture.

The relief families got nowhere with suspicious landlords, for although the government promised support, landowners feared they would end up furnishing relief clients. So case workers and clients together visited landlords, and, despite the scarcity of work stock, placed all families. It became impossible, however, to furnish both fertilizer and supervision, so many clients worked independently. The tenure arrangements varied: 15 clients farmed their own land, 19 paid no rent, 2 cleared land for its use, 2 others worked for the landlord, and 169 sharecropped for one-fourth of the corn and sorghum. Thirty-six families shared FERA mules, 18 used their own, 98 gave one-fourth of the corn and sorghum, 53 exchanged a day's work for the landlord for a day with the mule, and 2 used animals rented by the FERA.

These arrangements produced an average return of $133.23 per family, which, the report argued, "seems a small return for the efforts of six months until it is considered relatively." Had these clients not worked, they would have had no income, but with this stake and the food they raised, many could barter for other supplies and survive without government aid. "Most people are deeply in-grained with the instinct to exalt work," the report stressed. By re-quiring work the program had stifled criticism that originated when the federal government began relief work. The report concluded optimistically that the success "prepares the way for future progress of these people."

. The FERA boasted that the program salvaged the pride of poor people. Although they were inadequately housed, fed, and doctored, the government program had given them hope. From the material standpoint the relief work had been successful, but "from a spiritual standpoint it has yielded a rich harvest in in-creased hope, self-reliance and confidence." A symbol of this at-titude hung in Pittman's office, for he had obtained a client's patched shirt. "The shirt was taken from a colored client for dis-play purposes," the report noted, "not because it was so badly worn but because of the infinite care that had been taken to keep it patched." The shirt exemplified the tenancy system that had been torn and patched so many times as landlords and tenants bargained for the tattered returns from cash crops. Pittman recognized the amazing resilience in this client and directed the man's energies to the land. Increasingly federal agencies would shunt such people to cities and away from all that was familiar and remunerative.

The Franklin County program revealed how little experienced farmers needed to succeed in the country. Without growing cotton or tobacco, most of these families came out ahead primarily because the rehabilitation program gave them hope, and it supervised them as much as funds permitted. The government in these cases simply replaced the traditional furnishing system with impartial and en-thusiastic oversight. That these unlikely candidates succeeded raises questions about the operation of the old sharecropping system and the exploitation that characterized it, for even growing cash crops few tenants broke even at settlement time. The FERA program stressed an older form of economic relationships—barter and non-commercial crops. It took little to survive in depressed Franklin County, but to break out of the bonds of dependence it did take opportunity. If the FERA could produce such results, it raises seri-ous questions about the lost potential of the Extension Service and later of the Resettlement Administration and the Farm Security Administration.

Unfortunately, the Franklin County FERA success was, if not unique, one of the rare triumphs in southern problem counties. If there were no jobs outside agriculture, tilling the land offered the only hope for work for unemployed farmers. As the FERA attempted to apply emergency aid to farmers, the Agricultural Adjustment Administration (AAA) worked at cross purposes by reducing acreage. It did not take long for farmers to figure out that less acreage under cultivation would mean less tenants doing the cultivating. While the FERA in Franklin County turned away from commercial farming to rescue displaced farmers, the AAA commodity programs reconfigured the relationship between landlord and tenant ushering in a shift to wage labor and ultimately to mechanization.

The acreage allotment, the amount of a commodity that a farmer could grow, in most programs went to the landowner, and this robbed tenants of any bargaining power. In September 1933, tobacco farmer Maynard P. West of Axton, Virginia, attended a meeting in Martinsville. Landlords, he warned, would gladly reduce acreage, but they would also reduce the number of tenants they used proportionately. "I believe it would be just to allow a tenant to carry his allotment with him from farm to farm," West suggested, "and require Land lords to reduce their planting in accordance with the total indicated allotment allowed them and their tennants." This, he insisted, would give tenants a bargaining lever and offer protection from eviction. John B. Hutson, chief of the Tobacco Section of the AAA, rejected West's idea and pointed out that it "would cause landlords to bid for these tenants in order to increase the acreage of tobacco on their particular farm."

Even if West's idea had been implemented in the flue-cured tobacco area, small farmers would still bear the brunt of reduction. The AAA Rice Section awarded allotments to whoever farmed the land, regardless of tenure, just as West suggested for tobacco farmers. Still, the rice program generated problems. W. J. Lowe of Iowa, Louisiana, personified the ambivalence of many farmers about government intrusion. On the one hand, he resented government programs, but he also tired of carping landlords in the rice area. He suggested in the spring of 1935 that larger landowners reduce their acreage to help smaller growers. He envisioned a model farm of 640 acres that rotated a 300-acre rice allotment that "will fit one irrigation well, one tractor, six mules, one drill, one binder, one thrashing machine and a regular hired man." Farmers who had more than a 300-acre allotment should be cut until they reached the 300-acre level while smaller farmers should be built up to that figure. "It is no worse for the big farmer to come down to three hundred acres," he argued, "than it is to hold the little farmer in bondage so that he cannot rise to a profitable basis." Lowe resented that small farmers had to work under government programs drafted "by high powered politicians that probably never wore overalls or tilled the soil; especially when they are a thousand miles away running the farmers' business, and whom they have never met personally and discussed their views with." While complaining about how farmers had been "planned, checked, inspected, mortgaged, charged, taxed, denied and red-taped," his suggested program would further regiment rice farmers by government planning. Lowe's idea, however, ran counter to the AAA philosophy that generally favored larger farmers. Years later when reduced allotments shook the Louisiana rice area in the mid-1950s, farmers revived Lowe's ideas and suggested that the cuts be graduated according to size, like the income tax.

Both West and Lowe offered constructive ideas on protecting small farmers from the disruption that AAA programs set in motion. Although the AAA ignored the suggestions of both farmers, other forces unique to the commodity culture in both areas protected tenants from displacement. Because of the labor-intensive nature of growing tobacco and the protection given by the Tobacco Section to small growers, no massive displacement took place along tobacco road. The highly mechanized rice culture remained stable because of producer allotments and the prohibitive capital requirements needed to start farming rice.

The AAA cotton program, on the other hand, arrived in the South not only at the same time that the cotton culture haltingly edged toward mechanization, but it also attempted to force the same rules upon farmers with vastly different tenure arrangements in the delta, Black Belt, hills, valleys, and plains. Cotton farmers in Meriwether County, Georgia, had worked out a simple tenure arrangement that seemed to fit the needs of many farmers. Located southwest of Atlanta and only a county away from the Alabama line, the county achieved the dubious distinction of being a FERA problem area. Warm Springs, the most famous part of the county, had developed into a rehabilitation center for polio victims. Franklin D.

Roosevelt often visited Warm Springs, attracted by the soothing water that he hoped would restore his legs to strength. He ultimately invested a large part of his personal fortune in the center and set up the Warm Springs Foundation. He enjoyed meeting people in the community and often drove his specially equipped automobile through the countryside, stopping to drink moonshine, watch coon hunts, and discuss everyday problems. He owned a farm in the county and raised livestock and grew some crops. He often described himself as a farmer, both because of the Georgia farm and because of his upbringing in bucolic Hyde Park. If there was one part of rural America that Roosevelt knew, it was Meriwether County. Whether he ever measured his New Deal policies by that county remains problematical, but if he did observe the forces flowing from government programs, he must have taken pause.

Farm tenants comprised 75 percent of the 2,430 farm operators in the county, but census categories did not reveal a unique rental plan that characterized the county. Hidden among "other tenants" and even sharecroppers and renters, a substantial number of farmers paid a bale of cotton per plow in rent. . . . FERA officials estimated that from one-third to two-thirds of all farm tenants were bale-per-plow renters who cultivated about ten acres per plow and produced some four to five bales of cotton. One bale paid for fertilizer, one went to the landlord, and the two or three remaining plus the seed went to the renter. While the 40 percent acreage reduction affected most tenants in the cotton South, it devastated the bale-per-plow arrangement in Meriwether County. Under the AAA, one plow turned only five or six acres after allotment cuts, producing about two-and-a-half bales. After paying the landlord and settling for fertilizer, the renter would only have one-half bale left for his profit and would have been better off without a New Deal.

For example, when cotton sold for 8¢ a pound, a farmer stood to make from $80 to $120 on his two or three bales, and he also got about $75 seed money from five bales. Thus, a renter would earn from $155 to $195 a year per plow under the old arrangement. Under the AAA, with one-half bale that sold for 12¢, he earned $30 for the lint and $45 for the seed from two-and-a-half bales. His yearly earnings came to $75. Of course he got from $4 to $5 per acre for renting the other land to the government, but his yearly earnings did not reach $100. Even if the price of cotton had fallen to 6¢ a pound the renter would have earned from $135 to $165 under the old system.

While the AAA may have worked well in other areas of the South where landlords were fair with payments to tenants, the tenure system in much of Meriwether County turned into chaos. In this sense, the county served as a model, for throughout the South the standard formulas of the AAA seldom took local customs into consideration. Instead of rebuilding the South, ushering in a reign of justice and prosperity, or even putting more money into the hands of farmers, the New Deal in many ways destroyed the old structure and prepared the way for large scale farming. . . .

Some farmers expressed strong contempt for Roosevelt and, at least until forced to by law, refused to go along with acreage reduction. According to Nick Tosches's biography of singer Jerry Lee Lewis, Lewis's father Elmo rented land from Lee Calhoun, a wealthy relative, and he told Elmo "to pay no mind to that damn-fool New Deal cripple talking at people from out of a damn-fool radio." The president had taken the country off the gold standard, Calhoun complained, "but now the fireside-talking fool had gone too far, trying to take us off the dirt standard." So Elmo Lewis did not plow up any cotton in 1933. He took the earnings and bought every Jimmie Rodgers record ever made, got drunk, and sang along with the records. It took standardization with teeth to corral such a spirit.

III

As some of the foregoing examples suggest, analyzing the impact of AAA commodity programs throughout the South presents the historian with a complex set of problems. Each commodity program reflected the ideology of the administrator as well as the statutes. The Cotton Section's Cully Cobb unabashedly represented the planter class, and his rulings consistently came down on their side. As most students of the rural South know, after government payments reached landlords, an indeterminate amount trickled down to tenants. The attempts of the Southern Tenant Farmers Union to rectify this and other injustices have been recorded by several historians and participants. Cobb allowed landlords to evict unneeded tenants, turned his head at many abuses, set up an investigative arm

that passed most problems back to local committees that were composed of the very landlords that dominated local affairs, and fired
section employees who insisted on interpreting the terms of the
contracts favorably to tenants. With acreage cut by some 40 percent, landlords evicted some tenants, changed the status of others
to wage hands, and consolidated their operations.

I will offer only one example of how this program benefitted
the landowning class. In 1935 the AAA surveyed three plantations
in Arkansas to assess the impact of the New Deal. Each planter
took a different course in adjusting his tenant population, but all
streamlined the work force and used more wage labor than formerly. The report observed that sharecroppers were able to pay off
their debts by 1934 and credited it to the benefit of the AAA. Yet
the AAA had an even greater impact on the income of the landlord
on one of the plantations. While the tenants' share of cotton lint
rose from $16,000 in 1932 to $17,000 in 1934, the landlord's
share rose from $39,000 to $77,000 over the same years. Tenants
shared more returns from cottonseed over the three years, increasing from $3,000 to $5,000, but the landlord's share rose from
$7,000 to $20,000. From all products sold from the plantation,
the tenants' share rose from $22,000 to $30,000 while the landlord's share rose from $52,000 to $102,000.

The flue-cured tobacco program under the direction of John
B. Hutson furnished a sharp contrast to the Cotton Section. The
tenant problem had been eased in part by the flight of many tobacco farmers from the land before the New Deal began. When
markets opened in 1933, prices lagged at about ten or eleven cents
per pound. Hutson forged a settlement with the tobacco companies to raise prices to a parity level of seventeen cents in exchange
for a reduction in acreage the next year. He also protected small
growers with a minimum acreage allotment and constantly fine-
tuned the program to make it popular with all classes of farmers.
By 1934 farmers of flue-cured tobacco had become addicted to the
federal tonic and, except for the 1939 crop year, voted for federal controls at every opportunity. Tobacco, of course, was an extremely labor-intensive crop, and any hope of mechanization lay far
into the future. The restructuring that progressed in some cotton
areas due to tractors and later harvesters only reached tobacco road
in the 1960s. A well-run and popular program and an antiquated

work culture combined to preserve traditional relationships in the flue-cured tobacco area. . . .

By the mid-1930s, millions of southerners had tasted the New Deal tonic, and many had become addicted. The small doses of federal money and jobs blurred a central issue—what would become of farming as they had known it? Huey Long, senator from Louisiana, was skeptical of the New Deal and offered his own patent medicine. In a 1935 radio address, punctuated by the jingle "Every Man a King," Long charged that five million more Americans were on the dole than during the previous year and that one million more were unemployed. In rural areas, he charged, crop reduction had led to idleness and unemployment, but at the same time people were starving. He would allow farmers to grow as much as they wanted, and when a year's supply accumulated, farmers could take off a year, labor on public works projects, or attend school. He charged that the frenzied New Deal activity clouded the conservative nature of most programs. The New Deal, he joked in another broadcast, was like St. Vitus's Dance. Whatever the failings of Long's analysis, he understood that rural people had not benefitted all that much from the New Deal and that it was disrupting traditional farming patterns.

Yet rural people supported the New Deal, and ironically, those who profited least supported the president most faithfully. Part of this enigma can be explained by the fact that many people did profit from the New Deal, and even those who received only crumbs dreamed of other programs that they might qualify for. They also received a barrage of propaganda from New Deal spokesmen on the radio. Roosevelt's fireside chats were incredibly effective in boosting morale and claiming successes. The First Lady, several of her children, political advisor Louis Howe, cabinet members, and representatives from every agency explained the cornucopia of benefits bursting from Washington. Soap operas, moreover, allowed escape. The radio proved a magical agent of consensus, raising hopes and muting protest.

The benefit payments to landowners provide a clear example of the bias in New Deal rural aid. . . . In Leflore County, Mississippi, for example, two cotton plantations received nearly $23,000 in 1934. Since county farmers received $262,200 in AAA payments, these two plantations got almost 9 percent of the county payments. It is problematical how much of this trickled down to tenants. . . . Connecticut General Life Insurance Company from its Washington County holdings in 1934 received $35,000 and in 1935 $32,000. The firm had 179 cotton farms under AAA contract in 1934–35, yet it was not the largest holder of cotton farms by far. John Hancock Mutual Life Insurance Company listed 1,580 farms under cotton contracts. Metropolitan 1,141, Prudential 999, Aetna 705, Travelers 636, Union Central 609, General American 602, and several other companies had hundreds of farms. In all, fifty-five multiple landowners who reported 150 or more AAA contracts owned 10,858 cotton farms.

Most payments went to growers in the western areas of the cotton belt. Indeed, North Carolina and Georgia only appeared on the 1933 list, South Carolina did not have a planter who qualified, Louisiana remained on it two years and received $413,000, and Alabama planters only got $130,000 over the three years. In contrast, Mississippi landowners received $2.5 million, Arkansas $2.1 million, and Texas $1.2 million. . . . Perhaps the most significant aspect of the report was the revelation that some $7 million of AAA money went not to struggling farmers but to large corporations and landlords. In this respect, the New Deal propped up business interests and commercial farmers.

Because of the small size of tobacco farms, the Senate report revealed only two landowners that fell into the large categories. A Georgia farmer received $11,000, and a North Carolinian pocketed about the same amount. The report showed that large corporations held 1,045 tobacco farms, but it did not break the statistics into the type of tobacco grown on the farms. Anxious to reap the federal money, several life insurance company representatives inquired of the AAA if their papers were in order.

In the three southern rice-growing states, Arkansas had four contracts in the $10,000 and above category that yielded a total of $69,000, Louisiana had twenty-five that received $484,000, and Texas had eighteen that pocketed $412,000. Altogether, rice growers in the large categories received $9.4 million for cooperating with the 1935 program. Looked at another way, large cotton planters took almost 2 percent of all AAA money in the program while tobacco farmers took but 0.74 percent. Obviously, rice farmers were much larger operators, for they took over 16 percent of the large farm government payments. . . .

IV

Of all the elements of transformation, mechanization proves the most elusive to chart. In a sense, it was like a wave that had gained momentum since the turn of the century. Rice farmers . . . were highly mechanized, and only during World War II would they turn to combines and reach another stage. Tobacco farmers plodded along with their labor-intensive work cycle until the 1960s, and only in the last dozen years have they turned to harvesting machines.

Mechanization in the cotton belt started in Oklahoma, Texas, and the Mississippi River Delta and spread east, from the area less encumbered with the boll weevil and the legacy of plantation agriculture and sharecropping. Increasingly, farmers bought tractors to replace aging mules, and both tractors and mules coexisted simultaneously. Many commercial farmers took the first step toward mechanization in the 1930s, and they often used government money to purchase tractors. With an assured parity price, they could invest with some certainty of paying off their debts.

According to one study, each tractor displaced several families, and the 111,399 tractors introduced into cotton-growing states in the 1930s displaced from 100,000 to 500,000 families, or from a half-million to two million people. Of the 148,096 fewer farm operators over the 1930s decade, mechanization displaced from one-fifth to two-fifths, and AAA acreage reduction accounted for much of the remainder.

The combination of New Deal acreage reduction and increasing mechanization during the 1930s started a significant shift in southern farm organization. Two studies, one of Georgia and the other of several Arkansas counties, show how traditional tenure arrangements shifted due to the introduction of tractors. "With the rapid increase during the past few years of the use of mechanical equipment on Georgia farms," the report began, "complications have developed in the customary rental arrangements between landlords and tenants." The study concentrated solely upon the changing relationship between landlord and sharecropper, obviously the most significant sphere of tenure adjustment. As the report observed, the percentage of croppers dropped 39.6 percent in the decade of the 1930s, and mechanization pushed off more sharecroppers than had the earlier acreage reduction policies of the AAA.

The report began with the example of a farmer in the Georgia Black Belt who customarily ran ten tenant families and twelve mules. "He bought a tractor and tractor equipment for cultivating, displaced all 10 cropper families and sold 8 of his mules." He kept two mules to use in small fields, kept two of the families on as wage hands, and did all the tractor work himself. In other cases, landlords continued using sharecroppers for cash crops but utilized tractors to till "conservation crops" and hay for livestock. Most owners charged sharecroppers for tractor work such as breaking land and running rows. The cost varied; some landlords charged for the labor of the tractor driver, others for driver costs, fuel, and depreciation, and a few simply charged a flat fee per acre. The families retained either as croppers or wage hands were the more able farmers.

Other cases from throughout the state illustrated changes in tenure. One landlord furnished the tractor, equipment, fuel, and half the seed and fertilizer and divided the crop equally with a sharecropper. The landlord had formerly used three cropper families and farmed with mules. The tractor plan had been working for three years, and the report concluded that both landlord and share-cropper "are well pleased with the change." Most examples showed a basic pattern as landlords displaced tenants, bought tractors, and increased the acreage tilled by the remaining croppers. In some instances, the cropper's status had been eroded with wage work. On one farm, the cropper worked eighty-five acres as a cropper and sixty-five acres for wages. On another, "The cropper is cultivating 160 acres of cropland with the tractor which was previously worked with 5 mules and 5 wage families." In another case, the owner supplied the tractor and also allowed the cropper to do custom work in the community and paid him wages for the work.

In Georgia, the shift from mules to tractors did not require a large amount of capital. The study focused on a Newton County farm to illustrate the point. The landlord displaced two of his three cropper families, sold three of his four mules for $600, and part of his mule-drawn implements for $100. He purchased a tractor for $630, and equipment including a "disc plow, section harrow, planter, distributor, and cultivator for $387." After selling off the mules and equipment, it cost the owner $317 to make the shift. He continued to plant the same number of acres but used one cropper and a tractor. The report neither questioned mechanization nor speculated on the fate of dispossessed sharecroppers.

A 1938 study conducted jointly by the USDA and the Arkansas agricultural experiment station weighed the impact of tractors on plantations in the Arkansas, Red, and Mississippi river bottoms in Jefferson, Miller, and Phillips counties. Using interviews with planters, sharecroppers, and wage hands plus AAA data, the report covered 89 plantation operators and 423 sharecroppers and wage hands. Unlike the Georgia study that included small units and the entire state, the Arkansas study measured plantations that averaged over one thousand acres with over two-thirds of the land in cultivation, mostly in cotton. It pointed out several new trends in farm organization traceable to government programs and mechanization. Tenant displacement took place in two periods, it stressed, "from 1933 to 1934, when cotton acreage declined for the second successive year; and from 1935 to 1937, when there was a marked increase in the number of tractors used on the plantations."

Not only did some croppers leave farming but also landlords changed the tenure pattern, assigning remaining croppers "nominal cotton acreages" and paid them extra for wage work. Data from two additional Mississippi River counties, Chicot and Mississippi, being studied separately, paralleled that from the other three. These two counties had a 12 percent displacement of resident families from 1932 to 1938. Both counties were shifting from sharecroppers to wage labor. "The number of tractors employed on the plantations in these two counties," the report added, "has increased at a more rapid rate than the number used on the plantations in Jefferson, Miller, and Phillips Counties."

Yet the change to tractors progressed unevenly in the rich Arkansas cotton lands. In 1937 only fifty-six of eighty-nine plantations used tractors, and thirty-six of these had been using them since 1932. Only three had used tractors before 1926. Most landowners used tractors for breaking land and seedbed preparation, and they increasingly used them for hay crops. On traditional mule plantations, the number of "resident families" remained stable, but on tractor plantations they decreased by 9 percent from 1931 to 1937.

Families remaining on mechanized plantations became wage hands or sharecropped reduced acreage. The report stressed that the "economic displacement" due to changes in tenure status was "equally as important as the physical displacement of families previously noted." Further displacement, the report noted, had been "held in check by the inability, thus far, of plantation operators to mechanize the operations of cotton chopping and picking." Most planters kept resident families and hired seasonal labor for these chores, but the report predicted that the successful development of a cotton picker "will pave the way for further displacement of resident families."

Paul S. Taylor, who toured the country with his wife, photographer Dorothea Lange, observed the changes taking place in the southern cotton culture. . . . Before a special Senate committee studying unemployment and relief, he observed in 1938 that former cotton sharecroppers and wage hands increasingly ended up on relief rolls. Many had been displaced by tractors. "A planter in the Mississippi Delta, to cite an outstanding example," he testified, "purchased 22 tractors and 13 four-row cultivators, let go 130 out of his 160 cropper families, and retained only 30 for day labor." Senator James F. Byrnes, skeptical at this example, asked for the name of the planter, and Taylor replied that it was J. H. Aldridge who farmed near Greenville, Mississippi. Dorothea Lange had taken a photograph of one of the tractors at work in a field. Most of the displacement, Taylor noted, came in the flat and relatively boll weevil-free states of Texas, Oklahoma, and the Mississippi and Arkansas deltas where farmers could easily utilize machinery and profit from a lower cost of production.

Displaced workers, Taylor observed, "are forced into the towns in large numbers and drawn back onto the farms only for short seasonal employment at chopping and picking time." In June 1937 he had watched trucks roll into Memphis and take from one thousand to fifteen hundred laborers to chop cotton in the nearby Delta area. Most, he observed were former sharecroppers. "The burden grows of relief of unemployed farm laborers congregated in the towns and cities of the South." Increasingly, it became obvious that the combination of acreage reduction and mechanization was changing the face of southern agriculture. Partial mechanization with tractors began a structural shift that would be consummated with the perfection of the cotton picking machine. By

World War II the last major piece of the mechanization puzzle, the mechanical cotton picker, was ready to be put in place.

V

The irony of federal intrusion lay not in the fact that the government entered agriculture or that in the 1930s it took control of much of its planning, but rather that it created conflicting programs that largely ignored not only its own role and that of poor farmers but also that of technology. The painstaking studies of tenure, of moving people to more fertile land, and aiding a small percentage of marginal farmers largely ignored the emerging structure of the cotton culture. The scientific arm of the USDA worked to create a new mode of technological production while its social agencies sifted through plans to prop up the old structure. While such contradictions touched the rice and tobacco cultures more lightly, from the 1930s to the 1950s the cotton South metamorphosed from a labor-intensive culture to one that used machines and chemicals, and the production of cotton moved ever westward.

The impact of New Deal policies in the rural South proved complex, contradictory, and revolutionary. The AAA and federal rural programs often aided landowners more than tenants, traditional lending agencies more than borrowers. After years of promotion by implement companies and boostering by the Extension Service, by the mid-1930s southern farmers turned to machines. Despite the surplus laborers clogging the byways of the region, landlords invested their government money in machines and looked with satisfaction at the stable prices produced by government programs. The rural cycle attuned to nature became warped. Tractors prepared seed beds, planted, and plowed the cotton land, while wage hands poured in to chop out weeds and then pick the lint. The human contribution in crop production became fragmented. Many southerners, black and white, hesitantly left the countryside, paused in towns and cities nearby, and moved on out of the South never to return. They took little in the way of earthly goods, but they transferred a rich cultural heritage.

The forces that had begun at the turn of the century at last triumphed, and the South experienced its own enclosure movement. Neither those who left nor their neighbors who stayed behind shared the traditional relations with landlords that had typified southern rural life since the Reconstruction Era. The custom of landlords supplying housing, food, wood, pasture, and hunting and fishing rights receded into memory, and the twenty-seven government agencies, in part, took up the slack as paternalistic provider. In the 1940s, rural exiles found work in defense industries or in the army, and thus World War II, not the New Deal, rescued many victims of government programs and mechanization. The war gave them a job, a purpose. It also became a great divide. After fifteen years of depression and war, the vitality and spiritual reserves of rural southerners and their exiled kin and neighbors were low. They had believed that Roosevelt and the New Deal would bring the millennium, but instead many were ushered off the land and dispossessed of their work and communities. It would be another generation before these Americans and their descendants could look with nostalgia to the 1930s.

Jane De Hart

Democratizing Culture

Among the most innovative, troubled, and controversial of all the New Deal programs were those intended to employ out-of-work artists and underwrite public displays of art. These programs were scattered about the federal government. The Federal Emergency Relief Administration (FERA) and the Treasury Department undertook some, but the most important and best known were the four WPA arts programs: the Federal Music Project, the Federal Writers' Project, the Federal Theater Project, and the Federal Art Project. From these came a rich outpouring that included guidebooks for states and cities, innovative stage productions such as the "living newspapers," concerts across the country, and murals in post offices and public buildings from Newark's airport to San Francisco's Coit Tower.

As Jane De Hart explains in her essay, the arts projects were intended to accomplish more than provide work for unemployed artists. They would, their proponents envisioned, enrich American culture and inspire

Jane De Hart, "Arts and the People: The New Deal Quest for a Cultural Democracy," *Journal of American History*, 62 (Sept. 1975), 316–339. Reprinted by permission.

social reform. More important, De Hart argues, was the "quest for cultural democracy." Art should be "accessible"—it should be "for the millions"—and not confined to a privileged elite; it should express "national" values; it should make art a vital part of American life.

De Hart's essay suggests other important themes in common with other essays in this collection. One is the role of decentralized administration. "Arts for the millions" meant arts programs in community centers, and like the AAA, the Indian Reorganization Act, and other parts of the New Deal, the arts programs hoped to nurture community-based institutions sustaining writers and painters, orchestras and acting companies. Furthermore, as with the Indian Reorganization Act, the AAA, and other measures, realizing these larger aims proved extremely difficult.

Jane De Hart is professor of history at the University of California at Santa Barbara. She is the author of *The Federal Theater, 1935–1939: Plays, Relief, and Politics* (1967), the coauthor of *Sex, Gender, and the Politics of ERA* (1990), and co-editor of *Women's America.*

"Life is drab and ugly. Life can be beautiful" if only we can "reshuffle the constituent parts that formed the dreary design of our national life" into a "picture of democratic justice and spiritual beauty." The words are those of George Biddle, American artist, mural painter, and Groton schoolmate of that master reshuffler and reshaper of American life, Franklin Delano Roosevelt, and they reflect the faith of those who believed that inherent in the American dream of a more abundant life was the promise not only of economic and social justice but also of cultural enrichment—in short, "Arts for the Millions."

Individuals sharing that belief expressed it in a variety of phrases. "People's Theatre" was the term of those who saw in the federal theatre project the seeds of a national institution belonging to all the people. In the same spirit, Federal Art Project directors entitled a collection of essays on that project, "Art for the Millions." But it is the term "cultural democracy" which best encompasses the ideas and aspirations of a New Deal élite who sought to integrate the artist into the mainstream of American life and make the arts both expressive of the spirit of a nation and accessible to its people.

This quest for a cultural democracy did not originate in the 1930s but had been a deep and abiding preoccupation in American culture. Ralph Waldo Emerson put the question succinctly nearly a century earlier: "how to give all access to the masterpieces of art and nature, is the problem of civilization." Like Thomas Jefferson, he believed that in a young democracy wealthy patrons would be few. Therefore access to "culture and inspiration" could only come through public ownership of art "properties"—ownership by states, towns, and lyceums. Other cultural enthusiasts also looked to government. In a plea for public support of the theatre, Edward Everett Hale suggested that in the hands of the "wise and good" the theatre was a force for moral and social betterment; it was as deserving of public support as the schools. But in an era of modified laissez faire, plans for government supported drama did not materialize. Nor did the commissioning of paintings and statuary for the decoration of the Capitol usher in a broad program of federal patronage.

If the arts were to provide a necessary antidote to the vulgarization of life presumably characteristic of a democracy, access would have to be guaranteed by groups not associated with government, men of wealth and community standing who believed that they had a responsibility to foster the cultural life of the new nation. This genteel élite, along with artists themselves, tried to establish exhibition halls in academies, atheneums, and libraries in growing cities. Their efforts, however, were inevitably limited and frequently failures in the democratic sense because they did not take into account the sensibilities of the mass audience. Such limitations became especially pronounced in the post-Appomattox years when industrialization produced new élites and new social values among which was a concern for cultural acquisitions for the few rather than cultural edification of the many.

Not until the Progressive era brought a self-conscious renaissance in democracy would pioneering cultural spokesman again share an intense desire to make the theatre or the museum a genuine public institution open to all and meaningful to all. . . .

[T]he progressive thrust to integrate the arts and democracy would have had relatively little impact had it not been for the Depression and the creation of the New Deal cultural projects. As economic conditions worsened, private patronage virtually ceased, as did those peripheral odd jobs on which artists depended for subsistence. By the early 1930s, the question was simply this: were artists important enough to use the power of the federal government to shield them from a depression which, without federal interference, would surely force them into nonartistic activities. Many people were indifferent; others thought artists were not a matter of legitimate government concern. But a few New Dealers dissented. In 1933, Harry Hopkins began funneling Federal Emergency Relief Agency (FERA) funds to a few unemployed artists, actors, and musicians. The following year, Secretary of the Treasury Henry Morgenthau authorized the creation of a Section of Fine Arts, under Edward Bruce, which put visual artists to work decorating public buildings. And in 1935, a major relief appropriation created the Works Progress Administration (WPA) and nationwide work relief projects for visual artists, musicians, theatrical and literary people.

The task of Bruce and his staff at the treasury was to secure for federal buildings "the best art" this country could produce and to select artists to do that work solely on the basis of quality. But for the directors of "Federal One," as the four WPA cultural projects were known, humanitarian considerations were paramount— 90 percent of their clientele had to come from welfare rolls. Yet neither they, Hopkins, nor the President regarded these WPA projects as the simple relief measures Congress intended. Rather they were the means to more important ends: the fulfillment of a long-standing desire to bring together artist and people and to use the uplifting power of art to enrich the lives of ordinary citizens. Translated into New Deal terminology, this meant creating a nation of cultural consumers, for, if recovery were to be achieved in the arts as well as the economy, government would have to provide potential consumers access to the arts. Only through accessibility would people come to regard the arts, not as an expendable luxury, but as a community asset.

Although New Dealers shared this commitment to aesthetic accessibility, the nature of the commitment varied considerably. For the President, the conviction that people were entitled to cultural enrichment as well as economic and social justice stemmed in part from his concern for the quality of life in this country. Although Roosevelt himself had no real aesthetic sense, as a patrician who had been exposed to culture in childhood and to the stimulus of artists, musicians, and theatre people in later years, he assumed that classical music, legitimate theatre, and the masterpieces of art were a part of the good life. For Roosevelt, access to the arts seemed as logical as access to the ballot box or school house. Hopkins shared this assumption, but he also saw the arts as instruments of reform. In moments of idealistic fervor, Hopkins talked not only of carrying music and plays to children in city parks but also of using the power of theatre to spotlight tenements so as to encourage the building of decent houses for all people.

For Hopkins' four cultural projects directors, concern for the state of the arts was paramount, but even here the level of commitment was uneven. Henry Alsberg, with his state guides and heterogeneous assortment of writers, was perhaps least concerned with the need of a creative intelligentsia for a public. Music project director Nikolai Sokoloff was more so. A cultural élitist prepared neither by temperament nor training to exchange his conductor's baton for the role of musical evangelist, he nonetheless had 15,000 unemployed musicians for whom new employment opportunities had to be generated, and that brought a keen awareness of the need to expand the national audience. For the federal theatre's Hallie Flanagan, art project director Cahill, and their associates, "Arts for the Millions" became an ideological imperative. Neither director would restrict audiences to the traditional forms associated with "high" art—a decision indicative of the imagination and flexibility which would distinguish them both.

Whatever their differing perspectives, New Deal cultural enthusiasts shared with other liberals and some leftists a belief that the fine arts had become the property of the monied few to the detriment of arts, arts institutions, and the public. Painting, sculpture, even drama had become luxury items—superfluous and expendable. Museums, like the objects they exhibited, had become "fragments of the past . . . legacies from rich men's houses," instead of inviting, accessible public institutions. The ultimate loss was that of the American people, for, outside a few metropolitan centers, original works of arts, accomplished orchestras, and professionally competent theatre groups were few indeed. Roosevelt himself estimated that only one out of ten Americans had ever had a chance to see a "fine picture." The estimate was probably optimistic. . . .

Thus denied access to "high" culture, most of this nation's citizens subsisted on the aesthetically deficient pap served up as entertainment—a later generation would call it *kitsch*. Although

New Deal cultural enthusiasts rejected the cultural élitism of such critics of mass culture as José Ortega y Gasset or T. S. Eliot, they were well aware that by the 1930s the nation had become addicted to mass culture: movies, radio, the tabloid newspaper, *Life* magazine. Predictably, "high" culture had suffered. As Dwight Macdonald subsequently observed, there was a Gresham's Law in cultural as well as monetary circulation: "bad stuff drives out the good, since it is more easily understood and enjoyed." . . .

To put unemployed artists to work, the cultural resources of the nation would have to become accessible. Theatrical production units and symphony orchestras would have to be established in regional centers from which touring companies could be dispatched. Local art centers would have to be founded to house workshops and traveling exhibits. In short, the arts would have to be freed from a cultural milieu that kept them as "high" culture—a thing apart—and returned to the healthy channels of everyday life. This the "cleansing waters of the depression" now made possible.

The directors of New Deal cultural projects reflected on potential contributions. Flanagan and her fellow enthusiasts spoke of the federal theatre as a true people's theatre. Rejecting the idea of the stage as a place "where sophisticated secrets are whispered to the blasé initiate," she insisted that federal players could bring to huge new audiences not only the classics but also experimental plays, religious plays, dance drama, and children's theatre. More important, they could produce plays that would reflect regional and ethnic differences and plays that would be boldly relevant to contemporary problems. The other arts could do no less. Sokoloff believed that orchestras and chamber groups could take "fine music" to "the masses." And while Bruce and his associate Forbes Watson talked of the murals that would advance American art, improve the nation's taste, and weld its people into a whole, Cahill elaborated on the potential contribution of the federal art project: gallery tours, free art classes, exhibits that would bring the works of the graphic, easel, and sculpture divisions to the people and finally an allocation program that would keep art on extended display in public buildings across the country. But Cahill knew that exposure alone was not enough. . . .

If these Depression-born ventures were to achieve institutional permanence, the arts must not only be physically accessible but also intellectually and emotionally accessible. The arts must have social meaning if they were to elicit response. And it is in the probing of artistic process and response that Cahill in particular went beyond his New Deal colleagues in developing the concept of a cultural democracy.

For Cahill, an ardent follower of John Dewey, the key was primarily "process" and only secondarily "product." "Art," wrote the director of the federal art project, "is not a matter of rare occasional masterpieces. . . . [G]reat art arises only in situations where there is a great deal of art activity, and where the general level of art expression is high." To produce such a climate and, more important, to create the "free and enriching communion" of which Dewey spoke, Cahill, like his former professor, believed in the primacy and pervasiveness of experience. Real understanding of art, he insisted, came not from passive observation but from intense participation in the creative process. The task of the federal art project, therefore, was to make possible "democracy in the arts" through "community participation."

The public art of the mural provided unexpected opportunities for just such participation as onlookers queried painters about subject matter and technique, volunteered criticism and suggestions, and thus turned the production of a mural into a community endeavor. Still more valuable were those participation-oriented classes where sympathetic teachers in the progressive tradition neglected the principles of "correct" drawing in order to encourage the kind of experience that would make their students "eye-minded." Through project-sponsored classes in technique, media, and design, Cahill was convinced that aesthetic sensitivity could be enhanced, expressiveness encouraged, audiences created, and the quality of life improved.

The institutions which best exemplified the kind of physical and intellectual accessibility that would create an arts-conscious public were the community art centers. Physical symbols of the New Deal effort to decentralize the nation's cultural resources, they were scattered across the country in small cities where they were directed by qualified artists-teachers. An arts-conscious public would be born in these centers, Cahill believed, as children and adults, irrespective of technical fluency, became amateur artists. In the process of creation they would discover that art was not something preserved in elaborate institutions, but "beauty for use"—use in the "broadest human sense." In emphasizing artistic process and public response, Cahill groped for a definition of art which Dewey had supplied only the year before. By providing access to what the philosopher called "art as experience," the New Deal could perhaps create the mass audience—the hallmark of cultural democracy.

With access would also come the integration of artist and public—one of the sought-after goals of creative intellectuals throughout the 1930s. As the arts became necessary, so, too, would the artist. No longer an extraneous, alienated member of society, he would find his livelihood more secure. More important, his works, whether literary, visual, or performing, would change as communication with the public stimulated his imagination and inspired a deeper interpretation of life. The arts would become infused with a new vitality, commitment, and maturity. Watson would have said meaning; Flanagan, relevance; Cahill, use. What they envisioned were the arts "interwoven with the very stuff and texture of human experience, intensifying that experience, making it more profound, rich, clear, and coherent."

Such works could affect and even transform men's hearts and minds, it was hoped. They could also reflect the spirit of a nation. For New Deal cultural enthusiasts, who were also aesthetic nationalists, the promise of arts which were distinctly American was tantalizing indeed. With characteristic confidence, Hopkins predicted that from the federal theatre "a vital new American drama" would emerge. To fulfill that pledge, Flanagan urged directors to search for plays which probed America's past, its present, and the richness of its regional diversity. To New England directors she even suggested dramatization of portions of the New England guides. With equal zeal, the music project's Charles Seeger called for the integration of popular, folk, and academic music into a distinctively American idiom. As initiator of that superb pictorial survey of early decorative arts, the "Index of American Design," Cahill was concerned with the sources and development of American art. To be sure, he and his fellow directors never went to such lengths as Bruce, who confined section artists to realistic depictions of wholesome American themes, but neither would they have quarreled with the poster in a Massachusetts art center which proclaimed: "OUT OF THE SPIRIT OF A PEOPLE ARISES ITS ART." Indeed, such assumptions were basic to all who hoped that interaction of artist and public would evoke a quality which, however elusive, was unmistakably American.

The actual process of interaction—the precise nature of this new communication—was never spelled out. Nor was there any acknowledgment of the perennial tension existing between the artist's desire for rapprochement with society and the defiant individualism, which has so often culminated in social alienation and aesthetic privatism. There are reasons why limited theorizing was devoted to these questions. Administrators—and artists—are seldom aestheticians. Moreover, the belief that the union of artist and the people would create a revitalized American art was in the 1930s a rhetorical commonplace and almost an article of faith. It also reflected the renewed interest in national values and traditions which permeated American thought in this troubled Depression decade.

These three elements then comprised the concept of a cultural democracy: cultural accessibility for the public, social and economic integration for the artist, and the promise of a new national art. Inspired as much by commitment to the arts as to democracy, it was also part of the 1930s effort to create and document an American culture—and the word is used here in the anthropological sense. But whatever its inspiration, this quest for a cultural democracy was one which had to be pursued in a context complicated by relief, bureaucracy, and politics—and there, of course, was the rub.

The task of bringing "Arts to the Millions" was formidable. Physical access demanded decentralization—getting the arts out of a few metropolitan centers where artists had congregated and dispersing them across the nation. It also meant providing access to the millions who had never attended a museum, symphony concert, or a play—and to the thousands more who could no longer afford the price of a ticket. For culturally starved New Yorkers, these projects meant free concerts in the park, a new municipal art gallery, Shakespeare in the schools, and inexpensive tickets to such varied dramatic fare as Eliot's *Murder in the Cathedral* or the Orson Welles-John Houseman production of *Horse Eats Hat*.

White New Yorkers were not the only beneficiaries. With an absence of racism not always characteristic of other New Deal agencies, the cultural projects hired unemployed black artists and carried their work to an expanding black audience. Under WPA auspices, Harlem's old Lafayette Theatre again became a theatrical magnet with a variety of productions, including a resplendent *Macbeth* which ultimately played to 130,000 people. And at the Harlem Art Center children and adults encountered the works of black artists, often for the first time. A young black girl later wrote to WPA alumnus Jacob Lawrence: "Even though I have had a very limited acquaintance with art, I was immediately struck by the power of your paintings of Negro life. As soon as I saw them, there was a shock of recognition and the feeling that this is just right, just as it should be."

Cultural élitists might dismiss Lawrence and his fellow artists as "sorry daubers, ham actors, spavined dancers and radical scribners luxuriating on the dole," but elated New Dealers knew better. As similar encounters occurred, project directors found tangible evidence of vastly expanded audiences. But the shortcoming of the federal theatre, and to some degree the other cultural projects, was that this was still predominantly a metropolitan audience. Plans to send theatre companies and orchestras to the other areas of the nation foundered on WPA regulations prohibiting sending relief personnel across state lines. An attempt was then made to establish local projects where there were enough musicians or actors on relief to comprise a performing unit, but many such units had to be disbanded because of reduced appropriations. Thus the number of states producing WPA music and drama declined. Roosevelt and Hopkins repeatedly urged Flanagan and Sokoloff to tour, but touring was expensive, complicated, and unpopular in Congress. As one congressman so bluntly put it, the purpose of the federal theatre was to relieve distress and prevent suffering by providing employment; it was not to go "touring over the country, from place to place, charging admissions at cut rates in open competition with the theatrical industry. . . ." Thus economic distress, bureaucratic restrictions, and political opposition confined WPA's performing artists to a few major cities, inaccessible to millions of the people for whom these theatres and orchestras had been intended.

Access to the visual arts proved easier. Although 75 percent of art project personnel were employed in eight metropolitan areas, Cahill boasted of operations in thirty-eight states. These figures, of course, indicated community art centers. Manned by small staffs—sometimes only a single artist-teacher—gallery-workshops could be set up inexpensively throughout the hinterland. Beginning with North Carolina, Cahill oversaw the creation of over 100 centers throughout the country. Stretching from Salem, Oregon, to Key West, Florida, they were initially housed in vacant stores, abandoned restaurants and undertakers' parlors, and in the assorted garages and basements provided by local communities. Some quickly acquired spacious, well-equipped quarters, but all opened their doors to the entire community. "High-hatting," observed a *Time* reporter, was "taboo." As residents of middle America discovered in these centers opportunities to participate as well as observe, attendance figures climbed into the millions. Moreover, those who attended WPA exhibits were getting quality art. In addition to work by project artists, Washington headquarters circulated works on loan from such institutions as the Whitney, the Pennsylvania Academy of Fine Arts, the Denver Museum, and the American Federation of Arts. Perhaps more important, people grew to appreciate what they saw. Visitors to the Raleigh Art Center were a case in point. Objecting to an early exhibit of abstract and surrealist paintings from the Corcoran, they demanded what the center's director could only describe as "realistic paintings of the most saccharine type." Within less than a year, some of these viewers responded to a watercolor exhibit with a new openness to experimentation in subject matter and style. In similar centers across the country where art was becoming accessible, "Arts for the Millions" seemed a reality.

But to suggest that the New Deal quest for a cultural democracy had been realized would be folly. In 1939, a mere four years after its creation, the federal theatre was abolished by a hostile Congress amidst charges of subversion, inefficiency, and immorality. The other cultural projects were allowed to limp along into the war years, when they too were disbanded. Cultural enthusiasts failed to convince the Congress that support of the arts or the provision of access to them was a legitimate function of government. Cultural democracy never became public policy. Even tangible remains were few: paintings, graphics, and sculptures of varying quality on loan to public institutions, over one million dollars worth of theatrical equipment consigned to storage, and the seemingly endless boxes of records. For most Americans this federal foray into the arts was one of the more ephemeral episodes in an era of bread and circuses.

Yet even in terms of the WPA's quest for a cultural democracy, there were positive accomplishments. The New Deal had taken arts to the people—symphony orchestras and dance bands, classics and circuses, Rembrandt etchings and contemporary murals. The breadth of these offerings, especially in the visual arts and theatre, was in part a tribute to the eclecticism and flexibility of Cahill and Flanagan. As an expert in American art—folk and primitive as well as contemporary—Cahill was ideologically prepared to embrace both the fine and practical arts. And Flanagan, for all her emphasis on experimentation, applied WPA's label to everything from a modern dance version of a Greek classic to vaudeville, demanding only excellence in execution as a criterion. For Sokoloff, "real" music was, of course, classical music. Indeed, his determination to promote symphonies, operas, and chamber groups precluded any attempt to effect a synthesis, much discussed in music circles, which would have united a traditional "cultivated" musical orientation with the vernacular tradition—folk songs, jazz, and popular music. But Sokoloff, like his fellow directors, was confronted with artists of widely uneven talent and professional background. Thus necessity provided a powerful stimulus to aesthetic elasticity on all WPA cultural projects, and directors could take comfort in the fact that they were providing something for everybody.

For all this array of cultural goods, the overall emphasis was on "high" art as determined by the purveyors rather than the partakers of New Deal culture. To be sure, the federal theatre had its audience surveys on play preference; and on all projects attendance figures were regarded as a reflection of popular judgment. Yet the real arbiters of taste were a New Deal cultural élite. Some of them felt ambivalent about that fact; others did not. Those who were burdened with the day-to-day administration of problem-ridden projects never managed to come together to fashion a consensus as to what kind of art was compatible with a democracy. Yet underlying much of what they did was the conviction that they were influencing America's taste by providing access to "good" painting, drama, and music.

But could "good" art come out of "political leaf raking"? For cultural élitists—and most Republicans—the answer was an emphatic "no." Deploring "the rape of the walls," Alfred Stieglitz suggested that the government give unemployed artists their $28.30 per week, but keep them away from paint. Eva Le Gallienne's objection was more to the point. The founder and director of the Civic Repertory Theatre, Le Gallienne argued that an audience could be created for the theatre only if people were given a chance to see the theatre at its "very best." This she doubted a relief project could do. Bruce agreed, insisting that his treasury section's muralists would produce superior art precisely because his was not a humanitarian venture. Nor were WPA directors immune from doubt. They knew only too well that their projects were burdened with relief personnel whose talents—sometimes meager to begin with—had been eroded by age as well as prolonged unemployment. Too often they watched helplessly as their best people were lured away by private enterprise just as a new play was about to open or a difficult orchestral score readied for performance. But Flanagan, with characteristic zeal, always insisted that such difficulties were not insurmountable. Because she and Cahill tried to provide an atmosphere of freedom in which their most gifted people would work productively, their efforts were at least partially rewarded. The federal theatre, with its all black jazz version of *The Mikado,* its prolabor opera, and its experimental documentaries, was controversial and creative. Not all productions were as theatrically innovative or as professionally produced as *Swing Mikado, The Cradle Will Rock,* and the inimitable living newspapers, but much of what was produced did have aesthetic merit and audiences responded accordingly.

Precisely who the audiences were is more difficult to determine. One thing is clear: the New Deal cultural projects uncovered a vast audience and a seemingly diverse one. Although the data in the federal theatre's audience surveys is insufficient to warrant confident conclusions, audiences seem to have been predominantly middle class, even in Harlem, despite a conscientious effort to attract low-income groups. The effort was made. Union locals and WPA workers were encouraged to become regular purchasers of blocks of tickets, and directors of community art centers were constantly told to make their institutions centers for the entire community, the clear implication being that class, if not racial, barriers were to be transcended. This was at least in part a new audience. And while it was never fully representative of all the people, it certainly reflected that aspiration.

But what of the relationship between audience and artist? Basic to the hope for a cultural democracy was the desire not only to improve the quality of life for the American people but also to redefine the role of the arts and artists. With respect to the first—improved quality of life—intellectuals such as Lewis Mumford, Archibald MacLeish, and V. F. Calverton believed that New Deal cultural projects had succeeded brilliantly. In an open letter to Roosevelt, Mumford commended the President and his arts administrators for having found a potential solution to the problem of "how to use our collective wealth and individual leisure with dignity and sanity and permanent delight." Optimistic, of course. But even if one allows for the enthusiasm of contemporary "believers" and the puffery of official press releases, project records suggest that this WPA venture relieved the drabness of the Depression decade in ways that elude precise measurement.

What then of the no less ardent desire to integrate the artist into a society of which he and his art were an integral part? The conviction that this goal was necessary was fed by many sources. First, historical example: citing the drama—and audiences—of Euripides and Shakespeare, Flanagan frequently argued that great art flourished in conjunction with great audiences. Second, current unemployment figures: here was evidence of the consequences of the public's perception of art as an expendable luxury. Third, Marxist ideology: arts for the masses was no less a goal of the Artists' Union and Writers' Congress; moreover, such influential front groups did much to shape rhetoric and cultural goals in this so-called "red decade." Finally and most important, there was the widespread desire among artists and intellectuals to end the alienation from the public so pronounced in the 1920s. This, after all, was the decade of Carl Sandburg's classic affirmation: "The People, Yes." The task of these cultural projects then was to develop an understanding, appreciative public which would embrace the artist as a functional member of society. Such at least was the hope!

Some believed the goal had been realized. "The artists . . . engaged in these WPA projects," wrote Mumford, "have been given something more precious than their daily bread: they have at last achieved the liberty to perform an essential function of life, in the knowledge that their work had a destination in the community." The artist, he said, had been brought into "working relations with his fellow citizens."

But had he? The illusion of integration was certainly there. Reflected in official pronouncements, it emerged in the contemporary statements of some artists and in the nostalgic recollections of others. But if economic support for the arts is made the measure of this new relationship the picture changes considerably. The public was neither willing nor able to express a monetary commitment to culture. Some among the more affluent denied their support because of politics; others because, as patrons, they saw their influence eroded by new groups. Besides, WPA audiences often appeared to be poor, and, worse still, radical. Liberals, of course, approved the projects and attended performances. But as for building up the kind of sentiment for the projects that would have guaranteed congressional support, "We . . . [did], well, not exactly nothing," lamented Malcolm Cowley, "but not really enough to matter." As for "the people," most were never really convinced that the arts were essentially theirs. National Art Week did not, as the slogan promised, produce "A Work of Art for Every American Home," despite the fact that graphics sold for as little as $2.50. Indeed, in 1941, the major purchaser turned out to be the man whom Roosevelt had asked to serve as National Chairman of Art Week, Thomas J. Watson of IBM.

Scant success came of efforts to secure local support for arts institutions after federal funds had been withdrawn. In Minneapolis, Mobile, Roswell, New Mexico, and Salem, Oregon, successful efforts were made to perpetuate WPA beginnings. But elsewhere the picture was dismal. In Florida, thirteen of fourteen community art centers disappeared, as did ten centers in North Carolina, eleven in Oklahoma, four in Tennessee and Utah. Music fared little better. One enthusiastic historian of the music project cites twelve cities in which orchestras were established after World War II, presumably on the foundation laid by the music project. But of these twelve orchestras, six had musical predecessors which were independent of WPA. Although the project's existence may have been basic to the creation of the other six orchestras, precise relationships are difficult to determine. The number of surviving institutions seems pitiably small, but this is not surprising. In the heyday of the little theatre movement in the first years of this century, the attrition rate was also high. Institutional permanence seldom developed except in instances where technical expertise and genuine creativity were combined under highly effective leadership. Even then the struggle for survival was a rough one. The problem, however, was not simply one of local leadership or the lack of a "comfort class" capable of supporting the arts, although the relative poverty of this Depression decade should not be minimized. The process of institution building is inevitably a slow one. For New Deal cultural enthusiasts working within the confines of an emergency relief measure, there was simply too little time and talent and too many bureaucratic and political difficulties. Efforts to create indigenous local institutions were thus handicapped from the start by the very circumstances which made the opportunity possible. . . .

And what of the new national art which the integration of artist and society was supposed to produce? Aesthetic nationalists, both within and without the projects, found in this New Deal cultural foray the possibilities for a renaissance of the arts in America. Their hopes were matched by their rhetoric. An American artist and distinguished modernist, Max Weber, predicted "a great virile American art" that would be "epical, evocative, rich in plastic beauty and socially significant in content, the essence and nature of which will stem from our fertile and prolific national genius." Although his WPA colleague was more restrained, Yasuo Kuniyoshi insisted that New Deal cultural projects, in their effort to make art a "wanted commodity" supported by the whole people, had established "the beginnings of great American art."

The basis for all this optimism was real enough. Handicapped though they were, the directors of New Deal cultural projects had nonetheless sought to create the kind of environment in which a genuine art movement might flourish. Accordingly, many artists were encouraged to probe the American experience and search for roots in the folk tradition of the people, documenting the values and behavior of a culture in the throes of self-recognition. Indeed, Alsberg's writers and Bruce's artists were given no choice. But even WPA artists, who were free of prescriptions as to subject matter and style, turned to the American scene with a consistency that had little to do with the regionalist tenets of Thomas Hart Benton, Grant Wood, and John S. Curry and much to do with a sense of national rediscovery. The resulting output of Americana was overwhelming, as only a project-by-project survey can convey.

Figures in the visual arts alone are impressive, especially when one recognizes that most of these works were those of contemporary realists exploring some facet of the American scene. In the few months when the Public Works of Art Project had flourished,

Bruce reported an output of 15,663 pieces of art and craft. Oils, watercolors, and prints led the way, but there were also etchings, woodblocks, murals, mural sketches, sculptures, drawings, and poster paintings. Subsequent competition for section murals held under treasury auspices elicited 40,426 sketches in 1,906 competitions—all devoted to American themes. And on WPA art projects, reliefers produced 2,566 murals and 17,744 pieces of sculpture in addition to the oils, graphics, and various other forms of artistic production which were displayed in public buildings. They also produced 22,000 plates for the "Index of American Design." Superbly accurate copies of such objects as ship figureheads, cigarstore Indians, weather vanes, and quilts, the "Index" material . . . was the base for a great national art.

The writers' project was a no less prolific purveyor of Americana. In life histories—sometimes verbatim, sometimes impressionistic—project writers tried to capture the texture and particularity of ordinary people. In ethnic studies, they explored the groups which had gone into the making of a pluralist America. Afro-Americans came under special scrutiny as unemployed writers went throughout much of the South collecting narratives of former slaves and the material for special studies on the Negro in America. And state after state yielded folk material from both black and white. The project's most significant contribution, however, was 378 books and pamphlets which made up the guide series. These American Baedekers routed travelers to cities, tourist areas, places of local interest, scenic waterways, and highways. No mere collection of maps, each state guide included lengthy sections on history, geology, climate, racial makeup, industries, folklore, social life, arts, crafts, and culture. They were a road map for the cultural rediscovery of America, and, in Mumford's opinion, his generation's "finest contribution to American patriotism. . . ."

Even the music and theatre projects self-consciously emphasized the works of Americans, although both included in their repertoires the usual European classics. The music project had been in operation only a little over a year and a half when Sokoloff proudly announced that his musicians had performed compositions of nearly 14,000 American composers and this at a time when concertgoers had imbibed Walter Damrosch's prejudices against music written after 1900 by non-French composers. Perhaps more helpful to the younger musicians were the composers' forums which met weekly in New York and a few other cities for the presentation of new works before audiences eager to engage in critical dialogue. Even the anonymous songwriter received his due as music project copyists explored the nation's nooks and crannies transcribing the music of the folk: Creole ballads in Louisiana, bayou songs of the Mississippi delta, folk songs of the Appalachian hills, white and Negro spirituals of the Carolinas, Spanish songs of the Southwest, and liturgical music from the California missions.

Although American playwrights were harder to find in such numbers, the federal theatre found many who warranted production. Certainly there was nothing perfunctory about the search for plays by contemporary American dramatists who could deal with authentically native material. At Harlem's Lafayette Theatre, where the need for appropriate material was especially intense, even the National Association for the Advancement of Colored People became involved; Walter White wrote to Sherwood Anderson to inquire whether the author in fact had a script about Negro life which the Harlem unit might produce. Anderson, alas, did not, but the federal theatre managed to produce the works of virtually every contemporary American playwright of note; Eugene O'Neill and Paul Green were especial favorites. Moreover, in their eagerness to present works that probed the nation's history, diversity, and problems, they turned to pageants, musicals, dance dramas, and, of course, the living newspapers. Titles alone tell the story: *Valley Forge, Bonneville Dam, An American Exodus, Power, Triple-A Plowed Under, Injunction Granted.*

Despite all this aesthetic probing of the American scene, the United States failed to produce the kind of renaissance for which the nationalists longed. Critics did not acclaim a flowering comparable to that which had occurred in American literature in the 1920s, and there was no dramatic thrust toward cultural maturity, no sudden easing of the nagging sense of inferiority in the visual and performing arts. To conclude that this outpouring of Americana was mere aesthetic boondoggling, however, is to miss the mark. Quite apart from their immediate value, the vast quantity of "American stuff" amassed by these New Deal cultural projects constituted the raw material for new creative works. Artists and critics, noted MacLeish, need no longer assume that each artistic beginning in America was "a beginning *de novo*." Indeed, amassing the material was significant for artists such as Ralph Ellison and Ben Shahn. Ellison in his research for the New York City guide had so immersed himself in the Harlem of *Invisible Man* that his novel acquired a substance and authenticity lacking in many of the works associated with the Harlem Renaissance. In much the same fashion, the photographic trips around the country which Shahn made for the Farm Security Administration provided him with photographs as well as the mental images which dominated his subsequent works. If the act of amassing material was important, so, too, was the mode of presentation. In their efforts to let ordinary people tell their own stories or to dramatize evidence about contemporary problems, New Deal artists were taking part in the creation of a new genre, the documentary. Evident in film, photography, journalism, and broadcasting, as well as the arts, the documentary captured the "tone, mood, and concerns of a decade." It was, according to William Stott, distinctively "thirties America." And nowhere is it better exemplified than in the federal theatre's living newspapers. Combining factual data and live actors with such diverse techniques as loudspeakers, film clips, lights, and music, these documentary explorations of public issues stimulated the emotions as well as the intellect. Influenced by such disparate sources as the "March of Time" and the "agitprops" of the Russian Blue Blouses, the living newspaper nonetheless constituted the "most original" form of drama developed in the United States and as a product of the New Deal, it was quintessential people's theatre.

What then of this quest for cultural democracy? Scholars must conclude that it was only partially realized, perhaps because it was only partially articulated. New Deal cultural enthusiasts did bring arts to the people, even pioneering in a new genre that was eminently accessible. But most people never fully accepted the arts as a public right and personal necessity. And in the postwar climate of disengagement, the vision of integration which had once been so inspiring seemed as dated as a 1935 copy of *New Masses*. In a characteristic expression of rejection, the painter Adolph Gottlieb, once a proponent of cultural democracy, denounced the "sentimental attitude that longs for a reconciliation between artist and public in the false hope that the artist can, in some nebulous fashion, be in touch with the grass roots of human aspirations." The notion of an "organic society" within which the artist could exist harmoniously was, in his view, a "Utopian fantasy." As for aesthetic nationalism, Gottlieb and his fellow art project colleagues would soon agree that attempts to establish a national character for the American arts were, at best, "misguided." But these old visions and the economic crisis which spawned them had served Gottlieb and his compatriots better than they realized. To be sure, fundamental questions about the relationship between artist and public were never resolved in the 1930s—this had, after all, been a persistent problem. But by their very existence, New Deal projects provided, however briefly, symbolic legitimization of the arts and public patronage. More important, they provided the artist with a livelihood, an artistic milieu, and objective affirmation of his professional identity and worth. In short, they brought the two concepts of "culture" into greater association with each other and both into closer identification with the living concept of democracy; and that, in a nation historically so indifferent to its cultural resources, was a matter of no small consequence.

New Deals

Deadly floods on the Ohio River in 1937 produced this ironic scene in Louisville, Kentucky. The billboard suggests white America's vision of a mass consumption economy, while the line waiting outside a relief center portrays a starkly different reality for African Americans. The photograph was taken by Margaret Bourke-White and originally appeared in *Life* magazine. (Margaret Bourke-White, LIFE Magazine © Time, Inc.)

Lizabeth Cohen

Workers Make a New Deal

Older accounts of the New Deal almost always told the story of the 1930s from a national perspective. The focus was almost invariably on Roosevelt and Congress or on labor leaders such as John L. Lewis and the struggle to build the CIO. In these accounts, however, farmers, workers, and the unemployed—"grassroots America"—were portrayed as passive participants in the New Deal drama. They listened to Roosevelt's fireside chats, voted in elections, wrote an occasional letter of protest, worked for a relief program, but in no important sense did they shape the New Deal or make conscious choices.

In her prize winning book *Making a New Deal,* a study of Chicago's ethnic working class during the 1920s and 1930s, Lizabeth Cohen offers a dramatically different perspective. These workers and their families were largely uninvolved in city or national politics before 1933, but faced with the shock of the depression and the benefits of the New Deal, they began to affiliate with Chicago's—and Roosevelt's—Democratic Party and to join the CIO's newly formed industrial labor unions. These working-class families were "making" their own New Deal within their communities and factories. They were vital participants in a larger national story. In the chapter excerpted here, Cohen describes how ethnic and African American workers came to identify themselves as Democrats and to mobilize politically.

Lizabeth Cohen is professor of history at Harvard University.

In 1935, Mrs. Olga Ferk wrote a letter to President Roosevelt in which she complained that she was mistreated at her relief station, that she was only $19 behind in her government HOLC mortgage payments, not three months as accused, and that her son's Civilian Conservation Corps (CCC) paychecks were always late in arriving. "How long is this rotten condition going to last," she demanded of the president. "I am at the end of the rope. The Rich get Richer and the poor can go to—H—that is what it looks like to me. . . . Let's have some results." What is most striking about Mrs. Ferk's

From Cohen, Lizabeth, *Making a New Deal: Industrial Workers in Chicago, 1919–1939.* © 1990 by Cambridge University Press. Reprinted with the permission of Cambridge University Press and the author.

letter is that only a few years earlier, her expectation that the federal government should provide her with regular relief, a mortgage, and a job for her son and be efficient and fair about it would have been unimaginable. In the midst of the Great Depression, families like the Ferks were depending on the national government as once they had looked to their ethnic institutions and welfare capitalist employers.

Two years later, Sociology Professor Arthur W. Kornhauser and his assistants at the University of Chicago interviewed several thousand Chicago residents of diverse occupations to learn their opinions about the great controversies of the day. Their findings indicate that Mrs. Ferk's discontents were typical of semiskilled and unskilled workers. Three-fourths of them felt that working people were not treated fairly, whereas in the minds of almost everyone, wealthy businessmen had too much influence in running the country. Although these workers were not asked directly how they would solve the depression crisis, their point of view can be pieced together from responses to other questions. Chicago's industrial workers blamed the capitalist system, and particularly big businessmen, for the economic depression, yet for the most part they were unwilling to abandon capitalism in favor of a socialist system where government owned industry. At the same time, however, they advocated the strengthening of two institutions to rebalance power within capitalist society: the federal government and labor unions. Ninety percent of the sample of unskilled workers and 81 percent of the semiskilled favored Roosevelt's New Deal, whose programs represented to workers the expansion of federal authority. Three-fourths of these workers even went so far as advocating that the government play a role in redistributing wealth in the society. Clearly, Chicago's working people were seeking a powerful federal government that would work for them, not their bosses. The other institution that workers thought would bring about a more equitable capitalist society was the labor union. More than four-fifths of them endorsed strong labor unions to which all workers would belong. If workers were organized in unions and protected by a strong federal government, the "moral capitalism" that they had hoped for under welfare capitalism during the 1920s might finally prevail, these Chicago working people seemed to be saying.

Having lost faith in the capacity of their ethnic communities and welfare capitalist employers to come to the rescue, Chicago's industrial workers had found new solutions. By the mid-1930s, they, and their counterparts elsewhere in America, were championing an expanded role for the state and the organization of national-level industrial unions. State and union, workers hoped, would provide the security formerly found through ethnic, religious, and employer affiliation as well as ensure a more just society. Although most workers interviewed did not call for revolutionary change, it would be a mistake to assume that their commitment to a moral capitalism did not challenge the status quo. Too often retrospective analysis of workers' responses to the Great Depression falls into the trap of pigeonholing them as either radical or not, according to some external standard, without evaluating in a more subtle way how workers changed their attitudes over the course of the 1930s. Newfound faith in the state and the unions was not preordained. It required workers to make significant breaks with previous values and behavior and to adopt new ones. . . .

Voting in the State

It was not at all obvious that when Chicago's working people suffered misfortunes in the depression they would turn to the federal government for protection. During the 1920s, these workers had put little faith in government, particularly at the national level. . . . [T]o the extent that working people's social welfare needs were met at all, they were met in the private sector, by ethnic communities and welfare capitalist employers. Many workers looked warily on the expansion of state power, as they felt it was already interfering with their cultural freedom by legislating and enforcing Prohibition.

Most indicative of their disinterest in government, large numbers of Chicago workers failed to vote. In wards with high percentages of foreign-born workers, less than one-third of the potential electorate (people over the age of twenty-one) turned out for the presidential election of 1924, in contrast to 65 percent in native, middle-class wards. Many of these nonvoters could not vote because they were not citizens. Stiff citizenship requirements and a disinclination to naturalize kept them away. Others qualified to vote but did not bother to register or to vote even when registered. They simply did not find national party politics relevant to their lives. "I had cast maybe one ballot in a national election, before the mid-1930s," recalled steelworker George Patterson, an immigrant of Scottish birth who had become a citizen easily in the twenties with no new language to learn.

Even those ethnic workers who voted during the 1920s did not often identify politically beyond their local community. The kind of machine politics that flourished in Chicago during the twenties kept people dependent on a very local kind of political structure not tightly bound to any one major party. . . . Political parties were most visible in a community right before election time and then often disappeared. There were general patterns, of course, in the voting of blacks and "new immigrant" groups who dominated Chicago's industrial work force—blacks and Yugoslavs strongly Republican; Poles, Czechs, Lithuanians, and eastern European Jews frequently Democratic; Italians often split—but no party could count on a particular group's votes, except the Republicans on the blacks. It was a rare ethnic worker in Chicago who had a strong identity as either Democrat or Republican before the late 1920s.

All this changed at the end of the decade. Workers became drawn into an interethnic Democratic machine in Chicago under the leadership of Czech politician Anton Cermak that connected them not only to a unified Democratic Party on the city level but also to the national Democratic Party. . . .

The creation of a Democratic machine in Chicago under Mayor Cermak and his successor Mayor Kelly (who took office in 1933 after Cermak was killed by an assassin's bullet intended for President Roosevelt) has drawn much attention for how it paved the way for years of undemocratic rule by the Daley machine. What is lost in hindsight, however, is how voters actually felt about joining a citywide and national Democratic Party at the time. First- and second-generation immigrants still made up almost two-thirds of Chicago's population, and a large proportion of these came from eastern and southern Europe. After years of having little voice in either party, new ethnic groups finally felt that they had a party that represented them. When Republican candidate "Big Bill" Thompson made an issue of Cermak's eastern European origins in the mayoral race of 1931, a multiethnic alliance for the Democrats was clinched. Thompson's taunt,

Tony, Tony, where's your pushcart at?
Can you picture a World's Fair mayor
With a name like that?

and Cermak's retort ("He don't like my name. . . . It's true, I didn't come over on the Mayflower, but I came over as soon as I could") crystallized for ethnic Chicagoans how the Democratic Party had become the only party for them.

The best evidence that Chicagoans were becoming increasingly committed to the Democratic party is that the Democratic vote in both local and national elections mushroomed. By 1936, 65 percent of Chicago voters favored the Democratic presidential candidate, three times as many as had in 1924. In wards with large numbers of first- and second-generation ethnics, 81 percent supported Roosevelt in 1936, in contrast to 38 percent for Davis in 1924. Even more significant, these new Democratic voters, when white, were less often converted Republicans than new recruits, ethnic working-class people who had not voted during the 1920s. In their wards, there was a two-thirds increase in voter turnout between 1924 and 1936, with essentially all of these new participants voting Democratic.

Several factors explain why Chicago's ethnic workers were voting in record numbers, and overwhelmingly Democratic, during the depths of the Great Depression. To start with, more people were eligible to vote. In an immigrant district such as the one surrounding the Chicago Commons Settlement on the West Side, two-thirds of those over age twenty-one qualified to vote in 1930, in contrast to only one-third in 1920. Both the coming of age of the American-born second generation and the more than doubling of the numbers of foreign born who had become citizens, particularly women, were responsible. But eligibility is one thing, actually turning out to vote quite another. Starting in 1928, Chicago's ethnic workers participated more actively in the political process, and as Democrats, because of ideology not just demography. Finally by the 1930s, they felt like legitimate players in the political game. However undemocratic the one-party rule of Chicago's Democratic machine may have later become, it began as a democratic experience for many Chicago workers, giving them for the first time the feeling that the political process worked for them.

[There were other crucial reasons for the new commitment to party politics by ethnic workers.] Beginning with Al Smith's campaign as a wet candidate in 1928 and increasingly with Roosevelt in 1932 and particularly in 1936, workers felt that the policies of the national Democratic party were making a difference in their lives. "Before Roosevelt, the Federal Government hardly touched your life," explained one man. "Outside of the postmaster, there was little local representation. Now people you knew were appointed to government jobs. Joe Blow or some guy from the corner." For jobs, and a myriad of other services once provided by others, it soon became clear, workers looked increasingly to the state. John Mega, a worker at Western Electric who grew up in a Slovak family in Back of the Yards, watched this transformation in his own family's political consciousness: "Our people did not know anything about the government until the depression years." His father never voted. In fact, he stated, "In my neighborhood, I don't remember anyone voting. They didn't even know what a polling place was." Suddenly with the depression, all that changed. Mega's relatives were voting to send Democrats to Washington and counting on them for relief and CCC and Works Progress Administration (WPA) jobs. Because the Kelly machine identified itself so strongly with the New Deal, voters like Mega's family and neighbors did not feel they were favoring national over local government. They saw the Chicago Democrats as the conduit for Washington's largesse.

It is important to recognize, however, that the promise and impact of New Deal programs alone cannot explain workers' reorientation to the federal government. That they had personally helped put in power the Democrats in Chicago and in Washington mattered enormously. Voting was a gradual process teaching them that national politics was reciprocal. As workers took credit for electing the nation's political leadership, the state seemed less remote. Over time Chicago workers came to feel like national political actors who had earned rights by their political participation. When Celie Carradina's estranged husband refused to share his WPA pay with her in late 1935, this resident of Back of the Yards wrote to President Roosevelt for help on the grounds that "I hope you every way that I could doing election and I am going to do my best again" (*sic*). . . . Many others like Mr. and Mrs. Memenga threatened the president that if relief benefits did not improve, "we will think twice the next time [we are asked to vote for you]." Working-class voters in Chicago were coming to feel not only that their fate increasingly lay in the hands of New Deal officials but also that national office holders and bureaucrats owed them something for their votes. . . .

Black workers in Chicago were also voting in record numbers and more Democratic than ever before by 1936, but they arrived at this same destination via a very different route than did ethnic workers. Rather than being newcomers to the political process, blacks had participated actively in elections during the 1920s. When only a third of Chicago's ethnics were voting in 1924, over 50 percent of blacks did. At the most basic level, it was easier for blacks to vote in Chicago. The longest residency requirement they faced was a year to vote in state elections, whereas the minimum requirement for naturalization was over five years, and it usually took immigrants at least ten years to become citizens. No less important, voting mattered to blacks who had been kept from expressing their full citizenship rights in the South. Many immigrants, in contrast, were former peasants from eastern and southern Europe who had never even had the expectation of voting.

Blacks not only voted more than ethnics in the twenties but also displayed a strong loyalty to one party, the Republicans. In fact, Mayor "Big Bill" Thompson built his political career on the support of Chicago's black wards. Few blacks had been in the North long enough to forget the southern lesson that the Republican Party was the black's friend, the Democratic Party his racist enemy. . . .

Yet despite Chicago blacks' unfailing loyalty to the Republicans during the 1920s, by the late 1930s, they were securely in the Democratic camp. Nothing demonstrates so well the extent to which working people reoriented themselves politically during the 1930s as this shift of black voters from Republican to Democrat. Dependable voters in the twenties, blacks turned out in still larger numbers in the thirties. The 61 percent of eligible blacks who voted in 1932 grew to 70 percent by 1940. And blacks increasingly voted Democratic. With them as with ethnics, New Deal programs alone did not make Democrats. Local and national Democratic administrations complemented each other. Cermak, and even more so Kelly, wooed black supporters with traditional lures of the machine, like patronage jobs and benign neglect of illegal gambling, as well as with symbolic actions such as banning the film "Birth of A Nation" and ceremoniously naming boxer Joe Louis "mayor for ten minutes." In time, Kelly would even defend integrated schools and open housing, much to his own political detriment. . . .

There is no denying, however, that Kelly and Roosevelt's efforts to make Democrats out of Chicago's blacks were helped by New Deal programs. Despite charging that the NRA functioned more as a "Negro Removal Act" than a "National Recovery Act" and that relief and job programs discriminated against them, blacks found themselves dependent on whatever benefits they could wring from federal programs as they tried to cope with the ravages of the depression. "Let Jesus lead you and Roosevelt feed you" replaced "Stick to Republicans because Lincoln freed you." . . .

By 1937 black workers were giving . . . the same message as their ethnic peers: Our survival depends on a strong federal government, and the Democrats, both in Chicago and Washington, are the only ones who can give it to us. . . .

From Welfare Capitalism to the Welfare State

Voting in national elections and participating in the unemployed movement gave workers greater expectations for the state. Benefiting from New Deal programs made them dependent on it. Living as we do today in a world so permeated by the federal government, it is easy to lose sight of how much people's lives were changed by the expansion of federal responsibility during the 1930s. Even the conservative politicians of the late twentieth century who repudiate a strong federal government take for granted that working people will receive Social Security benefits upon retirement, that bank accounts will be insured by the Federal Deposit Insurance Corporation (FDIC), and that anyone who works will be assured a nationally set minimum wage. A world without these protections is hardly imaginable.

Despite the indisputable expansion of federal authority engendered by the New Deal, critics at the time, and even more so historians since, have nonetheless emphasized how improvisational, inconsistent, almost half-hearted the New Deal was. The reasons were varied. The Roosevelt administration was politically cautious, more oriented toward meeting emergencies than solving long-term problems, and most importantly, ambivalent, sometimes even fearful, about the growth of federal power that it was orchestrating. Critics rightfully point out that New Deal reforms failed to make the major social transformations, like the redistribution of wealth, that many progressives . . . hoped for. The American welfare state born during the depression turned out to be weaker than that of other western industrial nations such as England, France, and Germany. But a new direction nonetheless had been set. Most significant, workers made a shift from the world of welfare capitalism, where employers and voluntary associations cared, however inadequately, for their needs, to a welfare state, a reorientation that they would not easily reverse. This transition was particularly powerful for Chicago's workers because the basic services that they had looked to their ethnic communities and bosses to provide—welfare, security, and employment—and the depression endangered were taken over by the federal government. Although the New Deal may not have gone as far as many workers hoped it would, by providing welfare services, securing their homes and life savings, and offering them new jobs or reforming their old ones, the federal government played a new and important role in the lives of Chicago's working people.

The New Deal provided workers with federally funded relief programs, and eventually a permanent Social Security system, to take the place of the welfare previously dispersed by private organizations, often sponsored by their ethnic and religious communities. Federal assistance actually had begun through loans to the beleaguered states under Hoover's Reconstruction Finance Corporation. But it was the Federal Emergency Relief Administration (FERA), one of the first and most expensive creations of Roosevelt's New Deal, that regularized the national government's role in relief. Illinois was in such dire straits by the time Roosevelt took office in March 1933 that it became one of the first seven states to receive FERA funds. By the end of 1933, more than a third of Chicago's working population, including 44 percent of the city's blacks, looked to Washington for at least some of their keep, which put slightly more Chicagoans "on the dole" than was typical nationally.

It is true that FERA was designed as a shared undertaking between the federal government and the states. Of the $500 million first appropriated, half was intended to match dollars spent by the states, the other half as a discretionary fund for FERA's use wherever the need was greatest. But without a doubt, the national government shaped, and underwrote, this relief program. Between 1933 and 1935, the federal government provided 87.6 percent of the dollars spent on emergency relief in Chicago, in contrast to contributions of 11 percent by the state and 1.4 percent by the city. Even though state and local authorities administered the federal funds, everyone knew that the power lay in Washington. From the many relief recipients and unemployed organizations that lodged complaints against local relief operations directly with FERA chief Harry Hopkins or President Roosevelt to the caseworkers who feared Washington's reproof enough to beg clients not to write "as it causes . . . [us] a lot of trouble," it was generally agreed that the national government ruled relief. Mayor Kelly, in fact, fought efforts to return more of the administration of relief back to Chicago. The added patronage jobs were not worth the increased financial and social responsibility.

The alarm of the Catholic Church in Chicago over this expanded relief role for the federal government testifies to its radical implications. The church recognized just how undermining of previous loyalties workers' new dependence on the federal government could be. Beginning in the summer and fall of 1932 and with increasing intensity over the next year as federal funding of relief grew, private charities withdrew from offering the kind of welfare they had struggled to provide before the national government stepped in. With FERA requiring that only public agencies could distribute its funds, private expenditures for relief in Illinois declined from a high of $8.3 million in 1932 to only $942,500 in 1935. Most agencies were grateful to be relieved of carrying a burden they were ill equipped to handle and redirected their energies toward helping families with specialized, often psychological problems such as domestic discord, vocational maladjustment, and parent-child conflict. They were willing, moreover, to pay a price for their reprieve: that people would depend on the government the way they once had depended on them.

The Catholic Church, however, resisted this retrenchment. The Church hierarchy, which had long been working to consolidate its hold over Chicago's diverse Catholic population, mustered the considerable political clout it wielded in the city and in Washington, . . . and in August 1933 had its Central Charities Bureau and Society of St. Vincent de Paul named a unit of the Illinois Emergency Relief Commission (IERC), the state's distributor of FERA funds. In other words, the church became an agent of the government in distributing federal and Illinois relief dollars. Disregarding the outrage of Chicago social workers, who denounced the ploy as a violation of both professional standards and the constitution's separation of church and state all the way up the relief bureaucracy to FERA chief Hopkins, the archdiocese took comfort that needy Catholics would benefit from new government aid while still being accountable to the Catholic Charities, the St. Vincent de Paul Society, and the priest. The lengths to which the Chicago Catholic Church was willing to go to coopt this new federal welfare presence suggests how undermining it potentially was of workers' old dependence on private welfare agencies and benefit societies.

It has become almost an axiom among analysts of the Great Depression that Americans were ashamed to be on government relief because they saw dependency as one more sign, along with loss of work, that they had failed. The testimony of unemployed and underemployed workers that has survived from the Chicago experience, however, suggests a different story. Although some claimed to be too proud to go on relief and many preferred work relief to hand-outs, the vast majority defended the propriety of looking to the government for help. In the months before the federal government bailed out the struggling local relief effort, Thomas Jablonski complained bitterly, "America! What does America care for its children that it allows them to go hungry?" Another Polish-born Chicagoan argued for government intervention, "We are citizens of the United States, have been paying taxes . . . and are in dire need."

Chicago workers felt that their American citizenship, voting records, and even military service so entitled them to relief benefits that their letters to Washington often revealed anger against foreigners who had not "earned" the privilege. For example, William Bowles, "an unemployed ex service man" who served his "Country and State since 1916, in the Regular Army and National Guards until August 1932 . . . born a Republican, Democrat by choice" wrote Roosevelt to complain of poor treatment at his Black Belt relief office: "Foreigners go there and get anything they ask for. . . . I think I am entitled to a little more justice from these people."

Likewise, Edward J. Newman, who had worked thirty years for employers including U.S. Steel and International Harvester, asked the president for help securing the "food, coal and cloathing and the necessity of life which we are deserving of as good Americans citizen. . . . I cannot see where Americans comes first you say this in your speeches why dont we Americans get what we are intitled to" [*sic*]. . . .

These Chicago workers, like many others, were voicing new expectations for the state along with their prejudices. A social worker who had long held jobs in working-class districts of Chicago observed the change in attitude by 1934: "There is a noticeable tendency to regard obtaining relief as another way of earning a living. The former stigma attached to a family dependent on relief is gone and each family in a given neighborhood knows what, when, and how much every other family in a given neighborhood is obtaining from an agency. The men spend most of their time in the relief offices where they gather for recreational purposes while they await their turn to discuss their needs with the case workers." . . . Rather than feeling like beggars, workers felt they deserved benefits as citizens and more specifically for supporting FDR and the Democratic Party. It became more common for people to complain about the inadequacy and unsteadiness of relief benefits than to lament their own dependence on them.

Working-class people were more likely than middle-class ones to feel justified taking government relief during the thirties. An extensive survey of the Indianapolis population completed in 1941 indicated that a greater orientation toward independence made middle-class citizens more resentful of their need for relief than workers. An aide to Hopkins made a similar observation in a letter to him in 1934: "Clients are assuming that the government has a responsibility to provide. The stigma of relief has almost disappeared except among white collar groups." This situation concerned rather than pleased New Dealers, however. Ironically, the Roosevelt administration, which made federal relief possible, also began to teach people that they should feel ashamed to take it. Hopkins once admitted that in order to win acceptance of a work program to replace FERA, New Dealers "overemphasized the undesirability of relief." By the time recipients of federally funded WPA jobs got their official *Workers' Handbook* in 1936, they were being instructed:

What happens to us when we are on the dole?
We lose our self-respect. We lose our skill. We have family rows.
We loaf on street corners. Finally, we lose hope.

No sooner had workers shifted their dependence from the institutions of their local communities to the federal government than they began to be told·that the state that offered them a hand could also bite. That the government went out of its way to teach working-class people to feel ashamed for being "on the dole" suggests that workers felt differently.

The federal government's new involvement in providing welfare was not limited to emergency relief measures. The Social Security Act, signed by Roosevelt in August 1935, established a permanent system of unemployment compensation, old age insurance, and aid for disabled and dependent children. Despite all the limitations of the act—the exclusion of many kinds of workers, the regressive payroll tax method of funding it, the small benefits, the administration of much of the system by the states—it is important not to lose sight of the strong impression it made on workers who had never before been offered any security by the government. Social workers at the Chicago Commons Settlement were convinced that the residents of their neighborhood felt inspired by the creation of Social Security. "As the Social Security laws have begun to operate through the unemployment insurance act, the old age annuity and the old age pension, there has come to each individual a sense that he is joining with government and industry in an effort to build for the future," they wrote in the Commons Annual Report for 1937.

Social Security also influenced people's day-to-day decisions about their lives. For a worker like Florence Parise, the prospect of benefits sent her back to work at the Kennedy Laundry in 1937, a job she had left several years earlier. Suddenly there was a future in the job. . . . Before the New Deal, a family with someone out of a job, old, disabled, abandoned, and even dead was at the mercy of family, friends, and community charity. In contrast, under Social Security, with all its limitations, a family had the right to benefits from the government.

Welfare was not the only responsibility of Chicago's ethnic communities that the federal government took over during the 1930s. In the 1920s, workers had entrusted their future security, in the form of savings and home mortgages, to ethnic banks and building and loan associations. People had felt confident that their investment was safe with the neighborhood banker or association officer. When these institutions encountered rough times during the depression, however, anxious depositors saw many of them fail, and the federal government come to the rescue of those that survived.

The banks that managed to endure Chicago's banking crisis of the early 1930s and reopened after the "national bank holiday" called by the president and Congress were all licensed as solvent by federal or state authorities. Customers, moreover, were assured of the federal government's continued backing through the FDIC, established under the Emergency Banking Act of 1933. "I was saved 'cause Roosevelt that time was elected" was how Salvatore Cosentino remembered the banking crisis of the 1930s. . . .

Salvatore Cosentino, whose bank savings were preserved by government action, was also among the many Chicago people who had government help holding onto another valuable asset, his home. Cosentino's home was one of the more than a million in the nation saved from foreclosure by the Home Owners' Loan Corporation (HOLC), which offered long-term, low-interest mortgages to eligible homeowners in urban areas who were unable to meet the terms of mortgage holders and faced loss of their property. Between 1930 and 1936, one in every four nonfarm dwellings in the Chicago area had been foreclosed or refinanced by the HOLC, which saved more than half of the threatened homes through granting 45,500 loans between June 1933 and June 1936. . . .

Some critics have assumed that the HOLC was only helpful to the middle classes. A closer look proves that assessment incorrect. In a city like Chicago, many workers were homeowners, and in the midst of the depression, many of these people faced foreclosure. The HOLC, moreover, went out of its way to lend to owners of small and inexpensive homes. Sixty percent of the loans given in Chicago were in neighborhoods rated C or D in a system where A represented the most prosperous.

Chicago's factory workers, who had sacrificed so much during the 1920s to buy their homes, were very grateful to the federal government for protecting them from foreclosure. Their reaction when they were turned down for HOLC loans, moreover, reveals how quickly they came to expect this government intervention as a right due them, much like relief. "My children served in the recent

World's War, to make our United States a safe place to live in and protect our homes," complained Anna Cohen, a widow whose property was refused a HOLC loan because it included a store she rented out. Flory Calzaretta, disqualified on some other technical grounds, made a similar defense to President Roosevelt: "I am an American citizen for the past 30 years and my children were born in America, and as such I believe I am entitled to some consideration. Your Excellency made these loans possible for destitute cases just like mine." Barbara Ann Carter blamed foreigners for depriving her of a fair shake: "When we first applied and tried to get this loan over two years ago we found, by sitting there hours and hours that no one was getting any attention of loans but foreigners on the South Side." No sooner had the federal government entered the mortgage business than Chicagoans counted on it being there.

As the national government stepped in to help workers protect their homes, ethnic institutions charged with that function became even weaker. It has already been established that ethnic building and loan associations suffered terribly in both reputation and finances during the depression. But the HOLC helped make the limping building and loan association even lamer. Building and loan associations accused the HOLC of hurting their recovery by overlooking their distressed loans and bailing out larger, more established banks instead. "The HOLC is ruining some of our institutions by prejudice against foreign people operating them," S. C. Mazankowski, Secretary of the Father Gordon Building and Loan Association and a director of the Polish American Building and Loan Association League of Illinois, complained bitterly. A more likely explanation, however, was that the HOLC rejected many association loans on the grounds that they were poor risks, having mortgages with inadequate security behind them or reflecting too high a percentage of the appraisal. Mazankowski confirmed this when he further grumbled "Our institution received from the HOLC about 46 cents for every dollar we had in property." The source of the problem was that ethnic building and loan associations had served more effectively as community institutions with a social responsibility to their membership than as sound financial institutions. When the federal government began refinancing mortgages, it preferred the business practices of more stable, usually larger banks and thereby contributed to the demise of these smaller, often ethnic competitors.

In another way, the HOLC helped workers in the short run while hurting their ethnic and black communities in the long run. As part of its program, the HOLC sponsored a massive project rating all neighborhoods A through D or 1 through 4 so that property values could be assessed. Although the HOLC, with its government backing, was willing to give loans to people living in C and D areas, these ratings were later picked up by banks and used to discriminate against "declining" neighborhoods in granting mortgages and assessing property. Faced with fewer alternatives after the depression to the big banks that respected these ratings, workers became victimized for years by a "redlining" that originated with these HOLC classifications. My perusal of the Chicago HOLC Area Descriptions and Residential Security Maps indicates that judgments about neighborhood stability depended very heavily on race and ethnicity. Whenever foreign or black populations were observed, areas were automatically marked as "unstable." For example, a "blighted area of Poles and Lithuanians" near the stockyards received the lowest rating of 4 even though the report acknowledged that the "Lithuanian element" was thrifty and hence the neighborhood would probably "remain in a static condition for many years." Further deterioration was also unlikely, the report went on, because of "no threat, yet, of colored infiltration." Many Chicago workers saved their homes in the thirties thanks to the HOLC, but the biases of its rating system ensured that many workers would have the HOLC to blame when the property values in their ethnic and black neighborhoods later deteriorated.

Whereas once people had consigned their most valuable assets to the care of ethnic community institutions, they now sought protection from the state. A large group of unemployed families interviewed shortly before many of these federal programs went into effect universally expressed rage at the local bankers who had lost their money, urging that "they be treated like crooks." They exhorted the government to take their place in safeguarding savings and mortgages: "If things keep up like this and the government doesn't realize it, there's going to be trouble. It doesn't feel good to be kicked out of your house." Workers like these found tremendous comfort in the government's new activities. A hundredth anniversary book celebrating Polish contributions to Chicago, published in 1937, recognized that now Poles had someone outside their own community to thank for whatever economic success they could still claim eight years into the Great Depression: "With the aid of our splendid President, Franklin Delano Roosevelt, whose humanitarian interests resulted in HOLC and other security laws pertaining to homes, investments and savings, many thousands of homes and millions of dollars have been saved."

Industrial workers found the federal government not only ensuring their welfare and security during the New Deal but also entering a third area that had long been outside the provenance of the state, employment. This was territory that previously had belonged almost exclusively to private employers. In the first phase of the New Deal, the Roosevelt administration tried through the National Industrial Recovery Act (NIRA) to get employers to voluntarily submit to industrywide "codes of fair competition," setting shorter hours of work and compensatory wage rates for their workers in return for production quotas, higher consumer prices, and a relaxing of antitrust restrictions for themselves. The hope was that government-business cooperation would promote national economic recovery by stabilizing production and keeping as many people working as possible.

The voluntary character of the program, however, ensured that Chicago workers' experiences under the NRA varied tremendously. Some workers reported an improvement in working conditions. One of those, Agnes Castiglia, worked a forty-hour week instead of her usual forty-eight and earned two dollars more at the Traficanti Noodle Company. But others concluded that the NRA only legitimized hour and wage reductions. "I was getting $44\frac{1}{2}$ cents an hour. The NRA came into effect, we got cut to $41\frac{1}{2}$ cents an hour. That's the NRA," Frank Bertucci said cynically. And Antonio Palumbo, a cook at Brachs Candy Company, agreed: "NRA helpa the capitalist; didn't help the working-a-people" [*sic*]. Many workers shared Bertucci's and Palumbo's experience that spreading the work around meant less for each individual worker. To a large extent, people's feelings about the NRA depended on how committed their industry was to the program. Employer enthusiasm ranged widely from electrical manufacturers like Western Electric who cooperated to the meatpackers who never even adopted an industry code.

Overall, the NRA probably did more to heighten worker awareness that government could, and should, intervene in the private sector than to achieve concrete improvements. Letters from steelworkers in the Calumet region to President Roosevelt and NRA officials, for example, are filled with angry complaints of employer violations of the NRA and pleas for more direct intervention by Washington. In many cases, workers asked the government for protections, like minimum weekly hours and wages, that NRA legislation did not authorize. Before the NRA, it was unlikely that these steel workers would have brought complaints against their employers to the government. Similarly, . . . Section 7a of the NIRA, which required employers to let employees organize and bargain collectively through representatives of their own choosing, proved more meaningful for giving workers confidence that the government was behind them as they tried to organize than for establishing successful new unions. The NRA experiment in government-industry collaboration served mostly to whet workers' appetite for more state regulation of their working lives.

The federal government's involvement in employment extended to the creation of actual jobs, first as a part of relief and then, after 1935 with the WPA, in place of it. Job programs for the unemployed included the CCC, the Civil Works Administration (CWA), the Public Works Administration (PWA), the WPA, and the National Youth Administration (NYA). Although these programs are often remembered best for their contributions to the nation's cultural life—to art, theater, music, folklore, and so forth—the majority of the federal dollars went to employ manual laborers to renovate public facilities like parks, streets, sewers, and schools. Factory workers who had been let down by private industrialists now found themselves working for the government. Observers commonly reported that the unemployed preferred these federal job programs to straight relief payments. "It is *work* we want, not *charity*," Mrs. Ellen De Lisle told President Roosevelt in requesting jobs for herself and her sons to supplement her husband's WPA check. The government's job programs were not perfect. Workers vociferously complained about low salaries, uninspiring job assignments, and poor administration, including corruption. But as with relief, their gripes related more to these shortcomings in the programs than to their own dependence on them. A typical attitude was, "I gave the best part of my life to the American country, and I spent every cent I made here. They owe it to me to take care of me. If there is no regular work that I can pick up, they should find something for me to do."

A wide cross section of Chicago workers flocked to job programs—seventy thousand assembled before sunrise on November 23, 1933, to register for the CWA—but blacks were particularly eager. Blacks suffered from higher unemployment than whites and knew they would be the last recalled to jobs in private industry. The typical WPA wage of fifty-five dollars a month, purposely low to discourage workers from remaining too long on the government's payroll, was welcomed by blacks who had few other options. . . . By 1939, a third of all people employed by the WPA in Chicago were black.

Blacks depended on the government for jobs, but they complained bitterly to WPA officials that they were discriminated against, always being dealt the most menial work. A group of WPA workers reassigned to common labor while their white colleagues got clerical jobs wrote President Roosevelt, "In all of your speeches, you have given us the impression that you are a God-fearing man and believe in the equality of men. If that be the correct diagnosis of your character, then we would like for you to know that the officials of the W.P.A. of Chicago, Ill are not treating us as God's children, but as God's step-children." For many blacks the government proved no less discriminatory than private employers, except for one important difference: Blacks working in a federal job program had recourse. They could write to Washington to lodge complaints about their treatment locally, and in a surprising number of cases, action was taken. In many ways, being employed by the government during the New Deal gave blacks a taste of the kind of leverage they would demand during World War II when government and defense industries were compelled to practice fair employment. . . . Consequently, even though working on the WPA was far from perfect, it was one of the New Deal programs most responsible for orienting blacks toward the federal government. As Frayser T. Lane of the Chicago Urban League put it, the WPA revealed to black citizens "just what the government can mean to them. . . .

Fortune magazine asked Americans of all income levels in 1935, "Do you believe that the government should see to it that every man who wants to work has a job?" Yes, replied 81 percent of those considered lower middle class, 89 percent of those labeled poor, and 91 percent of blacks, whereas less than half of the people defined as prosperous shared this view. The editors of *Fortune* concluded somewhat aghast, "public opinion overwhelmingly favors assumption by the government of a function that was never seriously contemplated prior to the New Deal."

Workers were all the more enthusiastic about the government's new role in employment because their bosses deeply resented the state's intrusion into matters they considered their own prerogative. The evidence from Chicago argues powerfully against the "corporate liberal" analysis that the New Deal represented an effort by clever corporate capitalists to revitalize the economy with the help of a state that they dominated. Although industrialists may in the end have figured out ways of benefiting from reforms like the WPA, Social Security, and even the Wagner Act, they fought their introduction every step of the way. Organized business in Illinois managed to hold off the state legislation needed to implement various components of Social Security as long as possible. When the New Deal's most proindustry program, the NRA, was declared unconstitutional in May 1935, most employers breathed a sigh of relief, though they were to become much more antagonized by the next round of reforms, which included such hated legislation as the Fair Labor Standards Act of 1938. This law banned child labor and set a minimum hourly wage of $0.25 (gradually to be increased to $0.40) along with a maximum work week of forty-four hours (to be reduced within three years to forty hours) with time-and-a-half for overtime for all work related to interstate commerce. It was not so much these relatively low standards that bothered businessmen, but rather that the federal government was now empowered to intervene in matters that had long been out of its purview. "You have in these government attempts to control labor a tendency in the direction of a Fascist control of the worker, and through him of the industries, and through both control of the economic life of the country, and therefore control of its political life," an article in *Chicago Commerce* warned. Workers, however, viewed the state's growing involvement in their employment not as control but as needed protection against autocratic industrialists.

When workers needed welfare, security for their savings and homes, and better jobs during the 1930s, they increasingly looked to the government they had put in office, not to their old community institutions or bosses. The situation of a family like the Ferks, which opened this chapter, would have been unheard of in the previous big depression of 1921. Fourteen years earlier, rather than writing to President Roosevelt about their government relief, mortgage, and job, the Ferks would have been begging for handouts from family, friends, neighborhood shopkeepers, former employers, and ethnic or religious welfare agencies. President Harding's government would have offered them nothing, and they probably would never have thought to ask. The decline of community institutions with the Great Depression and the rise of an activist welfare state that people felt had a responsibility to them profoundly changed the survival strategies of families like the Ferks.

The Meaning of Worker Statism

Chicago workers felt they were making a new deal during the 1930s when they became invested in national party politics and a national welfare state. It is important to consider, however, just how new that deal was and exactly what it meant that they made it.

Workers' faith in the state grew out of old as well as new expectations. On the one hand, they wanted the government to take care of them in much the same paternalistic way as they previously had hoped their welfare capitalist employers and their ethnic communities would do. This dependence on a paternalistic state is most clearly seen in the way workers viewed President Roosevelt. For many workers, FDR was the federal government. In the election of 1932, people voted against Herbert Hoover. By 1936 they were voting for Roosevelt on the grounds that "He gave me a job" or "He saved my home." One unhappy husband who complained that his wife was now "wearing the pants" in the family reported that she rejected him on the grounds that now "F.D.R. is the head of the household since he gives me the money." As evident in the testimony presented in this chapter, distraught Chicagoans frustrated by the relief bureaucracy often appealed to Mr. and Mrs. Roosevelt for help. In enough instances to keep them asking, their appeals to "father" and "mother" Roosevelt were rewarded with action. Henrietta Malone was not alone in getting winter clothes out of her Chicago caseworker only after she had written the president. The files of New Deal agencies abound with letters, many on tattered pieces of paper in barely literate English, appealing to President Roosevelt for assistance. People found it easy to look to him, moreover, because he went out of his way to cultivate an image as a fatherly figure concerned for the needy.

Workers' feeling that Roosevelt was caring for them in much the same ways as their local communities and welfare capitalist employers had once promised to do helped personalize "federal power," which might otherwise have seemed so abstract. The woman who thanked the "government" for helping her out, saying "it sure is a blessing, too, to have sech *[sic]* a good government!" no doubt pictured Roosevelt personally making it all possible and rewarded him with her vote. Even when people became frustrated with specific New Deal programs, they retained their faith in government by remaining confident of the president. Lorena Hickok reported back to Harry Hopkins in May 1936 that FDR enjoyed what today might be called a "can't lose" status among workers and even the unemployed. They gave him credit for any effort to improve conditions while absolving him of responsibility for problems ("he means right"). . . .

Workers in Chicago and elsewhere in the nation were looking to the federal government as they never had before, but the shock of that transition was cushioned by the way that they used the president to personalize the state. It was a rare worker's home where a portrait of Roosevelt, whether a torn-out newspaper image or a framed color photograph, did not hold an honored place. Eleanor Roosevelt later commented that after the president's death, people would stop her on the street to tell her, "They missed the way the President used to talk to them. They'd say, 'He used to talk to me about my government.' " Martha Gellhorn's field report to Hopkins captured this strange and moving phenomenon, as true for industrial workers in urban Chicago as for the mill workers she visited in a southern textile town:

> And the feeling of these people for the President is one of the most remarkable phenomena I have ever met. He is at once God and their intimate friend; he knows them all by name, knows their little town and mill, their little lives and problems. And though everything else fails, he is there, and will not let them down.

At the same time that workers projected their old paternalistic expectations of ethnic community and welfare capitalism onto the state, however, they were developing a new and somewhat contradictory notion that they were entitled to benefits from the government. Alongside a pattern of dependence grew a new claim to legitimate rights. By voting, by becoming Democrats, by supporting Roosevelt, by being citizens, by serving in the military, by spending their money in America, for all these reasons and more that workers quoted in this chapter have articulated, working people felt justified in their new sense of entitlement. With this notion of rights, moreover, workers were moving beyond the hierarchical authority relationships implicit in paternalism, which made them dependents. As contributing members of society, they made no apologies for taking relief, social security, FDIC insurance, HOLC mortgages, and CCC and WPA jobs from the state.

This sense of entitlement lay at the heart of the social vision that workers endorsed during the 1930s, a vision that is easily overlooked when the only tests applied to worker politics are capitalist or anti-capitalist, moderate or radical. As Kornhauser discovered in 1937, workers advocated a form of political economy that can best be characterized as "moral capitalism." They did not reject private ownership of property but favored a form of capitalism that promised everyone, owner or worker, a fair share. A *Fortune* survey in 1940 was surprised to learn that "the man on the street wants more income than he has, but no more than that of many a government clerk." Apparently, American workers were dreaming neither of a dictatorship of the proletariat nor a world where everyone was a successful capitalist. Rather, they wanted the government to police capitalism so that workers really would get that "new deal" they deserved. . . .

Contrasting workers' expectations of the New Deal with those of the policymakers who created it introduces the issue of how distinctive working people's politics actually were. Workers' integration into the mainstream, two-party system could suggest that they had little ambition for a class-conscious politics. Indeed, industrial workers in Chicago were far from revolutionary; few voted Communist, and fewer still joined the Labor Party of Chicago and Cook County, which had a strong affiliation with the traditional craft unions of the Chicago Federation of Labor. But that does not mean that workers had no sense of themselves as members of a working class distinct from the middle and upper classes. As a worker told an investigator in another city during the 1930s, "Hell, brother, you don't have to look far to know there's a workin' class. We may not say so. But look at what we do. Work. Look at who we run around with and bull with. Workers. Look at where we live. If you can find anybody but workers in my block, I'll eat 'em. . . . Look at how we get along. Just like every other damned worker. Hell's bells, of course, there's a workin' class, and its gettin' more so every day." . . . By voting Democratic and supporting the New Deal, many workers felt that they were affirming rather than denying their class status. American society was polarized enough in the midst of the Great Depression that workers could feel that supporting a sympathetic mainstream party like the Democrats was a way of pursuing their class interests. Many even went so far as to consider the Democratic Party a workers' party.

One might wonder if workers were deceiving themselves in believing that the Democratic Party really had their interests at heart. But many of their experiences reinforced that view. Foremost was the political language that Roosevelt used. It was the president of the United States, for example, not some rabble-rousing radical, who pledged himself when accepting his party's nomination in 1936 to take on the "economic royalists" who were fast creating a "new industrial dictatorship" that autocratically set the conditions of labor. "Private enterprise" had become "privileged enterprise." At many other times as well, workers heard Roosevelt lash out at their bosses and commit himself to protecting "the common man" and woman. The Republicans only helped FDR's image as the working person's president, determined to turn things upside down, by lambasting the New Deal as a dangerous break with the past, "one that is alien to everything this country has ever before known."

This political rhetoric affected workers so powerfully because it fit well with the world they knew in Chicago. By the election of 1936, Chicago was polarized into political camps with definite class identities. In their factories, workers and their bosses were almost always on opposite sides. "Thes companys shure dont want you President" *[sic]*, one steelworker wrote Roosevelt. Eva Barnes learned that lesson the hard way. She arrived at her job assembling radios one day wearing a big Roosevelt button. When she was told to take it off and refused, "they said, 'You're for Roosevelt, you get out, you don't get a job.' " Other Chicago employers made their preferences clear from the start by putting Alf Landon leaflets, which denounced FDR, into workers' pay envelopes.

As workers took stock of political allegiances beyond their workplaces, in the city as a whole, they could not help but notice that even a place as Democratic as Chicago divided along class lines. In 1936, 81 percent of those with family incomes under a thousand dollars a year voted for Roosevelt, as did 79 percent of those earning one to two thousand dollars; in contrast, only 46 percent of people with family income over five thousand dollars pulled the lever for Roosevelt. Cutting it another way, FDR won 82 percent of unskilled and semiskilled worker votes and only 32 percent of major business executives and 39 percent of a white collar group like engineers. Neighborhoods where well-to-do native whites resided were conspicuous Republican strongholds. A soloist at the elite Fourth Presbyterian Church of Chicago recalled getting up to sing at services the Sunday before election day in 1936 and looking out into a congregation of a thousand: "It was a sea of yellow. Everybody was decorated with large yellow Landon sunflower buttons. Just the impact of the thing suddenly made me realize there is such a thing as class distinction in America." . . .

Workers' identification with the Democratic Party does not mean that they did not recognize some of the limitations of the New Deal and try to push it farther to the left. In many ways the National Labor Relations Act, Social Security, and other prolabor legislation like the Fair Labor Standards Act were testimony to the power of working-class voters who pressured for progressive state action. . . . But workers' ability to achieve much of the relief and security they sought through the Democrats, as limited as some of that legislation turned out to be, reinforced their sense that they had an important voice in the party. Though workers were participating in mainstream politics, they felt they were joining with men and women of other ethnicities and races to get themselves, as workers, a new deal.

Of course, the Democratic Party was not a labor party explicitly committed to pushing an essentially anticapitalist trade union agenda in the political arena. The Democrats had to keep happy a broad-based coalition, including conservative southerners and antiurban rural interests, which made all their programs less progressive than they might have been. And Roosevelt, despite a rhetoric of class carefully tuned to scare some people and win others, had some very traditional ideas about who should hold power in American society. The result, as mentioned earlier, was that the New Dealers showed more ambivalence toward using the state for reform than their working-class supporters and explicitly rejected— through, for example, the regressive way they structured new tax laws and social security—workers' vision of a moral capitalism that would redistribute American wealth. The paradox of workers' politicization through the Democratic Party during the 1930s was that they became invested in a party that they felt served their interests much more than it did. Workers learned to live in the American version of the welfare state so well that they accepted inequitable programs like unemployment insurance, which let states set variant and inadequate benefits, without voicing much criticism of the New Deal. To the extent that the New Deal perpetuated inequalities and offered some people more of a "raw" than a "new" deal, workers themselves bear some responsibility.

Workers nonetheless made an enormous shift during the thirties from the world of welfare capitalism to a welfare state. When their welfare capitalist employers and ethnic communities who had promised to care for them in the 1920s let them down in the crisis of the Great Depression, workers found a new protector in the state. In time, as they began to participate more in national politics, they grew to feel that that protection was something they deserved. The depression, rather than turning workers against the political system, as many at the time feared it might, tied workers to it more tightly than ever as they became party voters and the beneficiaries of government programs. It is very possible that the New Deal's impact should be measured less by the lasting accomplishments of its reforms and more by the attitudinal changes it produced in a generation of working-class Americans who now looked to Washington to deliver the American dream.

Nancy J. Weiss

Why Blacks Became Democrats

A majority of African Americans who voted in the 1932 election remained loyal to the Republican Party by casting their ballots for Herbert Hoover. Four years later, however, they voted overwhelmingly for Franklin Roosevelt and Democratic candidates, and this realignment of black voters has proven to be the most enduring legacy of the New Deal coalition.

Weiss, Nancy, *Farewell to the Party of Lincoln: Black Politics in the Age of FDR*, Copyright © 1983 by Princeton University Press. Reprinted by permission of Princeton University Press.

Historians have often asked why black voters became Democrats. Why vote for Roosevelt when FDR had bowed to the pressure of white southerners by refusing to endorse antilynching bills, legislation to ban the noxious poll tax, or any other civil rights measure? Why vote the New Deal when the NRA, the AAA, and the CCC accepted discriminatory and segregationist practices? Why abandon the Republicans when programs such as the AAA were encouraging the displacement of black tenant farmers and sharecroppers from southern plantations?

In the selection that follows the historian Nancy Weiss attributes black America's political conversion to both the symbolic and the tangible benefits of the New Deal. In spite of the discrimination and the refusal to embrace equal rights, Roosevelt, his wife Eleanor, and the New Deal programs paid more attention to African Americans than had any previous administration since Reconstruction.

This selection is drawn from Weiss's book *Farewell to the Party of Lincoln: Black Politics in the Age of FDR* (1983).

Perceptive observers recognized the paradox in the outpouring of black support for the New Deal in the election of 1936. One need not be a diehard Republican to wonder at the marriage between a black electorate and a Democratic party that seemed purposefully to evade any important issue that smacked of race. How could a President who sidestepped on antilynching legislation, seemed outwardly unperturbed by disfranchisement and segregation, and presided over relief programs rife with discrimination, win an overwhelming majority of black votes, and, in so doing, transform the political habits of black Americans for decades to come?

New Deal racial attitudes and discriminatory practices certainly mattered. Black spokesmen—publicists, politicians, leaders of the organizations for racial advancement, and others—protested vigorously against them. But that protest related more to the ritual of black leadership than it did to actual expectations about realizable progress. Positions of national leadership among blacks were few and thus hotly contested; since the late nineteenth century, competition for them had turned on different approaches to racial advancement. For black spokesmen not to have articulated and fought for a racial agenda would have been unthinkable. No newspaper with any pretensions of speaking for the race could have failed to flay the Roosevelt administration for its shortcomings on racial issues. No leader could keep any standing among his colleagues or constituency if he failed to set forth prescriptions for remedying the impact on blacks of racial violence, disfranchisement, and discrimination.

But to read the rhetoric of black spokesmen on racial issues as a predictor of black electoral behavior in 1936 is to misunderstand the process by which most blacks made their political choices. In making sense of those choices, one needs to remember two essential points. First, the racial expectations of most blacks fell considerably short of the protest voiced by black spokesmen. And second, the key to black electoral behavior lay in economics rather than race.

It is hard to know whether black leaders in the 1930s honestly expected the Roosevelt administration to do more than it did to move toward racial justice. They certainly *hoped* that the administration would do better, but if there was a gap between their public assertions and their private expectations, it has not been recorded. Most ordinary blacks, however, did not expect great strides toward racial advancement. There was no reason for them to—the federal government had not done anything significant for the particular benefit of blacks for as long as most of them could remember. Racial expectations and racial consciousness were considerably more limited then than they became in the postwar era. Robert Carter doubtless spoke for many blacks when he reflected on his own attitudes in the 1930s: "I shut out of my mind the fact of Roosevelt's personal racism—his views—never looked at them, and I think few blacks did. Maybe at that time we weren't as aware and weren't as demanding of white conduct."

Far from being surprised at the failure of the New Deal to embrace a racial agenda, most blacks in the 1930s remarked on how much attention the Roosevelt administration seemed to be paying to them. The administration made unprecedented gestures toward the race. Although trivial, perhaps, in comparison to inaction on lynching, disfranchisement, and discrimination in relief, such gestures struck a responsive chord. In the judgment of Rayford W. Logan, who cast his first vote for Roosevelt in 1936: "Negroes had been so depressed, so frustrated, almost having given up hope, that nearly anything would have created substantial support. . . . The outlook was so bleak . . . that little things counted a great deal. . . . Apart from questions of policy, treating Negroes as human beings was a very significant factor." Despite the fact that Roosevelt had done very little for blacks as a racial minority, he had managed to convey to them that they counted and belonged. In the light of inattention from previous administrations, even the limited racial recognition of the New Deal seemed to many black Americans to be a token of hope. . . . [I]n the words of Clarence Mitchell, "when you start from a position of zero, even if you move up to the point of two on a scale of twelve, it looks like a big improvement."

The same kind of logic applied to discrimination in New Deal programs. No one condoned it. Most black people knew that they were getting less economic assistance than whites, and most of them needed more than they got. But the point was that they got something, and that kept many families from starving. The simple reality that blacks were not excluded from the economic benefits of the New Deal was a sufficient departure from past practice to make Roosevelt look like a benefactor of the race. "Discrimination or not, *we were participating,*" insisted Charles Matthews, who became one of the first black Democratic ward chairmen in Newark. "We were a part of the economic and social fabric of the community. We started working." The Reverend Samuel Proctor spoke to the same point. The CCC may have been segregated, he said, but blacks could get into CCC camps. The WPA may have been discriminatory, "but before that blacks had no bread. Black folk have never been so crazy as to wait for things to be perfect."

As this testimony illustrates, racial concerns were not paramount in shaping the response of blacks to the New Deal. Symbolic racial gestures did not cause the shift of blacks to the Democratic party in 1936. Nor did the limitations in the New Deal's record on race significantly retard that shift. In voting Democratic in 1936, blacks did not vote for reasons of racial advantage. Rather, they behaved like most other poor people in the United States. In short, they responded to the New Deal on economic rather than racial grounds.

To black intellectuals and activists who sought to comprehend the "Negro problem" and to devise effective strategies for racial progress, the relative importance of race and class was perhaps the central question of the 1930s. In their behavior at the polls, the masses of black Americans made clear where they stood on the race-class debate. The New Deal had failed to act on the racial agenda of the 1930s. But racial concerns had to be fitted into a scale of priorities, and there was overwhelming agreement among most blacks that economic problems were even more pressing than specifically racial concerns. The struggle to survive took precedence over the struggle for equality. And in the struggle to survive, many New Deal programs made a critical difference.

Blacks in the 1930s spoke eloquently to the point. "I know me and my children would have starved this winter if it was not for the Presendent," wrote a woman in Memphis. "Me and my people have been able to live through the depression with food shoes clothing and fuel all through the kindheartness thoughtfulness and sane leadership of Roosevelt," wrote a mother of ten in Columbus, Ohio. "He is the greatest man I ever saw in the White [House]," declared "A Converted Roosevelt voter" in Kentucky, whose home had been saved from foreclosure. "Has done moore for the poor people than any President in my time." "You see dis new house," an elderly former slave told an interviewer, "de flower pots, de dog out yonder, de cat in de sun lyin' in de chair on de porch, de seven tubs under de shed, de two big wash pots, you see de pictures hangin' round de wall, de nice beds, all dese things is de blessin's of de Lord through President Roosevelt." A popular song summed up the case:

> Roosevelt! You're my man!
> When the time come
> I ain't got a cent,
> You buy my groceries
> And pay my rent.
> Mr. Roosevelt, you're my man!

It was no wonder that such economic assistance paid large political dividends to the Democratic party. An election board official in Columbia, South Carolina, reported that every Negro that he had registered so far had said that he would vote for Roosevelt, because "Roosevelt saved them from starvation [and] gave them aid when they were in distress." A black leader in Chicago said the same thing: "Mr. Roosevelt gave us work and bread. Our people will respond by giving Mr. Roosevelt most of their votes." As a woman at a Baltimore political meeting expressed it, "Yes, I'm gonna vote for Roosevelt, because when I was slipping and sliding in the mirey clay Franklin Roosevelt put my feet on the solid rock of the WPA." From Springfield, Ohio, a WPA worker wrote, "I was suffering when you took your seat, but now I eat and live so much better that I am intising everybody I can to vote for you. . . .

I . . . don't think it is fair, to eat Roosevelt bread and meat and vote for Gov. Landon." . . .

Blacks looking back on the 1930s gave the same kind of explanation for the attraction of blacks to the Democrats. In the words of the president of the Phelps-Stokes Fund, Franklin Williams, "It was not civil rights, it was jobs" that brought blacks into the Democratic party. Blacks became Democrats because the "Democrats had a program that was going to help the underprivileged, or the poor, more than the Republican party," said the Harlem political leader, Lloyd Dickens. Countless blacks echoed the sentiments of the Washington taxicab driver who explained that he voted Democratic because the Democrats "favor the little man, and I've been a little man all my life."

All of this testimony speaks to an important point: if the economic benefits of the New Deal attracted black voters, it follows that the economic status of those voters influenced, even determined, their support for the Democratic party. To put it simply, blacks who were suffering the most from the Depression had the least to lose in leaving the Republican party. And they stood to gain the most from the tangible assistance of the New Deal. Of course, most blacks felt the effects of the Depression; few of them in the 1930s were really well-to-do. But insofar as one can draw meaningful distinctions of economic condition within the mass of lower and lower-middle class blacks, a consistent pattern appears: Democratic voting grew faster in the poorer black neighborhoods.

This same point—that the highest-status blacks were the most reluctant to embrace the Democratic party—also shows up clearly when one examines what people said about their political allegiances. The first national survey to document party identification among blacks, conducted in 1937, revealed that 44 percent of those questioned thought of themselves as Democrats. But the pattern was strikingly different among the black elite: 71 percent of the professionals, businessmen, civic leaders, and others who were included in a leading biographical encyclopedia, published in the same year, still called themselves Republicans.

In light of all of this evidence, the black embrace of the Democratic party in 1936 becomes comprehensible as a pragmatic political response. At a time when the Republican party offered no more than rhetoric and tradition, the Democrats were delivering tangible economic assistance. No matter that it came through no special concern for the plight of blacks—blacks could still benefit as part of the one-third of a nation ill-housed, ill-clad, and ill-nourished that the New Deal was designed to assist. Call it what you will—"a 'bread and butter' vote," a pragmatic vote, a vote for the lesser of two evils—blacks in 1936 marked Democratic ballots in spite of the party's record on race, in trade for the economic benefits that came their way under the New Deal.

And yet, for some blacks there was more to it than a pragmatic political calculation. Earl Brown, the black reporter who covered the campaign for the *New York Herald Tribune,* understood what was happening. "It was a kind of a religion to vote for Roosevelt in '36," he reflected; "—this was no longer politics." In New York City, Brown saw black voters lining up at the polls at 9:30 on the night before the election, "standing in that line to vote for Roosevelt." At campaign rallies, the display of Roosevelt's photograph or the mention of his name "was sufficient to evoke wild cheers and applause."

In short, blacks not only voted for Franklin Roosevelt—they idolized him as well. They hung his picture—often a full-page campaign photograph cut out of a newspaper—beside that of Christ or Lincoln on the walls of their homes. "Every black home you went into, you saw a picture of Franklin Roosevelt, *framed,*" Basil Paterson remembered. "It was the damnedest thing." "I have the President's picture in a light," a woman in Philadelphia explained; "every time it lights up [my son] knows it is the man that is good and helping us to live." Black people named their children for the President. Harlem Hospital welcomed Franklin Delano Wilford, Franklin Delano Kulscar, Donald Roosevelt Evans, Roosevelt Little, and dozens of Eleanors, Franklins, and Delanos besides. Harold Rome captured the phenomenon in "F.D.R. Jones," a song he wrote for a Broadway revue in 1938, *Sing Out the News:*

> Come right in Benjamin Franklin Brown!
> Abraham Lincoln Smith, set yourself right down!
> There's a new hero here,
> He's the man of the year,
> Mr. Franklin D. Roosevelt Jones!

"I wrote the number," Rome later recalled, "because we wanted to say Hurrah for F.D.R. . . . Since blacks seemed to name their children for famous men they admired, this was a good way to do it. . . . During the run of the show, I received quite a few birth announcements of new F.D.R.s."

So many black Americans loved Franklin Roosevelt. They told him so in the handwritten letters penciled on scraps of lined paper that poured into the White House. The grammar and spelling were often very poor, but the message was clear. "You must be a God Sent man," a black Mississippian wrote in 1934. "You have made a great change since you have ben President. . . . You ben Bread for the hungry and clothes for the naked. . . . God Save the President." Or, as a woman in Texas put it in 1935, "It seem lak we got a unseen Eye watchin' an' studyin' our troubles an' lookin' after 'em. . . . I feels lak he's jes' another Moses God has done sent to head His chillun. . . . I'se restin' easy case I know he's got his han' on de throttle an' his eye on de rail." Letters to newspaper editors told the same story: Roosevelt was "the greatest man living today," "the greatest President America has ever had."

To these people, Roosevelt was a man larger than life, one vested with superhuman qualities and capable of outsized accomplishments. He was "a man of brain, common sense and 'guts,' " "endowed with Natural Abilities . . . unfathomable experiences . . . and superior qualities," "a big man, in the biggest job this country has ever had . . . the skipper of the greatest ship that has ever traveled this old ocean." He had "tackled the depression, . . . kicked the wheels of industry into renewed life, . . . bucked the strength of powerful figures and . . . run the gauntlet of public criticism." He was "the all-American President, qualifications—triple threat."

The images recurred again and again: paternity, royalty, and deity. Roosevelt was a father figure, a king, a messiah, "America's Salvation," "a God sent man." "You are to us as Jesus is to the rightous"; "I think Mr. Lincoln was raised up by de Lord, just like Moses, to free a 'culiar people. I think Mr. Roosevelt is de Joshua dat come after him." To many blacks, Roosevelt's reelection was "a matter of religious principle," for he had been "a Savior to our race."

Millions of white Americans were also captivated by Roosevelt and shared the perception of him as omnipotent leader and savior of a country in terrible distress. But the adulation on the part of blacks is worth remarking for two reasons. Not only were black Americans singling out a white President as their personal hero; many of them were also doing so in plain defiance of the facts of where he stood on race.

The hero-worship is easily comprehended. In part it reflected the novelty of attention from the White House. W. J. Trent, Jr., put it this way: "It was the first time in our lives that the Great White Father was concerned about us—or doing something to aid us." In part, as Clarence Mitchell grasped, it reflected the nature of the assistance Roosevelt had rendered: "When you've struggled all of your life to keep a little patch of land that's a farm or buy a house and a Depression comes so that you're going to lose it, necessarily a person who leads you out of that difficulty is someone that you not only cherish yourself but that you pass on to your children and their children as an example of greatness." In part, too, it signified a sophisticated understanding of the relative priorities of economics and race. "It was an indication of the folk wisdom on the part of Negroes that they worshipped the Roosevelts in spite of the fact that FDR never clearly defined civil rights goals," Kenneth Clark said. "This might be a reflection of their intuitive understanding that problems of racial equality had their roots in economic problems, and that, once the political power of the federal government had been harnessed for the attainment of economic equity, its use for the attainment of racial justice became inevitable."

But the adulation also reflected the paucity of black heroes. "You have to understand that [blacks] had no other symbol," Ralph Metcalfe—himself something of a symbol at the time as an Olympic runner—explained; "as a result, they naturally supported [Roosevelt] because he came forth with programs for their benefit." "Till relatively recently all our heroes were white anyway," Basil Paterson reflected. At a time when "there were very few [black] heroes to be found," it was no wonder that blacks shared the heroes of white America.

But to perceive that hero as a special friend of blacks took a real leap of faith. Those blacks with the best perspective on the President knew better. Walter White [of the NAACP] saw him clearly: perhaps Roosevelt was free of the prejudice that afflicted some of his close advisers, surely he was eager "to secure . . . the full fruits and benefits of democracy" for everyone, blacks included. However, he was never willing to take political risks in behalf of the race. White's colleague, Roy Wilkins, put it succinctly: "Mr. Roosevelt was no friend of the Negro. He wasn't an enemy, but he wasn't a friend."

But for those not close to Roosevelt, it was easy to form different perceptions. Blacks, like other Americans, were susceptible to the "almost mystical" effect of the Roosevelt personality, and the President often came out looking "above any kind of fault so far as blacks [were] concerned." Not only was he without fault, but he was a friend, a beneficent protector, affirmatively and personally concerned with the welfare of the race. These attitudes closely mirrored those of unemployed whites. E. Wight Bakke, who studied the unemployed in New Haven in the 1930s, found "a growing conviction that Roosevelt honestly has the interest of the workers at the basis of his policies." As Roy Rosenzweig pointed out, even though "the substance of the New Deal was often meager for many of the poor and out-of-work, its programs and rhetoric persuaded many to look to Roosevelt to resolve their problems."

The inconsistency between the image that blacks held of Roosevelt's beneficence and the reality of the treatment that blacks experienced during his administration posed no logical problems. The slights, the injustices, and the rank discrimination in the administration of relief were surely the products of less well intentioned underlings who acted in contravention of the President's wishes. If Roosevelt knew how badly blacks were being treated, correspondent after correspondent insisted, he would surely set things to rights. Again, precisely the same attitude was characteristic of working-class whites, who, Robert S. McElvaine has found, "sincerely believed that the president was a friend of the masses and that he was trying to assist them" and accordingly "tended to blame all their problems on Roosevelt's subordinates, who were charged with failing to carry out the president's good intentions."

Distance was one of the factors that gave Roosevelt such a favorable image in the eyes of blacks. The other main ingredient that made Roosevelt a hero was his wife. Up close or at a distance, the First Lady's image stayed constant: here was a genuine friend of blacks. Her sympathetic ear in the heart of the administration made the critical difference in conveying a sense of caring; and her racial involvements made many blacks believe that the President was more interested in racial justice than he actually was. Roosevelt was "the front man," she was "the doer," Roy Wilkins observed; "the personal touches and the personal fight against discrimination were Mrs. Roosevelt's; that attached to Roosevelt also—he couldn't hardly get away from it—and he reaped the political benefit of it." "I used to say," Pauli Murray summed up, "that there were two presidents in that White House, and that Roosevelt was so successful because people were voting for Eleanor as well as they were voting for FDR."

The combination was nearly irresistible: real economic assistance, Eleanor's genuine concern, the President's magical personality—no wonder Roosevelt came out a hero. As if to seal the legitimacy of the judgment, blacks transferred to Roosevelt the adulation that had previously been reserved for Abraham Lincoln. The imagery was familiar: Lincoln, too, had been widely perceived by blacks as a hero, a father figure, a savior, and a messiah. No matter that emancipation had been declared as a war measure and that Lincoln had explicitly stated that he would maintain slavery if he could thereby save the Union. To blacks, he was the Great Emancipator, enshrined ever afterward as the special champion of the race. A similar disjunction between perception and reality operated in the case of Roosevelt. No matter what his racial intent, Lincoln was the father of emancipation; no matter what *his* racial biases, Roosevelt was the father of the New Deal. That made him the second emancipator, the inheritor of Lincoln's mantle, "the best friend the Negro American has had in the White House since Abraham Lincoln," "the Modern Abe Lincoln of the race." That the economic emancipation of the New Deal may have been as flawed as the freedom accomplished through the Thirteenth Amendment somehow escaped comment.

Identification with the President played an important part in the politicization of black Americans. Roosevelt was a magnetic symbol of political authority, one who drew those who identified with him into a positive identification with the larger political system. The South Carolina woman who wrote, "I don't know what Republican or Democrat means but I know one thing true I never get any where untill you taken your seat," spoke to an important point. Identification with Roosevelt was a way station on the road to greater political awareness. That awareness grew because he per-

sonified a government that impinged directly on the lives of ordinary people in unprecedented ways.

Most blacks knew the story of Sylvester Harris, the Mississippi farmer who called the White House in distress over the
prospect of losing his farm. Somehow, he got the President on the
wire. "These white folks down here is gwine take my farm," he
told Roosevelt, according to a popular version of the conversation.
"I hear you wouldn't let them do it if I asked you." Roosevelt
promised to look into the situation, and a government loan saved
Harris's property. The uniqueness of Roosevelt's personal intervention in the Harris case was really beside the point. What mattered was the habit of looking to the White House to solve the
problems of ordinary people.

By repeatedly appealing to the President for assistance, blacks
unconsciously exemplified the new relationship that was emerging
between the government and the American people. "Mr. President
give us some place where we can make us a living"; "I am asking for
help help help, please help I am in need"; "Please Sir get me in
shape to farm"; "President Roosevelt, Honored Sir . . . I appeal to
you for help in the name of the Lord." No matter that Roosevelt
himself rarely answered. By responding to those appeals, at least
in many cases, with significant assistance, the New Deal began to
change popular perceptions of the possibilities of federal power.
The remark of an elderly former slave summed up the transformation. "I gits along pretty good," she said. Her family lived nearby
and helped to care for her. But now there was something new: "De
government helps me out. It sure is a blessing, too—to have sech
a good government!" Government became immediate, its impact
tangible, its activities relevant. Blacks, especially, had been shut out
of national politics—disfranchised, discriminated against, their
racial concerns unheeded, and their needs far removed from the issues that held center stage in Washington. The New Deal changed
all that: now what happened in Washington vitally affected the lives
of blacks as it did other Americans. As a result, blacks, like other
Americans, found themselves drawn into the political process.

The shift to the Democratic party, therefore, was part of
the larger process of politicization that was changing the political
habits of black Americans. The New Deal not only changed the political affiliation of the black electorate; it also increased black
interest in political participation. In part the change was one of

attitude. A black laborer captured the transformation in the making. His fellow workers, he said, had "talked more politics since Mistuh Roosevelt been in than ever befo'." But attitudinal change was only a small aspect of the politicization that was occurring. The New Deal brought out new black voters at the same time that it swung blacks who were already voting away from the Republican party. Hence the experience of blacks fits both of the models which political scientists use to explain the New Deal realignment: the conversion of previously Republican voters to the Democrats, and the mobilization of "previously apolitical citizens," who simultaneously entered "the political arena and acquire[d] a party identification.". . .

Part of the new black electorate came from men and women newly concerned about politics, people who were of age but who simply had not voted before. Part of it came from blacks who were just coming of age in the 1930s. It was more difficult for older blacks, who either remembered slavery and Reconstruction/Redemption themselves or were the children of people who did, to support the Democratic party.

For younger blacks, though, especially those in the North, and more especially the children of the Great Migration who came to political maturity during the Depression, it was much easier to perceive the Democrats as a viable political alternative and much less persuasive when the Republicans invoked the rhetoric of Lincoln and emancipation. These young people proved especially susceptible to the appeal of Franklin Roosevelt. Black college students were typical of their age group in their enthusiasm for Roosevelt. The admiration was shared "even among the left-wing," recalled Kenneth Clark, then a student at Columbia University. Doyle L. Sumner, in the 1930s a Sierra Leonean studying at Hampton Institute, remembered the student body listening attentively to radios during Fireside Chats, the campus devoid of other activity. Forty years later, Sumner could still feel the Roosevelt magic: "If you told me that I'd meet Roosevelt in heaven," he said, "I'd go—he'd do so much good there." Louis Martin reflected that as a student at the University of Michigan in the 1930s, he was "among those young kids who were just absolutely mesmerized by Roosevelt." Less shackled than their elders by ties of sentimentality and tradition, this "new generation" of blacks was freer to vote on the basis of issues and merit. Thus such cities as Chicago, Cleveland, Detroit, Philadelphia, Pittsburgh, and New York, where two-fifths of the potential black electorate in 1940 had reached voting age during the Depression, were political gold mines for the Democratic party.

Disfranchisement makes it difficult to use conversion or mobilization as meaningful indices of the politicization of blacks in the South. Even there, however, blacks shared in the increased political activity and interest that came with the New Deal. In communities throughout the region in the 1930s, black citizens began to organize to claim their franchise. New groups emerged to promote voter registration, urge payment of the poll tax, and encourage blacks to go to the polls. . . . The obstacles were formidable: complicated registration requirements, poll taxes, white primaries, and outright intimidation kept blacks from registering or attempting to vote. Still, the efforts showed some results: the number of registered blacks in Atlanta grew from less than 1,000 in 1936 to 2,100 in 1939; in Miami, where only 50 blacks were on the voting rolls through most of the 1920s and 1930s, 2,000 had qualified by 1940; in Tampa, where barely 100 blacks had voted in 1934, 2,500 were registered by the time of the general election in 1940.

No one mistook the politics of the new voters. The registrar of Macon County, Georgia, who did his best to block blacks from voting, observed that blacks in his area had turned Democratic "since Roosevelt became Santa Claus." "Every nigger is another vote for Roosevelt," declared a justice of the peace in Greene County, Georgia. "You ask any nigger on the street who's the greatest man in the world," exclaimed the secretary-treasurer of the Greene County Democratic committee. "Nine out of ten will tell you Franklin D. Roosevelt. Roosevelt's greatest strength is with the lower element. That's why I think he is so dangerous.". . .

One cannot help but wonder whether those whites who objected to the politicization of blacks in the 1930s fully imagined the array of "dangers" that politicization eventually brought. The growing interest of blacks in politics, their involvement in the Democratic party, and their new sense that the political process could be responsive to their needs became essential underpinnings of the drive for civil rights. The political habits established during the New Deal had repercussions far beyond their immediate consequences in the 1930s.

Graham D. Taylor

The Native American New Deal

One of the most interesting examples of the New Deal's reformist zeal and its commitment to encouraging grassroots governing was the Indian Reorganization Act of 1934 (the Wheeler-Howard Act). This "Indian New Deal" was intended to end the tragic policies of the Dawes Act of 1887 which had tried to assimilate Native Americans into white culture. The results were both economically and culturally bankrupting, and had left many western tribes destitute.

In an effort to reverse these trends, Roosevelt and his secretary of the interior, Harold Ickes, named John Collier as the new Commissioner of Indian Affairs. The dynamic Collier quickly set about an ambitious effort to reform—once again—the federal government's policy toward Native Americans. Collier hoped to improve the economic well-being of Native Americans but he also wanted to rekindle tribal self-government. The effort to make the tribes important governing units reflected both a growing appreciation for the richness of Native American culture and the New Deal's commitment to nonbureaucratic means of governing. As Graham D. Taylor points out in his essay, however, the "tribal alternative to bureaucracy" was difficult to implement and achieved only mixed results.

Taylor's analysis provides an interesting illustration of what Ellis Hawley has described as the "antibureaucratic impulse" within the New Deal. It also provides important comparisons between the New Deal for Native Americans and the New Deal for African Americans and the industrial working class.

Graham D. Taylor is professor of history at Dalhousie University in Halifax, Nova Scotia and the author of *The New Deal and American Indian Tribalism: The Administration of the Indian Reorganization Act, 1934–1945* (1980).

In November, 1933, John Collier, the newly installed Commissioner of Indian Affairs, circulated questionnaires among a number of leading anthropologists and other scholars who were presumed to have some knowledge about Indian social and political organi-

From "The Tribal Alternative to Bureaucracy: The Indian's New Deal, 1933–1945," by Graham D. Taylor, *Journal of the West*, vol. 13, no. 1 (January 1974). Copyright © 1974 by Journal of the West, Inc. Reprinted with permission of Journal of the West, P. O. Box 1009, 1531 Yuma, Manhattan, KS 66505-1009, USA.

zations. The circular included questions about the specific political systems of various tribes and observed changes in the structure of political leadership. The response was disappointing. As one anthropologist ruefully admitted, since "most anthropologists in this country have been comparatively uninterested so far in the practical problems of Indians . . . fewer satisfactory responses will follow the questionnaires than could be expected." This general ignorance about Indian political systems was to have a marked effect on the execution of the New Deal reform program.

While information about changing political and social conditions was sparse, there was abundant evidence that the traditional policies of the Bureau of Indian Affairs had failed to achieve stated goals and had left Indians mired in poverty and despair. The Indian policies associated with the Dawes Act of 1887 and subsequent similar measures had unwittingly spawned in the Bureau a frightening example of an arrogant, corrupt, and undirected bureaucracy. These policies can be summarized by the terms of assimilation and allotment.

The basic premise underlying the assimilation policy was that Indians were at some lower stage in the evolutionary scale, and had to be forced to discard their barbaric customs and embrace those of the dominant white society. The Bureau sought, not entirely successfully, to eradicate traditional Indian religious and social customs and ceremonies. Indian children were taken off the reservations to boarding schools where they were given rudimentary training in industrial skills. Meanwhile, the Bureau assumed almost total control over Indian civil and economic life, displacing the traditional tribal leaders.

Allotment policy was more complicated. In keeping with the premises of assimilation, the traditional Indian system of tribal ownership of lands and other resources was regarded by the framers of the Dawes Act as backward. Indians were to be introduced to the concepts of private ownership and the American family farm. The initial Act of 1887 provided that the Bureau would hold tribal lands for a maximum of twenty-five years, and then distribute 160 acres to each family head. After allotment the remaining reservation land would be opened for public sale. . . .

These policies had a devastating effect on a people already badly demoralized by a century of exploitation and conquest. A study made by the Brookings Institution for the federal government in 1928 determined that Indian landholdings had diminished from 139,000,000 acres in 1880 to less than 48,000,000. Since the Bureau had failed to provide its wards with training in farming, many Indians sold or leased their lands to neighboring white farmers. . . . [O]n some reservations in the Northern Plains states more than eighty percent of the Indians owned less than five acres of land. During the 1920s the agricultural depression contributed to Indian poverty: in 1928, fifty-five percent of all Indians had a per-capita income of less than two hundred dollars per year, and only two percent earned more than five hundred dollars per year.

The assimilation policy was equally disastrous, although more difficult to measure in its impact. Younger Indians raised in boarding schools returned to the reservations alienated from both white and Indian cultures. Poorly trained for industrial vocations, they were equally unprepared for farming. Alcoholism and petty crime posed a constant problem for Bureau agents on the reservations. Among Indians of all ages diseases, such as tuberculosis and trachoma, persisted despite efforts in the 1920s to improve medical conditions. The frightening incidence of biological decline was an indicator of the cultural disintegration induced by these policies.

The policies were bad enough; administration was often even worse. Most Indian agents and reservation superintendants were honest—instances of outright fraud had diminished by the 1890s—but the agents often treated their wards in an arbitrary and paternalistic manner. Moreover, the Bureau only occasionally attempted to act as protector of the Indians against the predatory schemes of Western business and political interests. Top positions in the Bureau were usually given to politicians with little interest or understanding of Indian problems.

The administrative system was top-heavy: agents on the reservations had to refer all but the most routine questions to Washington for decision. This lack of opportunity for responsibility plus low salaries prevented the Bureau from acquiring the best administrators. Indians, even those with education, were barred from taking high positions in the Bureau.

Probably the most pervasive problem was the apparent capriciousness, the lack of continuity in administration. "There is no Indian tribe whose memory is not filled with the recollection of the constantly fluctuating policies of successive Commissioners and

Secretaries of the Interior," John Collier pointed out to a Congressional committee in 1934, "and the situation is one under which Indians cannot be expected to work in earnest to build up a stable domestic government."

The existing structure of policies and administration of Indian Affairs had clearly failed, and during the 1920s a movement for reform developed in the wake of a particularly blatant effort by Interior Secretary Albert B. Fall and others to deprive the Pueblo Indians of their traditional lands. The Herbert Hoover Administration brought a reform-minded leadership to the Bureau under Charles Rhoads at the same time that the Brookings Institution released its important critique of the existing system.

Under Rhoads the Bureau abandoned the boarding school system and medical facilities were improved. Stimulated by proposals in the Brookings report, Rhoads in 1929 drew up a program for the complete overhaul of the Indian Bureau. The most significant elements in the proposed program were: (1) the gradual diminution of the allotment process and encouragement of tribal consolidation of landholdings; (2) the establishment of tribal councils on reservations with the authority to tax lands leased to white farmers; (3) the establishment of tribal corporations to manage tribal resources, drawing on the tribal funds held in trust by Congress, and upon a government loan program.

These proposals . . . were never formally proposed in a bill to Congress. . . . Even the initial steps taken by the Rhoads administration to assist the Indians were soon engulfed by general economic conditions.

. . . [T]he failure of the Bureau under Rhoads to produce a new Indian program left the field open for bolder experimenters, such as John Collier, spokesman for the militant American Indian Defense Association. In 1933, President Franklin D. Roosevelt, on the recommendation of secretary of the Interior Harold Ickes, appointed Collier as Commissioner of Indian Affairs.

Collier brought to the Bureau a background not only in Indian reform, but also experience in the urban community center movement in New York. . . . From this experience he had acquired a strong belief in the potentiality of the local community to play an active role in making important decisions affecting national as well as local social and economic arrangements. He clearly saw in the designing of a new Indian program an opportunity to apply directly on a large scale the concepts developed by community organizers in the period of the First World War.

The Indian program was not the only New Deal program in which emphasis was placed on community participation. In the Department of Agriculture, M. L. Wilson, Howard Tolley and others were developing ideas about the integration of local rural communities into the federal agricultural policy process. Similar approaches were advanced by leaders in the Soil Conservation Service and the Tennessee Valley Authority. But these ideas were most fully developed and applied by the Indian Service during the 1930s. . . .

The bill was introduced in Congress by Senator Burton K. Wheeler of Montana and Congressman Edgar Howard of Oklahoma, chairmen, respectively, of the Senate and House Committees on Indian Affairs. It was an omnibus bill with provisions for the termination of allotment and restrictions on further sales of Indian lands. It established a revolving credit fund of $10,000,000 for tribes to use in the purchase of new lands. Other sections provided Indians the right to take positions in the Bureau, and authorized the Interior Department to purchase lands for landless Indians. . . .

The heart of the new Indian program was the part of the bill dealing with tribal self-government. On reservations where more than forty percent of the land had not been alienated a referendum would be called to determine whether the tribe—or tribes—desired to come under the Act. If they chose to do so they would be entitled to draw upon the revolving credit fund and could prepare a tribal constitution. The constitution also had to be approved in referendum by a majority of the authorized tribal members. Under the approved constitution officers of the tribal council would be elected and the elected government could establish business corporations to manage resources such as timber, minerals and tribal lands. . . .

During the debates on the bill Senator Wheeler encountered opposition from Western politicians . . . who maintained that the Bureau could easily manipulate Indian voting through organized minorities. To counter this objection Wheeler added a provision requiring approval in referenda by a majority of all potential voters rather than simply of those who came to the polls. This requirement, more stringent than those for most state and national political elections, was the source of endless disputes and delays since many Indians who had left their reservations and even those removed from tribal life for more than a generation could demand inclusion in the voting. . . .

The most controversial element in the Bureau proposal empowered the tribal governments to force reservation landowners, white and Indian, to sell their lands to the tribe (or exchange the land for shares in the tribal corporation) for the purpose of consolidation. Most of the reservation lands were in the Great Plains states and were more suitable for large scale farming or grazing than small individual family farming. . . . [P]ressure from Western landowners and from Indians who had leased productive mineral resources on their allotments persuaded Wheeler to remove the provision from the bill. Collier later mourned the loss of this measure as "a major disaster to the Indians, the Indian Service and the program."

The Wheeler-Howard Bill which was signed into law as the Indian Reorganization Act on June 28, 1934, thus constituted a compromise between the views of reformers in the Bureau of Indian Affairs and the Western interests represented in Congress. In the political sphere the final bill encouraged far more activity among Indians than its original designers may have intended. The requirement of two referenda and absolute majorities in each election set the stage for major struggles in tribes such as the Navajo and Blackfeet where control over important land and mineral resources were at stake. In the economic sphere the range of authority available to tribal governments had been limited, and a flexible approach to Indian economic organization had been eliminated. But most of the elements of the original concept remained, reflecting the influence of both the Indian reform movement of the 1920s and the earlier movement for urban community organization and participation.

From 1933 to 1945 the Bureau of Indian Affairs under Collier compiled an impressive record of administration under the Indian Reorganization Act. During these years more than one hundred tribes acquired some measure of self-government, the first most had experienced since the end of the Indian wars in the nineteenth century. Indian landholdings were increased by 7,400,000 acres, and more than $12,000,000 was drawn from the revolving fund to help finance tribal enterprises in livestock, lumbering, land and water reclamation, and encouragement of the tourist trade; of these loans less than two and one-half percent was in default in 1945, and most loans had been repaid in full.

Yet, measured against this record of success in improving the material condition of Indians was the fact that an indigenous sense of participation in, and support for the reforms had not taken place. Some of the major tribes actively resisted the introduction of the Reorganization program: the Five Civilized Tribes of Oklahoma lobbied successfully for their exclusion from the Wheeler-Howard bill in 1934, as did the Iroquois in New York State. The Navajos of Arizona and New Mexico, the largest single tribal group in the United States, rejected the program by a close vote in referendum in 1935.

Even among the tribes who embraced reorganization the ideas of tribal interest and Indian cultural self-consciousness were slow to take root. During the decade that followed Collier's departure from the Bureau, Western Congressmen devised a new policy called "termination" under which the federal role in the management of Indian lands and properties would be rapidly eliminated, reservation lands not tribally owned would be made available to private buyers, and Indians would vote on whether or not to retain the tribal governments and corporations. This plan, which revived in a new form many of the problems of the allotment policy, encountered less than whole-hearted resistance from the Indians. While most official tribal spokesmen opposed termination, many Indians were indifferent and some supported the proposal.

One of the basic aims of the Indian's New Deal had been the regeneration of a strong tribal identity to resist the encroachments of neighboring communities and capricious shifts in government policy toward Indians. The failure of tribal leaders to mobilize opposition to termination indicated the limits of the reorganization program in developing a strong tradition of Indian self-determination.

There were several factors which critically affected the development of the Indian Reorganization program but were beyond the control of the Bureau officials responsible for its administration. First, there was the growth of Congressional opposition to Indian reform and its effect on budgetary appropriations for the reorganization programs.

During the first three years of the program appropriations for the Bureau rose by $14,000,000. By 1938, however, charges of mismanagement of the Indian programs and a deficit-conscious Congress blocked further increases. Appropriations declined precipitously in 1941 and the next two years by more than $5,000,000.

These shifts could be explained in part by the broader political and economic situation, particularly the 1938 recession and the advent of American entry into World War II in 1941. During the same time, however, Congressional criticism of the reorganization program was increasingly vocal. Senator Wheeler, who had never wholeheartedly endorsed the plan, became disenchanted with the Bureau in general and Collier in particular. In 1937 Wheeler introduced a bill for the repeal of the entire program. Although Collier successfully lobbied against this and three similar bills during the next six years, his critics in Congress were persistent and their frequent investigations provided a forum for white and Indian opponents of reorganization to expound on the inefficiencies and socialistic tendencies of the program.

A second factor was the impact of World War II on the development of tribal self-government. We have already noted the drastic reduction in appropriations. The approach of war also led to cutbacks in Bureau personnel and a consequent loss of momentum in the reorganization effort as some of the more energetic field representatives left the Bureau. Most important, mobilization stripped the tribal councils of their most talented and vigorous leaders who left for the armed forces or joined the tide of rural people to the new wartime industrial centers.

The basic problem of reorganization, however, derived less from external circumstances than from ambiguous and even mistaken assumptions about the structure of Indian communities and the development of spontaneous and effective self-government among the Indians. This problem related to the definition of the tribe, the essential unit of government under the Act.

The Wheeler-Howard Act defined a "tribe" as "any Indian tribe, organized band, pueblo, or the Indians residing on one reservation." While flexible, this definition was not very helpful to administrators, given the fact that neither the new Bureau leadership nor most anthropologists could provide adequate information about existing political institutions among the Indians. In practice, therefore, the reservation became the focus for organization. . . .

This approach created much confusion and unanticipated problems. Many of the reservations in the Great Plains and Southwestern states were populated by a congeries of unrelated Indian groups who often did not speak the same language and shared nothing except mutual antipathy toward some other group of Indians in the past. This was the case at Fort Berthold Reservation in North Dakota where Mandans, Arikaras and Gros Ventres resided together simply because they had banded for mutual defense against the Dakota Sioux a century before. Another example from the Southwest was found on the Mescalero Apache Reservation in Arizona where two traditionally hostile elements of the same band had been forced by the Bureau to live in uneasy coëxistence.

Situations of this sort impeded the progress of reorganization, particularly after a tribal council had been organized as factions tended to divide along traditional lines. One of the first "tribes" to establish a council was at Flathead Reservation in Montana, composed of members of the Salish and Kootenai groups along with remnants of other bands, none of whom shared any common language or tradition other than hostility toward the Blackfeet. Eight years after the chartering of the Flathead council in 1935, J. H. Holst, a field observer from Washington, found that adequate representation of the two major tribal groups on the council never had been satisfactorily resolved; consequently, plans for the development of the more than adequate resources of the reservation had not been made by the council.

Even on reservations inhabited by a people sharing linguistic and cultural ties, similar problems emerged. Years of powerlessness had eroded the sense of responsibility and interest in civic affairs of the traditional leaders, and the advent of reorganization brought to light the deep fissures that had developed in Indian societies. Factionalism was widespread: Indians divided on the issue of reorganization along a variety of lines, ranging from political and religious affiliations to personal and family vendettas. In many ways, of course, Indians differed little in their political behavior from their white neighbors who also brought their religious and social prejudices to the political polls. The problem for the Indians, however, was that their political performance directly affected the rate at which they acquired control over their own resources.

The misapplication of the tribal concept by Bureau administrators related to a deeper problem. The whole program was based on the revival of traditional tribal institutions with leaders who could gradually be integrated into organizations for the management of Indian resources. Yet in practice the institutions established under the Reorganization Act were built along Anglo-American lines, with electoral districts, voting by secret ballot, tribal presidents, vice-presidents and committees—the paraphernalia of American political tradition transferred to a people whose experience with those institutions was remote or non-existent.

The result in many cases was that older full-blood Indians and their leaders were further demoralized while younger men, often of mixed-blood background rose in the new councils. J. H. Holst, commenting on the program on the Sac and Fox Reservation in Iowa, dealt succinctly with this problem:

> For a long time the old system of local government under headmen has been breaking down. Most of the old men have held tenaciously to the traditional system while the young, trained in school and in closer contact with the whites, have gradually adopted the new ways. Re-organization has tended to emphasize this cleavage and set up irreconcilable groups. This is not a new thing or one peculiar to this reservation. It is . . . a difficult problem among all real Indian groups.

At best this situation generated much rivalry among Indians on the council over inconsequential matters. At worst it could corrode any existing tribal self-consciousness and lead to bitter struggles for power, particularly where tribal resources promised potential wealth.

The Blackfeet in Montana provide a striking example. Oil was discovered on the reservation shortly before the new program was introduced and a faction of younger men of mixed blood moved rapidly to secure control over the tribal council which had responsibility for the mineral lands. They invested the revenues from mineral leases in tribal enterprises whose share-holders were for the most part mixed-blood. The full-blood faction protested to the Bureau that there was clear discrimination in establishing voting districts for the council. Although the Bureau kept out of the dispute a report made in 1945 concluded that "the Indian Reorganization Act has placed a legal tool in the hands of the ruling clique . . . that more or less formalizes the struggle for control on a plane that makes full-blood resistance almost an act of treason."

In fairness to the Bureau we must add that Collier attempted to bring the knowledge of anthropologists into the reorganization process despite the disappointing results of his initial survey. In 1935 the Education Division was established under Willard W. Beatty to provide incoming Bureau personnel with a background in the various types of Indian cultures and to stress that administrators should adapt the program to these situations. A more ambitious effort was the applied anthropology staff which provided special assistance in tribal organization. Budget cuts after 1938, however, according to Collier, forced the Bureau to curtail this project.

Ultimately the reorganization effort failed to achieve its goal of reviving cultural and communal unity. This failure was not simply the result of administrative mistakes bred by ignorance and haste. The designers of the program chose to focus their activities on the tribe, a once potent but now relatively declining and hence artificial institution in Indian life, rather than seeking to identify and work directly with existing Indian communities.

This crucial point was made by an Indian in 1942. Archie Phinney, a Nez Pérce who brought to the Bureau a background in anthropology with Franz Boas, discussed the general implications of reorganization in the course of a report on Chippewa tribal organization. After noting that, as was the case for many other Indians in the Great Plains states, "tribal" unity had no relationship with the actual situation, Phinney went on to point out that the sponsors of the program had failed to recognize or exploit the potential for spontaneous and enduring participation at the community level:

> A study of the relations between the elected representatives and their constituents will show a growing democratic centralism which kind of detachment can never lend itself to the creating of wide community participation in tribal affairs. . . . The efforts of the Indian Organization staff in the past years have been directed mainly toward the strengthening of tribal council government. . . . But this achievement is empty of the result most needed—the reinforcement of community life. . . . The basic problem is how to stimulate the development of initiative and responsibility on the community level, within local groups, for only on this level, below the council, can

there be any real Indian participation, and any real exercise of whatever new powers the Indian Bureau may want to transfer to the Indians. . . .

There were experiments with the community alternative. They were scattered and never part of a systematic program but they received a good deal of complimentary attention in the Bureau's house organ, *Indians At Work*.

One of the most successful cases of effective tribal organization in the Southwest, for example, emphasized a local community approach. The Pueblo Indians had a tribal council but most of the routine decisions were made at the village level by elected community bodies. When Pueblo lands were found to be subject to excessive grazing the Bureau sent representatives to each of the villages and worked out equitable procedures for herd reduction and land improvement, which was accomplished on a gradual basis between 1935 and 1940. This situation contrasted sharply with the experience of the neighboring Navajo tribe in the same period where stock control policies encountered vehement resistance and culminated in the complete disillusionment of the Indians with the reorganization program.

An equally striking example of community development under the sponsorship of local Bureau officials took place in the Great Plains region, on the Sioux Reservation at Pine Ridge, South Dakota. When the initial plans for consolidation and recovery of tribal lands for grazing encountered the usual obstacles, and a vocal full-blood minority emerged to contest the authority of the tribal council, the local Bureau agent decided in 1938 to establish a model community at Red Shirt Table. Community meetings were held, a local committee composed of mixed-bloods and full-bloods was formed, and advisers were brought in from the Extension Service, the Soil Conservation Service and other federal agencies to help design a land-use plan. To prevent friction among the Indians, community projects were divided: full-bloods established a livestock coöperative while the mixed-bloods designed and developed an irrigated gardening project and a housing construction enterprise. By 1943 the Red Shirt Table Development Association had established enough community cohesion to demand special representation on the Pine Ridge tribal council. . . .

There were, however, limits on the extent to which the community approach could be applied. The legacy of the allotment period—scattered kinship lands and huge tracts of alienated lands in the most productive areas of the reservations—left a situation in which few communities could be expected to effectively plan the use of their major, often their only resource. The legal restriction of incorporation to the tribal level hindered the development of new enterprises since Indians could get credit only from the federal government, and then only through the tribal councils. By the time that Bureau leaders had begun to actively consider the community alternative the exigencies of wartime mobilization had significantly reduced their share in the federal budget, their manpower in the field, and even the local leaders who might have made the program work.

This analysis may seem unrelievedly negative. It is not meant to be. Collier's administration did more to improve the physical and psychological conditions of Indian life than any administration before or since. Even to militant Indian spokesmen of the present, like Vine Deloria, Jr., the Collier period marked the one instance in the grim history of relations between the Indian and the white governments where a genuine and farsighted effort was made to bridge a cultural chasm and allow the Indians to build a new society on the foundations of traditional institutions.

At the same time, we must recognize the weaknesses of the reorganization program as it affected Indian communities, for this subject is relevant not only to the subsequent history of the Indians, but also to some broader conclusions about the dynamics of community organization under government sponsorship.

Observers of the Indian Reorganization effort and other New Deal experiments with community organization concluded that communication between Washington policy-makers and their field agents often broke down. . . . [C]ritics maintained that Bureau officials on the reservations continued to regard Indians as incompetent wards of the state. Despite their willingness to initiate reorganization, reservation agents misinterpreted the local situation and therefore "screened the instructions they got from Washington."

Bureau records for this period do indicate these problems existed. Washington observers found local officials narrowly defining the rights and authority of tribal councils, frequently vetoing tribal legislation, and seeking to retain supervision over tribal resources.

The records, however, do not reveal a systematic attempt by local officials to undermine reorganization goals. Some agents maintained a paternalistic attitude while others worked actively to promote Indian participation. There are no clear-cut patterns in this area, and even where agents opposed reorganization goals, the tribal councils vocally asserted their rights, particularly on such issues as the licensing of traders and leasing of mineral resources.

Moreover, the Indian position was consistently defended and promoted by the Washington Bureau, which frequently acted as an appellate court in these disputes. Bureau leaders, such as Willard Beatty, William Zimmerman, William Brophy and Kenneth Meicklejohn, shared Collier's view that tribes be given free rein consistent with existing economic limitations. After Collier's retirement Brophy and Zimmerman continued his policies in the face of growing Congressional criticism. To augment their position *vis-a-vis* the local agents, Washington leaders maintained a number of traveling field observers, many of them Indians with backgrounds in anthropology, such as Archie Phinney and D'Arcy McNickle. These field observers provided an often critical, but necessary and influential view of developments in the reorganization program.

The program's major problem was not the administration but the underlying idea, the focus of the effort. For some Indians the tribal connection still had some importance despite almost a century of systematic uprooting; for many it did not. On the other hand, Indians still lived in small, relatively isolated communities and demonstrated a willingness to work together when provided the opportunity. These were not traditional communities nor had they existed long enough with a self-consciousness of shared needs to be considered a "natural community" by the standards of contemporary social theory. The potential, however, existed.

Designers of Indian Reorganization only gradually realized that these communities could determine the future of American Indians. As a result the reforms disintegrated, allowing a revival of bureaucratic control and Congressional exploitation. The assertion of Indian self-determination is left to a new generation of Indians.

Winifred Wandersee

Women and the New Deal

Women have played major roles in all twentieth century reform movements, and the New Deal was no exception. Not only did Eleanor Roosevelt redefine the role of the First Lady and the secretary of labor, Frances Perkins, become the first woman to hold a cabinet office, but women were crucial in staffing the many relief agencies and in lobbying for the social-welfare programs. Their involvement grew out of a tradition of women's activism on behalf of improving working-class conditions known as *social feminism*. But despite the prominent place of women in the New Deal, rarely did the Roosevelt administration advance a feminist agenda. As in the case of African Americans, it did not seek to eliminate discriminatory laws and regulations, and it rarely sought to advance women's issues. Instead, the New Deal's women's network sought to aid women by providing new forms of "security" for families, raising wages for workers, and ending the depression. As a result, however, the New Deal and the depression years were a mixed legacy for women. The new systems of Social Security and unemployment insurance, as Linda Gordon has recently argued and as Winifred Wandersee notes in this selection, reinforced female dependency and gender barriers. Most jobs available to women were not covered by the new programs, and hence benefits were extended to most women only as part of a family headed by an employed husband.

Winifred D. Wandersee wrote *Women, Work, and Family Values, 1920–1940* (1981).

Until very recently, it would have been difficult for any historian to have given an account of American women and how they related to the New Deal, and in fact, few would have considered the topic worthy of attention. In spite of the fact that women of the 1930s had acquired the vote, that the "new woman" of the 1920s had made her colorful imprint on American values, and that women reformers participated in public and private welfare agencies across the country, the New Deal era was, nonetheless, the only major pe-

From, "A New Deal for Women: Government Programs, 1933–1940," by Winifred D. Wandersee. From *The Roosevelt New Deal*, edited by Wilbur J. Cohen. (Austin: Lyndon B. Johnson School of Public Affairs, 1986), © 1986 by the Board of Regents, The University of Texas.

riod of reform since the American Revolution that did not include a strong feminist component. Furthermore, traditional historians of the New Deal have been prone to ignore the presence of women in Washington, aside from a polite recognition of Frances Perkins and, very occasionally, Molly Dewson or Mary Anderson. Even the recent historians of women have tended to slight the New Deal era and emphasize the more dramatic advances of World War II.

Yet in the last few years, several important studies have appeared that attest to women's active participation in the events of the 1930s, and to the fact that although their experience was not necessarily "feminist" per se, it was nonetheless distinct from that of men and worthy of its own historical account.

What can we learn from these recent studies—about the New Deal, about women's historical experience during the 1930s, and about a historical profession that has dissected in minute detail every aspect of the New Deal but has waited for nearly fifty years to evaluate the role of women in this watershed event? The current generation of historians that seeks the answers to these questions is primarily female and basically feminist. That is, the writers have tried to interpret history as if it were something experienced by women, in a manner distinct from that of men. The approaches have varied, emphasizing work, reform, feminism, and family. But the record that is emerging from this wide range of issues indicates clearly that the significance of women's interaction with the New Deal has been greatly understated in the past.

Basically, women's experience during the 1930s can be divided into three broad categories: work and family life under the pressures of economic crisis; the debate over feminism and careerism; and the New Deal itself, its impact upon women, and the role that women played in creating and carrying out the reforms of the New Deal. It is this last category of concerns that is the focus of this paper. Although the decade of the thirties was a time of economic stagnation, stress, and deprivation for women as well as for men, on the whole, the New Deal opened more doors than it closed. Furthermore, as a broad program of public policy reform, the New Deal was, in fact, the culmination of more than three decades of social feminism. It was the social reformers' "finest hour," as Secretary of Labor Frances Perkins quite clearly stated in June of 1940, when she read in a newspaper that the Republican Party convention had adopted all the social security programs in its platform. "God's holy name be praised! No matter who gets elected we've won."

What had been won, from Perkin's point of view, was a long struggle for industrial and social insurance programs that stretched back to the early years of the Progressive era. This struggle was carried on largely, though not exclusively, by the social feminists. But if social feminism achieved a victory in the form of the New Deal, the emphasis of that victory was certainly upon the social rather than the feminism. And herein lies the irony of this success. . . . The reform program of the New Deal, to the extent that it focused upon the problems of women, served to reinforce traditional notions of what women could and should do. Perhaps it was inevitable that the reformers would adhere to the societal pressures that were characteristic of the era, but the consequence, nonetheless, was a concrete and theoretical limitation upon the advancement of women and the cause of feminism. Thus, the New Deal was a catalog of contradictions that paradoxically represented great advances for women in some areas, while severely limiting their long-range opportunities by reinforcing age-old stereotypes.

A crucial issue for women during the 1930s was the tension between work and family—a tension which has characterized women's domestic and economic experience since the origins of the industrial era. Kessler-Harris notes in her recent study *Out to Work* that the Depression delivered to women a curious double message. On the one hand, it imposed economic pressures on the family that pushed women into wage work. On the other hand, it fostered a public stance that encouraged family unity and urged women, in the interest of jobs for men, to avoid paid work for themselves.

The reforms of the New Deal reflected a similar ambiguity. The programs for women were an honest and sometimes creative attempt to meet the needs of women workers, but they were based upon limited views of women's roles and their long-range place in the labor market. Finally, women leaders themselves, as reformers and feminists, contributed to that ambiguity. . . .

The classic example is the National Industrial Recovery Act (NIRA), which established codes covering about one-half of all employed women—mainly those in manufacturing, trade, clerical work, communications, and certain large service groups. Many women not covered by the codes were working in occupations in which the worst conditions prevailed, such as domestic service, laundries, dressmaking, and public service. At the other end of the occupational spectrum were the 1.5 million women in professional services who were also neglected by the NIRA codes.

More to the point, although the NIRA codes did cover many women in industry, they also reflected the general view that women needed less money than men. By September 1, 1934, there were 233 NIRA codes, and 135 of them fixed minimum wage rates for women below those of men. The differences ranged from 6.3 percent lower in three cases, to as much as 30 percent lower in several cases. However, in most cases the difference was from 10 percent to 20 percent.

The establishment of NIRA codes had a much more complicated effect than the rather simplistic fact of wage discrimination. . . . [T]he codes succeeded in raising minimum wage levels dramatically. They also reduced the average number of hours worked for all workers, but particularly for women and other low-skilled, poorly paid, hourly employees. For instance, in the textile industry, where hours had been particularly long, they declined by 25 to 28 percent. Of course, this was a mixed blessing. Shorter hours usually resulted in lower weekly wages. Also, the better-paid workers often had their wages reduced to benefit the lower-paid workers.

The labor clause of the NIRA, Section 7a, and its successor, the Wagner Act, both had a somewhat ambiguous impact upon women workers. The Wagner Act, often considered the most far-reaching piece of labor legislation ever signed by a President, revitalized the labor movement and encouraged the formation of the CIO in 1935. . . . [T]he organizing drive through both the AFL and the CIO had a definite impact upon woman workers. The estimated number of women affiliated with unions increased fourfold during the 1930s. Major women-hiring industries that were affected included textiles, paper and paper products, cigar and confectionary manufacturing, restaurants, and laundries. The major thrust of the CIO was, of course, toward heavy industry. The automobile and the rubber industries were the most significant of those organized by the CIO as far as women workers were concerned. About 20 percent of the rubber workers were women. They had suffered severe wage reductions and extended hours earlier in the decades, but the recognition of the United Rubber Workers increased the wage rate twofold and made prevalent the eight-hour-day. On the other hand, the contract also designated "men's jobs and women's jobs," with women's wages averaging 20 percent less than men's.

So, although women workers in major CIO-organized industries gained improved work standards and job security along with their male colleagues, discriminatory features were a part of most contracts. Wage differentials, sex-defined job categories, and separate seniority lists were accepted practices, and furthermore, some unions opposed the hiring of married women. Also, women continued to play a very minor role in union leadership.

The special position of women, both on the job and in the organized labor movement, was a reflection of the public debate which characterized societal attitudes toward women and work in the 1930s and which was carried on at another level through governmental programs. Therefore, the New Deal programs for unemployed women were never as far-reaching as those for men. Tentative and short-range in their goals and objectives, they reflected an honest concern with the special problems of women, but an unwillingness to see the problems as more than temporary.

The Federal Emergency Relief Administration, the National Youth Administration, and the Works Progress Administration (WPA) all had programs geared to the special needs of women. The programs tended to emphasize job skills that would prepare the women as domestic servants or housewives, but they did little to prepare them to compete on the job market. An article in the September 1938 *Women Worker* reported that more than one-half of the 372,000 women employed on WPA projects were working on projects such as canning and sewing. They made garments and supplies to be distributed to relief clients and to hospitals and other public institutions. They preserved, canned, and dried surplus food for needy families and for school lunch projects.

Many of the women involved in work relief under WPA were in a special program set up in July 1937 called the Household Service Demonstration Project. The program provided training for women who were seeking domestic employment, but it also provided for the employment of women who acted as teachers and demonstrators in the courses. Some seventeen hundred women were involved in giving a two-month training course in methods of cooking and serving food, care of the house, care of children, washing, ironing, and marketing. A survey of the project, done in December 1939, showed that in the more than two years of operation, twenty-two thousand women had received training and eighteen thousand trainees had been placed. Those who were not placed had either dropped out of the training course, found employment, married, or left the community. For those who stuck with the full course, placement was almost 100 percent.

The WPA also employed another thirty thousand women on housekeeping aid projects. Women who were good homemakers but had no other skills were sent into the homes of needy families to help out in times of illness or other distress. In addition, during the 1937–38 school season, eight thousand women were employed on school lunch projects.

Of course, women were employed in the various professional projects as well as those emphasizing menial domestic work. In fact, their occupational distribution was much more favorable than their male counterparts. Women on WPA projects were more likely to be placed in a white-collar occupation than were men. Almost 40 percent of all clerical workers and of all professional and technical workers were women. And surprisingly, women had as large a proportion in the category of project supervisors and foremen as men. These three categories together occupied nearly a third of all WPA women workers.

The statistics indicate that women workers, as a whole, were underrepresented on WPA projects, although this was the work relief agency most sympathetic to the needs of working women. Only 17.5 percent of all WPA workers were female, at a time when women made up about 24 percent of the total labor force and their unemployment rates were comparable to men's.

The major programs directed at youth—the Civilian Conservation Corps and the National Youth Administration (NYA)—focused most of their efforts, training, and funding on the needs of young men. Although women were included, at least in the NYA, they were never the primary object of concern. For example, the resident educational camps, established first under the Federal Emergency Relief Administration and later transferred to the NYA, reflected a class and sex role bias that steered young women into limited channels of achievement and ignored their potential for higher achievements. Also, the educational camps were in existence for only about three years, and reached less than ten thousand young women.

Thus, the New Deal addressed the problems of women, but it tended to further relegate them to their traditional roles, thereby reinforcing their already low economic status. The employment of women on relief projects was seen as a temporary necessity, geared toward their basic economic survival. The New Deal reformers saw a woman's long-range security as linked to her position in the family and supported by the primary family wage earner.

Nowhere was this commitment to family security more evident than in the most important piece of New Deal legislation, the Social Security Act of 1935. Under the terms of this legislation, adults who did not work for wages were not eligible for Social Security. Therefore, women who chose marriage over employment gave up government protection as well as their careers. The implication was obvious. The security of women was dependent upon men. Also, Social Security excluded many occupations that employed women, such as domestic service, farm labor, and educational, charitable, and hospital personnel. The exclusion of domestic workers left one-third of all married working women outside of a social welfare program. On the other hand, there was an Aid to Dependent Children (ADC) component to Social Security. In fact, some local WPA officials tried to take advantage of ADC by switching women from work relief to ADC as quickly as possible. The women themselves tended to prefer work to cash relief, and in a few cases they actually protested with sit-down strikes at welfare offices.

Interestingly enough, the Social Security Act, as much as any part of the New Deal, was the creation of the social feminists, and as such it reflected their attitudes toward the poor, the welfare state, and the role of women. However, most of the studies that deal with Social Security give little consideration to the feminist-reformer aspect of the issue. Clearly this key piece of legislation not only laid the foundations for the social welfare state, but it institutionalized female economic dependency and reinforced attitudes about women's traditional role that were to affect women's economic lives for decades to come.

It is perhaps unrealistic to suppose that government policies, programs, and projects of the 1930s would work toward the elimination of the sex role biases that were so thoroughly ingrained in the American social and occupational structure. Yet given the fact that women played such a large role in initiating, formulating, and implementing the New Deal, it is somewhat surprising that there was not a more aggressive stance taken on the potential of women—and a more creative effort to move beyond conventional stereotypes of women's role. The generation of women who were behind the New Deal were the first group of women to play an active and influential role in policymaking. Yet although they developed a network of support among themselves, and were directly concerned with women's issues, they seldom defined themselves as feminists. Their attitude was that of the social feminists of the Progressive era, and, of course, many, if not most, began their careers during that era. They were primarily concerned with the need to protect women and children caught in a harsh, competitive world. The hardships of the Depression understandably increased rather than decreased that tendency.

Historian Susan Ware has pointed out in her study *Beyond Suffrage: Women in the New Deal* that the experimental, reformist atmosphere of the New Deal encouraged and facilitated progress for women, particularly those who pursued careers in public life. The women who came to Washington during the New Deal era were able to rise to positions of power and prominence in many of the new government agencies. They came from similar backgrounds, with similar career patterns, and many of them knew each other from social welfare and reform activities going back to the Progressive era. The interaction of these women, on both the personal and professional level, formed a "network" which became an important force in enlarging women's influence in the New Deal.

. . . [W]omen in the New Deal network took an active interest in furthering the progress of their sex. They recruited women for prominent government positions, demanded increased political patronage, and fostered an awareness of women as a special interest group. Although promoting the advancement of women always remained a central concern of the network, the women identified themselves as social reformers rather than feminists. They pursued social welfare goals benefiting both men and women. Ware argues that they also advanced the cause of women by taking on new and unprecedented roles in the public sphere. Yet they neither set an example for future generations—at least not one that was imitated—nor broke down the sexual stereotypes of their day that governed economic activity, vocational training, and public policy.

Even recognizing the humane concern that the New Dealers had for women, children, and youth, the question must be asked: why did they not play a more aggressive role in breaking down sexual barriers and advancing the cause of feminism from their position of public influence? The answer lies partly in the general conditions which underlay the climate of opinion in the 1930s. The Depression was in itself a problem of such immediacy and magnitude that feminism as an issue and an ideology was remote from the concerns of most social reformers. Thus even limited benefits for women were seen as victories. The New Deal broke new ground in establishing employment, training, and welfare programs for women, and the reformers themselves were willing to accept that half-loaf. In part this was typical of the time and the temperament of the New Deal, but it was also partly related to the personal characteristics of the women in the New Deal Network. As her biographer notes, Frances Perkins's career was built on the premise that in daily work there was no essential difference between men and women. She was widely quoted for her remark that being a woman in government was a handicap "only in climbing trees."

This rather cavalier dismissal of the many slights that Perkins endured on a regular basis was quite typical of this generation of reformers. Ware points out that the women in the network naively believed that since they had done so well in government, conditions would continue to improve for women who wanted to pursue careers in government and politics. Eleanor Roosevelt stated in the *Democratic Digest* in 1938 that "the best way to advance the equal rights of women is for every woman to do her job in the best possible way so that gradually the prejudice against women will disappear."

This kind of public feminism was perhaps adequate for those women who had strong individual talents and particular social and professional advantages. But such an approach was not going to produce basic changes for women in American society, no matter how impressive an example was being set. Because the women in the New Deal network were exceptional, they failed to question women's second-class status in American society. They never delved deeply into the causes of discrimination against women; they never challenged the stereotypes of "women's nature." And finally, because their own political impact was so dependent upon individual contributions, it was difficult to institutionalize even the limited gains that were won in the 1930s.

The lack of feminist consciousness within the New Deal network can also be attributed to the split in the postsuffrage women's movement between the social reformers and the equal rights feminists. Susan Becker addresses this issue in her book *The Origins of the Equal Rights Amendment,* in which she argues that the National Women's Party (NWP) was the only "true" feminist organization in the United States during the interwar period. Party members kept feminism alive during these years, alerted women to the legal and economic discrimination that they faced, and probably prevented many of these discriminations from becoming worse. In formulating the Equal Rights Amendment, NWP feminists pointed the way to a future potential equality before the law.

But the NWP's legalistic approach to feminism, with its unbending commitment to the Equal Rights Amendment, lost it many supporters among the social feminists and tended, perhaps, to give feminism a bad name among those who saw the need for protective legislation for women when the security of family life had failed them. Furthermore, the relationship between women's work and family values was the primary issue for most working women of the Depression years. To gain a wide base of support, the feminist ideology would have had to adapt to the basic fact that the great majority of American women were committed to a traditional pattern of family life that had little to do with equal rights or "careerism."

To a certain extent, the lack of a strong feminist consciousness among New Deal reformers can be attributed to a simple expediency—a desire to cooperate and consolidate the gains that had been made among this first generation of women in government. These gains had often been made for those less fortunate than themselves. Certainly expediency was characteristic of some of the members of the so-called Negro cabinet, in particular Mary McLeod Bethune, head of the Negro's division of the National Youth Administration. B. Joyce Ross, in a recent article on Bethune, points out that Bethune adopted a pragmatic approach to desegregation and equal treatment of blacks. In her efforts to advance Negro interests in the New Deal agencies, Bethune necessarily had to accept limited progress in overall racial equality; in the presence of white audiences, she often spoke the language of the "accommodationist."

In fact, in some ways, the experiences of blacks and of women in the New Deal are parallel and provide a good opportunity to compare the advances, the benefits, and the overall impact of expanded governmental activity upon two groups traditionally outside of the mainstream of American politics. In both cases, there were definite, though limited, gains. In both cases, old stereotypes were reinforced and certain structural inequities became an accepted part of the trappings of the New Deal welfare state— inequities that were to remain as unresolved issues to haunt future generations.

One historian has said, "Not even with the benefit of historical perspective is it a simple exercise to untangle the web of beneficial and victimizing effects of New Deal legislation." Certainly this is true, but it is nonetheless the task of the historian to move beyond the traditional interpretations of the New Deal which note its "pragmatism," its lack of ideological rigidity, and its peculiar inability to challenge existing mores and values, to consider an equally interesting question: why was one-half of the population pragmatically dismissed from mainstream America, and why has it taken American historians so long to address this issue?

Suggestions for Further Reading

Reference Works

An excellent reference guide with essays on legislation, events, ideas, and prominent New Deal figures is Otis L. Graham, Jr. and Meghan Robinson Wander, eds., *Franklin D. Roosevelt: His Life and Times, An Encyclopedic View* (1985). Also valuable is James S. Olson, ed., *Historical Dictionary of the New Deal: From Inauguration to Preparation for War* (1985).

Histories of the New Deal and the 1930s

Among the classic studies of the New Deal are Arthur M. Schlesinger, Jr., *The Age of Roosevelt: The Crisis of the Old Order* (1957); *The Coming of the New Deal* (1959); *The Politics of Upheaval* (1960) and William Leuchtenburg, *Franklin D. Roosevelt and the New Deal* (1963). Paul Conkin, *The New Deal* (1992) and Barton Bernstein, "The New Deal: The Conservative Achievements of Liberal Reform," in Barton Bernstein, ed., *Towards a New Past: Dissenting Essays in American History* (1968) are important studies critical of the New Deal. Conservative critiques have drawn less attention in recent years, but see Robert Higgs, *Crisis and Leviathan: Critical Episodes in the Growth of American Government* (1987) and Gary Dean Best, *Pride, Prejudice, and Politics: Roosevelt versus Recovery, 1933–1938* (1991).

Historians and social scientists continue to argue that the New Deal was dominated and shaped by business and corporate interests and the demands of a stable system of industrial capitalism. Recent works that make this argument include Colin Gordon, *New Deals: Business, Labor, and Politics in America, 1920–1935* (1994); Thomas Ferguson, "From Normalcy to New Deal: Industrial Structure, Party Competition, and American Public Policy in the Great Depression," *International Organization* 38 (1984): 41–94; Rhonda Levine, *Class Struggle and the New Deal: Industrial Labor, Industrial Capital, and the State* (1988).

Several first-rate histories of the New Deal have appeared in recent years. The best is Anthony J. Badger, *The New Deal: The Depression Years, 1933–1940* (1989). Roger Biles, *A New Deal for the American People* (1991) is also a fine study. Robert S. McElvaine, *The Great Depression: America, 1929–1941* (1984, 1994) is excellent on the social and cultural history of the 1930s. *Anxious Decades: America in Prosperity and Depression, 1920–1941* (1992) by Michael E. Parrish is a valuable overview of the 1920s and 1930s.

The New Deal continues to be the subject of provocative new interpretations and analyses. The best of these studies include: Barry Karl, *The Uneasy State: The United States from 1915 to 1945* (1983); Alan Dawley, *Struggles for Justice: Social Responsibility and the Liberal State* (1991); Jordan A. Schwarz, *The New Dealers: Power Politics in the Age of Roosevelt* (1994); Alan Brinkley, *The End of Reform: New Deal Liberalism in Recession and War* (1995); Ronald C. Tobey, *Technology as Freedom: The New Deal and the Electrical Modernization of the American Home* (1996); and the essays in Steve Fraser and Gary Gerstle, *The Rise and Fall of the New Deal Order, 1930–1980* (1989).

There are also many edited collections with excellent essays and analyses of the New Deal. In addition to *Rise and Fall of the New Deal Order,* see: John Braeman, Robert H. Bremner, David Brody, eds., *The New Deal: The National Level* and *The New Deal: The State and Local Levels* (1975); Robert Eden, ed., *The New Deal and Its Legacy: Critique and Reappraisal* (1985); Harvard Sitkoff, ed., *Fifty Years Later: The New Deal Evaluated* (1985); Wilbur J. Cohen, ed., *The Roosevelt New Deal: A Program Assessment Fifty Years After* (1986); Stephen W. Baskerville and Ralph Willett, eds., *Nothing Else to Fear: New Perspectives on America in the Thirties* (1985); and William E. Leuchtenburg, *The FDR Years: On Roosevelt & His Legacy* (1995).

On the "origins" of the New Deal and the transition from Hoover to Roosevelt, see: William E. Leuchtenburg, "The New Deal and the Analogue of War," in John Braeman, Robert H. Bremner, and Everett Walters, eds., *Change and Continuity in Twentieth Century America* (1964); Robert Himmelberg, *The Origins of the National Recovery Administration: Business, Government, and the Trade Association Issue, 1921–1933* (1976); Elliot A. Rosen, *Hoover, Roosevelt and the Brains Trust: From Depression to New Deal* (1977); Susan Estabrook Kennedy, *The Banking Crisis of 1933* (1973); and David E. Hamilton, *From New Day to New Deal: American Farm Policy from Hoover to Roosevelt, 1928–1933* (1991).

Two older but still valuable historiographical essays are: Jerold S. Auerbach, "New Deal, Old Deal, or Raw Deal: Some

Thoughts on New Left Historiography," *Journal of Southern History* 35 (1969): 18–30 and Richard S. Kirkendall, "The New Deal as Watershed: The Recent Literature," *Journal of American History* 54 (March 1968).

Biographies

The best scholarly biographies of Roosevelt that cover the pre-New Deal and New Deal period are: James MacGregor Burns, *Roosevelt: The Lion and the Fox* (1956); Frank Freidel, *Franklin D. Roosevelt:* vol. I *The Apprenticeship* (1952); vol. II *The Ordeal* (1954); vol. III *The Triumph* (1956); vol. IV *Launching the New Deal* (1973) and Freidel's one volume study *Franklin D. Roosevelt: A Rendezvous with Destiny* (1990). A splendid brief biography is Patrick J. Maney, *The Roosevelt Presence* (1992). On Roosevelt's life before the depression, see Geoffrey C. Ward, *Before the Trumpet: Young Franklin Roosevelt, 1882–1905* (1985) and *A First-Class Temperament: The Emergence of Franklin Roosevelt* (1989). On Eleanor Roosevelt, see: Joseph P. Lash, *Eleanor and Franklin* (1971). For a discussion of Roosevelt biographies, see John Whiteclay Chambers, "Biographers and Public Reputation," in *Franklin D. Roosevelt: His Life and Times,* pp. 27–38.

Biographies of New Deal leaders include: George T. McJimsey, *Harry Hopkins: Ally of the Poor and Defender of Democracy* (1987); Graham White and John Maze, *Henry A. Wallace: His Search For a New World Order* (1995); Jeanne Nienaber Clarke, *Roosevelt's Warrior: Harold Ickes and the New Deal* (1996); Jordan A. Schwarz, *Liberal: Adolf A. Berle and the Vision of an American Era* (1987); George Martin, *Madam Secretary: Frances Perkins;* John A. Salmond, *A Southern Rebel: The Life and Times of Aubrey Williams, 1890–1965* (1983); Michael E. Parrish, *Felix Frankfurter and His Times: The Reform Years* (1982); John Kennedy Ohl, *Hugh S. Johnson and the New Deal* (1985); J. Joseph Huthmacher, *Senator Robert F. Wagner and the Rise of Urban Liberalism* (1968); and Richard Lowitt, *George W. Norris: The Triumph of a Progressive, 1933–1944* (1978).

Politics

A good overview is John M. Allswang, *The New Deal and American Politics* (1978). Important studies of voting behavior and the formation and nature of the New Deal coalition include: Kristi

Andersen, *The Creation of a Democratic Majority, 1928–1936* (1979); Gerald Gamm, *The Making of New Deal Democrats: Voting Behavior and Realignment in Boston, 1920–1940* (1989); Allen J. Lichtman, "Critical Election Theory and the Reality of American Presidential Politics, 1916–1940," *American Historical Review* 81 (1976); David Plotke, *Building a Democratic Political Order: Reshaping American Liberalism in the 1930s and 1940s* (1996); Sidney M. Milkis, *The President and the Parties: The Transformation of the American Party System Since the New Deal* (1993).

On the formation of the "conservative coalition," see: James T. Patterson, *Congressional Conservatism and the New Deal: The Growth of the Conservative Coalition in Congress, 1933–1939* (1967). On the Republican Party in the 1930s, see Clyde P. Weed, *Nemesis of Reform: The Republican Party During the New Deal* (1994). On the transformation of the presidency, a recent work is Matthew J. Dickinson, *Bitter Harvest: FDR, Presidential Power, and the Growth of the Presidential Branch* (1996).

Two books on the New Deal and the cities are: Mark I. Gelfand, *A Nation of Cities: The Federal Government and Urban America, 1933–1965* (1975) and Bruce Stave, *The New Deal and the Last Hurrah: Pittsburgh Machine Politics* (1970).

Business-Government Relations and the NRA

The classic analysis is Ellis W. Hawley, *The New Deal and the Problem of Monopoly: A Study of Economic Ambivalence* (1966, 1995). Colin Gordon's *New Deals* is well-argued and challenging. On the NRA, see Robert Himmelberg, *The Origins of the National Recovery Administration;* Bernard Bellush, *The Failure of the NRA* (1975); Donald Brand, *Corporatism and the Rule of Law: A Study of the National Recovery Administration* (1988); James P. Johnson, *The Politics of Soft Coal: The Bituminous Industry from World War I Through the New Deal* (1979).

On other aspects of the New Deal and business, see: Michael E. Parrish, *Securities Regulation and the New Deal* (1970); Ellis W. Hawley, "A Partnership Formed, Dissolved, and in Renegotiation: Business and Government in the Franklin D. Roosevelt Era," in Joseph Frese and Jacob Judd, eds., *Business and Government: Essays in 20ᵗʰ Century Cooperation and Conflict* (1985); and Thomas K. McGraw, *TVA and the Power Fight: 1933–1939* (1971).

Labor

There is an extensive literature on the New Deal and labor. See Irving Bernstein's *The Turbulent Years: A History of American Workers, 1933–1939* (1969) and *A Caring Society: The New Deal, the Worker, and the Great Depression* (1985); David Brody, *Workers in Industrial America* (1993); Melvyn Dubofsky, *The State and Labor in Modern America* (1994); Lizabeth Cohen, *Making a New Deal: Industrial Workers in Chicago, 1919–1939* (1990); James A. Gross, *The Making of the National Labor Relations Board, 1933–1937* (1974) and *The Reshaping of the National Labor Relations Board* (1981); Steven Fraser, *Labor Will Rule: Sidney Hillman and the Rise of American Labor* (1991); and Robert H. Zieger, *The CIO, 1935–1955* (1995). Works more critical of the intent and impact of New Deal labor policies include Stanley Vittoz, *New Deal Labor Policy and the American Industrial Economy* (1987); Christopher L. Tomlins, *The State and the Unions: Labor Relations, Law, and the Organized Labor Movement in America, 1880–1960* (1985), and Karl Klare, "Judicial Deradicalization of the Wagner Act and the Origins of Modern Legal Consciousness, 1937–1941," *Minnesota Law Review* 62 (March 1978): 265–339.

Farm Policy, Reform, and Rural America

A fine introduction is Theodore Saloutos, *The American Farmers and the New Deal* (1982). Other works include Richard S. Kirkendall, *Social Scientists and Farm Politics in the Age of Roosevelt* (1967, 1982); Donald Worster, *The Dust Bowl: The Southern Plains in the 1930s* (1979); Anthony J. Badger, *Prosperity Road: The New Deal, Tobacco, and North Carolina* (1980); David Hamilton, *From New Day to New Deal;* Pete Daniel, *Breaking the Land: The Transformation of Cotton, Tobacco, and Rice Cultures since 1880* (1985); Jack Temple Kirby, *Rural Worlds Lost: The American South, 1920–1960* (1987); Mary W. M. Hargreaves, *Dry Farming in the Northern Great Plains: Years of Readjustment, 1920–1990* (1993); Michael W. Schuyler, *The Dread of Plenty: Agricultural Relief Activities of the Federal Government in the Middle West, 1933–1939* (1989); Van L. Perkins, *Crisis in Agriculture: The Agricultural Adjustment Administration and the New Deal, 1933* (1969); Christiana M. Campbell, *The Farm Bureau and the New Deal: A*

Study in the Making of National Farm Policy, 1933–1940 (1962). Excellent on the economic consequences of New Deal farm policy is Sally H. Clarke, *Regulation and Revolution in United States Farm Productivity* (1995).

Books examining New Deal efforts to combat rural poverty include: Sidney Baldwin, *Poverty and Politics: The Rise and Decline of the Farm Security Administration* (1968); Paul K. Conkin, *Toward a New World: The New Deal Community Program* (1958); Donald S. Holley, *Uncle Sam's Farmers: The New Deal Communities in the Lower Mississippi Valley* (1975); Paul Mertz, *New Deal Policy and Southern Rural Poverty* (1978); Brian Q. Cannon, *Remaking the Agrarian Dream: New Deal Rural Resettlement in the Mountain West* (1996).

On class struggles in agriculture, see Cletus E. Daniel, *Bitter Harvest: A History of California Farmworkers, 1870–1941* (1981); Devra Weber, *Dark Sweat, White Gold: California Farm Workers, Cotton, and the New Deal* (1994); Donald Grubbs, *Cry from the Cotton: The Southern Tenant Farmers Union and the New Deal* (1971); David E. Conrad, *The Forgotten Farmers: The Story of Sharecroppers in the New Deal* (1965).

Fiscal Policy

Herbert Stein, *The Fiscal Revolution in America* (1969, 1990) is the standard work. Albert Romasco, *The Politics of Recovery: Roosevelt's New Deal* (1983) is very good at explaining the political obstacles to recovery policies. The best study of New Deal tax policy is Mark H. Leff, *The Limits of Symbolic Reform: The New Deal and Taxation* (1984). On the role of the Reconstruction Finance Corporation, see James S. Olson, *Saving Capitalism: The Reconstruction Finance Corporation and the New Deal, 1933–1940* (1988).

Much has been written in recent years on the role of economists in shaping economic policy. See, for instance, William J. Barber, *Designs within Disorder: Franklin D. Roosevelt, the Economists, and the Shaping of American Economic Policy, 1933–1945* (1996); Theodore Rosenof, *Economics in the Long Run: New Deal Theorists & Their Legacies, 1933–1993* (1997); Richard P. Adelstein, " 'The Nation as an Economic Unit': Keynes, Roosevelt, and the Managerial Ideal," *Journal of American History* 78 (June 1991): 160–87; and Dean L. May, *From New Deal to New Economics: The American Liberal Response to the Recession of 1937* (1981).

On the American economy during the 1930s, the persistence of the depression, and the economic consequences of New Deal policies see Michael Bernstein, *Great Depression: Delayed Recovery and Economic Change in America, 1929–1939* (1987), Lester V. Chandler, *America's Great Depression* (1970), and Peter Fearon, *War, Prosperity & Depression: The U.S. Economy 1917–1945* (1987). On the U.S. and world economies, see Barry Eichengreen, *Golden Fetters: The Gold Standard and the Great Depression, 1919–1939* (1995); Charles Kindleberger, *The World in Depression, 1929–1939* (1979); and John A. Garraty, *The Great Depression* (1986).

Relief

The best starting place is James T. Patterson, *America's Struggle against Poverty, 1900–1980* (1981). See also Williams R. Brock, *Welfare, Democracy, and the New Deal* (1988); Bonnie Fox Schwartz, *The Civil Works Administration, 1933–1934: The Business of Emergency Employment in the New Deal* (1984); William W. Bremner, "Along the American Way: The New Deal's Work Relief Program for the Unemployed," *Journal of American History* 42 (1975), 636–52; John Salmond, *The Civilian Conservation Corps, 1933–1942: A New Deal Case Study* (1967); and Richard Lowitt and Maurine Beasley, eds., *One Third of a Nation: Lorena Hickok Reports on the Great Depression* (1981).

There is a large literature on the New Deal arts programs. It includes Richard D. McKinzie, *The New Deal for Artists* (1973); Jane De Hart Mathews, *The Federal Theater, 1935–1939: Plays, Relief, and Politics* (1967); Jerre Mangione, *The Dream and the Deal: The Federal Writers' Project, 1935–1943* (1972); Monty Noam Penkower, *The Federal Writers' Project: A Study in Government Patronage of the Arts* (1977); Marlene Park and Gerald E. Markowitz, *Democratic Vistas: Post Office and Public Art in the New Deal* (1983); Karal Ann Marling, *Wall-to-Wall America: A Cultural History of Post-Office Murals in the Great Depression* (1982); Kenneth J. Bindas, *All of This Music Belongs to the Nation: The WPA's Federal Music Project and American Society* (1995).

Welfare and Social Security

Roy Lubove, *The Struggle for Social Security, 1900–1935* (1968); W. Andrew Achenbaum, *Social Security: Visions and Revisions* (1986); Theda Skocpol and John Ikenberry, "Expanding Social

Benefits: The Role of Social Security," *Political Science Quarterly* 102 (1987): 389–416; Daniel Nelson, *Unemployment Insurance: The American Experience, 1914–1935* (1969); Edward Berkowitz and Kim McQuaid, *Creating the Welfare State: The Political Economy of Twentieth Century Reform* (1992).

In recent years Social Security and the New Deal social welfare system have been criticized for reinforcing and institutionalizing gender inequality. See Linda Gordon, *Pitied But Not Entitled: Single Mothers and the History of Welfare, 1890–1935* (1994) and Gwendolyn Mink, *The Wages of Motherhood: Inequality in the Welfare State, 1917–1942* (1995).

Region, State, Locality

James T. Patterson's *The New Deal and the States: Federalism in Transition* (1969) initiated a now burgeoning literature on the New Deal at the state and local level. For a survey of the works since Patterson, see Anthony J. Badger, "The New Deal and the Localities," in Rhodri Jeffreys-Jones and Bruce Collins, eds., *The Growth of Federal Power in American History* (1983). See also *The New Deal: The State and Local Levels;* Charles H. Trout, *Boston: The Great Depression and the New Deal* (1977); Jo Ann E. Argersinger, *Toward a New Deal in Baltimore: People and Government in the Great Depression* (1988); D. Jerome Tweton, *The New Deal at the Grass Roots* (1988). For regional studies, see Richard Lowitt, *The New Deal and the West* (1984); Roger Biles, *The South and the New Deal* (1994); James C. Cobb and Michael V. Namorato, eds., *The New Deal and the South* (1984).

Late New Deal

Alan Brinkley's *The End of Reform* is the major work on the late New Deal, but much work has been done on this period. A fine review essay is Maurizio Vaudagna, "Recent Perspectives on the Late Thirties in the United States," *Storia Nordamericana* (1989): 161–90. Other works include Richard Polenberg, *Reorganizing Roosevelt's Government: The Controversy over Executive Reorganization, 1936–1939* (1966); Barry D. Karl, *Executive Reorganization and Reform in the New Deal: The Genesis of Administrative Management, 1900–1939* (1963). For insightful discussions on the idea of a "third" New Deal, see Karl's *The Uneasy State;* John W.

Jeffries, "The 'New' New Deal: FDR and American Liberalism, 1937–1945," *Political Science Quarterly* 105 (Fall 1990): 397–418; and Otis Graham, "Franklin Roosevelt and the Intended New Deal," in Thomas E. Cronin and Michael Beschloss, eds., *Essays in Honor of James MacGregor Burns* (1989).

Statebuilding, Antistatism, and New Deal Planning

In addition to Karl's *The Uneasy State* and the essay by Ellis Hawley in this volume, see Kenneth Finegold and Theda Skocpol, *State and Party in America's New Deal* (1995); Theda Skocpol, "Political Response to Capitalist Crisis: Neo-Marxist Theories of the State and the Case of the New Deal," *Politics and Society* 10 (1981): 155–201; Margaret Weir and Theda Skocpol, "State Structures and the Possibilities for 'Keynesian' Responses to the Great Depression in Sweden, Britain, and the United States," in Peter B. Evans, Dietrich Rueschemeyer, and Theda Skocpol, eds., *Bringing the State Back In* (1985); Alan Brinkley, "The New Deal and the Idea of the State," in *The Rise and Fall of the New Deal Order;* and Otis L. Graham, Jr., *Toward a Planned Society: From Roosevelt to Nixon* (1976).

Constitutional Revolution

Peter Irons, *The New Deal Lawyers* (1982); Ellis W. Hawley, "The Constitution of the Hoover and F. Roosevelt Presidency During the Depression Era, 1930–1939," in Martin Fausold and Alan Shank, eds., *The Constitution and the American Presidency* (1991).

On the "court-packing" plan, see the essays in William Leuchtenburg, *The Supreme Court Reborn: The Constitutional Revolution in the Age of Roosevelt* (1995); Michael Parrish, "The Hughes Court, the Great Depression, and the Historians," *Historian* 40 (1975): 286–308; Richard Maidment, "The New Deal Court Revisited," in Stephen Baskerville and Ralph Willett, eds., *Nothing Else to Fear: New Perspectives on America in the Thirties* (1985).

African-Americans and the Struggle for Equal Rights

Major works include Nancy J. Weiss, *Farewell to the Party of Lincoln: Black Politics in the Age of FDR* (1983); Harvard Sitkoff, *A New Deal for Blacks: The Emergence of Civil Rights as a National Issue* (1978); Nancy Grant, *TVA and Black Americans: Planning for the Status Quo* (1990); and Patricia Sullivan, *Days of Hope: Race and Democracy in the New Deal Era* (1996).

Women

Susan Ware has written: *Beyond Suffrage: Women in the New Deal* (1981); *Holding Their Own: American Women in the 1930s* (1982); and *Partner and I: Molly Dewson, Feminism, and New Deal Politics* (1987). See also Alice Kessler-Harris, *Out to Work: A History of Wage-Earning Women in the United States* (1982); Lois Scharf, *To Work and to Wed: Female Employment, Feminism and the Great Depression* (1980); Susan D. Becker, *The Origins of the Equal Rights Amendment: American Feminism Between the Wars* (1981); Winifred D. Wandersee, *Women's Work and Family Values, 1920–1940* (1981); Linda Gordon, *Pitied But Not Entitled: Single Mothers and the History of Welfare, 1890–1935* (1994).

New Deal and Native Americans

Important works include Donald Parman, *The Navajos and the New Deal* (1976); Kenneth R. Philp, *John Collier's Crusade for Indian Reform, 1920–1954* (1977); Graham D. Taylor, *The New Deal and American Indian Tribalism: The Administration of the Indian Reorganization Act, 1934–1945* (1980); Laurence M. Hauptman, *The Iroquois and the New Deal* (1981).

New Deal Critics

Major works include Alan Brinkley, *Voices of Protest: Huey Long, Father Coughlin and the Great Depression* (1982); David H. Bennett, *Demagogues in the Depression: American Radicals and the Union Party, 1932–1936* (1969); George Wolfskill, *The Revolt of the Conservatives: A History of the Liberty League, 1939–1940* (1962); R. Alan Lawson, *The Failure of Independent Liberalism, 1930–1941* (1971).

New Deal Legacy

William E. Leuchtenburg, *In the Shadow of FDR: From Harry Truman to Bill Clinton* (1993); Fraser and Gerstle, eds., *The Rise and Fall of the New Deal Order, 1930–1980;* and Eden, ed., *The New Deal and Its Legacy.*